PENROSE MEMORIAL LIBRAI

C0-APG-133

CITY, TOWN AND COUNTRYSIDE
IN THE EARLY BYZANTINE ERA

Edited by
Robert L. Hohlfelder

EAST EUROPEAN MONOGRAPHS, BOULDER
DISTRIBUTED BY COLUMBIA UNIVERSITY PRESS
NEW YORK

1982

HT
115
.C57
1982

EAST EUROPEAN MONOGRAPHS. NO. CXX

Byzantine Series, No. 1

PENROSE MEMORIAL LIBRARY
WHITMAN COLLEGE
WALLA WALLA, WASHINGTON 99362

Copyright © 1982 by Robert L. Hohlfelder
Library of Congress Card Catalog Number 82-70731
ISBN 0-88033-013-9

Printed in the United States of America

P NRROSE MEMORIAL LIBRARY
RECEIVE

SEP 2 1 1983
83-4540
ACQUISITIONS DEP'T

CONTENTS

iii

PREFACE

With this inaugural volume, a new monograph series on Byzantine studies begins, the *East European Monographs: Byzantine Series.* One might ask if there is a legitimate need for such a venture. I think there is. Marketing considerations continue to reduce traditional publication outlets for research in fields as specialized as ours. Increasing costs often require a significant author subvention, usually sought from universities with diminishing resources for such projects. When financial exigency causes institutional retrenchment, support for humanistic research is frequently an early casualty. For beginning scholars and for those whose research assumes inconvenient size, either too long or too short for a standard book, the problems are greater. Moreover, if a manuscript is accepted, production time from initial submission to final copy is increasing. Today, the opportunities for timely publication of original research on Byzantium are limited. There is little solace in looking to the immediate future for change. Tomorrow may well be worse.

The *East European Monographs: Byzantine Series* hopes to address some of these problems and invites both younger and more established scholars to submit their research for prompt consideration. This series plans to publish studies on all aspects of Byzantine civilization but with an emphasis on non-traditional and interdisciplinary approaches and with more attention paid to the value of the research than to its length.

Without sacrificing quality, the *East European Monographs: Byzantine Series* promises the community of Byzantine scholars an expeditious and inexpensive publication alternative for important new research on Byzantium and the world in which it flourished. I would like to end my prefatory remarks with a statement of appreciation to Professor Stephen Fischer-Galati, a colleague of mine at the University of Colorado and editor of the *East European Quarterly* and the *East European Monographs*, for supporting this effort. The extraordinary success of his monograph series, from which this one evolves, has been nothing less than remarkable. May its derivative fare as well! I would also like to thank Professors Peter Topping and Gary Vikan of the Center for Byzantine Studies, Dumbarton Oaks, for their encouragement at a seminal stage of this project. Finally, I wish to express my gratitude to Professor Giles Constable of the same institution for his good advice and counsel on the difficulties of launching an enterprise such as this one. With luck, this series may avoid some of the pitfalls he so kindly outlined.

Robert L. Hohlfelder
Boulder, Colorado
1 August 1982

INTRODUCTION AND ACKNOWLEDGMENTS

On October 26, 1979, a program bearing the same title as this volume and organized by the editor was conducted at the Fifth Annual Byzantine Studies Conference held at Dumbarton Oaks in Washington, D.C. Response to the papers presented during this session was enthusiastic. Numerous conference participants suggested at the time that these communications should be published as a unit if at all possible. The Program Committee of this conference and particularly its chair, Professor Gary Vikan, was also actively encouraging such efforts. I proceeded to contact the panel members about a collaborative project and other speakers from different sessions who had offered topics that seemed appropriate for an anthology to be entitled *City, Town and Countryside in the Early Byzantine Era*. Five of the articles presented here grew from papers presented at this symposium. The other contributions were solicited from scholars working in the general field of early Byzantium.

It is the intent of this volume, and of the original session as well, to provide scholars with diverse professional training and intellectual interests with an opportunity to share their particular insights on the early Byzantine era in a common forum. The individual articles of this anthology are important contributions to their respective fields of scholarship. In content, geographical purview and methodology, their scope is broad. The subject matter ranges from Byzantine aesthetic proclivities to city street widths and spans the Empire from Greece to Palestine. In addition, these specialized essays may gain from their grouping. Prepared by distinguished historians, archaeologists and philologists, they elucidate aspects of both the diversity and the commonality of the early Byzantine experience. Collectively, the articles of this volume may suggest ways in which different scholarly paths of investigation can compliment and augment one another in understanding an important transitional age of history.

The publication of this collection would not have been possible without the generous support of some of the institutions of the contributors. In this regard, I would like to thank the University of British Columbia, the University of Calgary, the University of Colorado, the University of Michigan the University of Maryland and University of New Mexico for their financial assistance for this project.

Robert L. Hohlfelder

1

CONTINUITY AND CHANGE: THE PRACTICAL GENIUS OF EARLY BYZANTINE CIVILISATION

Barry Baldwin

(University of Calgary)

For the sake of reasoned and reasonable limits, this study is confined to the period from the fourth to the seventh centuries. The chosen termini are treated with some elasticity, to permit mention of themes which straddle them, or authors whose work helps to illumine the chosen topics.

Unlike Krumbacher, Beck, and others,[1] I take Byzantine literature to begin before the age of Justinian. Neglect of the fourth and fifth centuries obscures the continuity of much social and literary tradition from imperial Rome to imperial Byzantium. It is a truism that in many ways Justinian marks the real beginning of Byzantine history. But in others, his age is an end. As Romilly Jenkins[2] observed, Byzantine authors enjoyed a widely educated and widely diffused audience up to the sixth century. By the revival of the ninth, after the intervening tumults and darkness, that audience had shrank to being largely a metropolitan one. And overall, at least in some genres, there was a decline in literary activity after the sixth century.[3] In Greek as well as Latin where Stein[4] on Corippus succinctly summed up the situation: "pour quelques siècles, la dernière épopée latine."

This holds good for Byzantine knowledge and appreciation of classical art as well as literature. According to Mango,[5] there is not one

1

ecphrasis of ancient art between Justinian and the twelfth century. He further maintains that there was no Byzantine collector of antiquities after the fifth century; this is more problematic,[6] but there was certainly a notable dearth of them. This development may be partly connected with the fact that at least one great art collection was destroyed by fire in the fifth century: the burning of the palace of Lausus in 475 will have reduced what there was to see for Byzantines of all classes—statues, unlike books, could be both education and entertainment for the illiterate—and weakened the immediate inspiration for Byzantine artists and writers of ecphraseis. Especially as no emperor after Justinian appears to have imported fresh supplies of antique statues.[7] Hence, considerable debasement of taste and knowledge in later ages was the result, leading to a dichotomy between uneducated superstitions and more sophisticated appreciation. A single example will suffice. One of the more engaging fantasies of the *scriptores originum Constantinopolitanarum*[8] is the claim that bronze figures of mosquitoes and other pests kept these plagues out of the city until Basil I broke them. A nice thought, unfortunately refuted by epigrams of Paul the Silentiary and Agathias on mosquito nets (*AP* 9. 764–6)!

It is not only the art historian who is informed by statues about Byzantine tastes and attitudes. The ecphrasis of those in the Zeuxippus Baths by Christodorus of Coptos, comprising Book Two of the Greek Anthology, is tedious as a poem but instructive in its content. It seems a warranted assumption that Christodorus enumerates *all* the collection, not just a sample.[9] His description is consonant with that of Cedrenus,[10] who says that the Zeuxippus was full of statues of *sophoi*, rhetors, poets, and men famous for courage. In view of the large number of Byzantine epigrams on statues and paintings of saints, charioteers, and dancing-girls, it is worth remarking the absence of all of these from the gallery of Christodorus. Christ does not here rub shoulders with pagans, as he does, for instance, in the chapel of the Roman emperor Alexander Severus.[11]

Of the men of letters immortalised in this ancient equivalent of Madame Tussaud's Waxworks Museum, poets slightly outnumber the writers of prose. A striking contrast to the later literary enthusiasms of Photius and his circle.[12] It is hardly surprising that Homer receives by far the fullest description (311–50). Notable absentees from the gallery of poets are Aeschylus, Sophocles, and Aristophanes. Euripides is there (32–5), whilst Old Comedy is represented by Cratinus (357–60), a procedure also followed by John Lydus who (*De Mag.* 1. 41. 3) exemplifies the genre with Cratinus and Eupolis, not Aristophanes. Here we have a good example of shifting Byzantine taste: this seeming vogue for Cratinus did not last solidly enough to allow the survival of any complete play. Prose writers not there include Polybius, Plutarch, or indeed any representative of the Second Sophistic.[13]

Some of the individual representations are a trifle bizarre. Why, for instance, is Julius Caesar, one of the very few Romans present, squeezed in between Chryses and Plato?[14] Perhaps the collection had become as crowded as those in some modern art galleries. And a few Byzantine eyebrows, not to mention modern ones, should have shot up on reading that Alcibiades was a giver of good counsel (85), albeit this is a great deal less egregious than a later mediaeval claim that he was *formosissima mulier apud Graecos*![15] Sometimes an individual is included for contemporary propaganda purposes. Pompey, another rare Roman in the collection, is not juxtaposed with Caesar as he ought to have been, but spotlighted near the end of the poem in order to glorify Anastasius and *his* Isaurian victories (398–406), a theme to which Christodorus also devoted an epic poem.[16]

The collection includes two Roman statesmen and two Roman writers. Such equipoise may or may not be accidental. Caesar and Pompey are balanced by Apuleius and Virgil. The latter's presence is not too surprising; he is one of the very few Latin writers in whom Greeks had always displayed overt interest.[17] Christodorus' decision to round off his poem with Virgil may reflect either his own enthusiasm for him or general Byzantine taste. That the Roman poet was actually read is made clear not only by the extant papyrus texts but by the statues of characters from the *Aeneid* in the Zeuxippus collection, specifically Dares and Entellus (222–7) and Creusa (148–54).[18] Apuleius is more of a turn up for the book. He is treated as a philosopher (303–5), the most respectable guise he could have for average Byzantine taste and morality. This is not a unique appearance by Apuleius in the period: he is one of the Roman authors adduced by John Lydus.[19] But interest in him was neither widespread nor enduring. No papyrus texts have yet turned up; and unlike Virgil, with whom he is reasonably familiar, the lemmatist to Christodorus' poem knows nothing of Apuleius.

Unlike the Palace of Lausus which contained such ancient masterpieces as the Cnidian Aphrodite, the Zeuxippus statues basically resemble a teaching collection. Visual pleasure for the less bookish is provided by the three different statues of Aphrodite and representations of the pugilists Dares and Entellus. When he is not expatiating on these,[20] Christodorus has little interest in the artists or artistry of the statues, apart from interminable repetition of the standard cliché that they looked to be alive. There is both reality and unreality in this cultural clutter. Thus, Homer dominates the poets, as he will throughout Byzantine history.[21] But at the very same time that Christodorus was writing, a contemporary high official and poet, Marianus of Eleutheropolis, was turning out iambic paraphrases of Hellenistic hexameter poets for those who could not cope with the originals.[22] This development, somewhat akin to that modern abomination, Coles' Notes to the Classics, prefigures the abandonment of the hexameter for epic by such as George of Pisidia.

A typical Byzantine mélange, then, this Hellenic marble backdrop to the Roman pleasures of the baths. Baths themselves, along with inns, restaurants, gardens, and houses, were some of the other permitted pleasures that evoked epigrams from Byzantine poets. Such amenities were not restricted to the capital. Baths are celebrated not only in Constantinople (*AP* 9. 614, 618, 619, 624, 625), but also in both large provincial towns (*AP* 9. 628: Alexandria; 9. 631: Smyrna) and small ones (*AP* 16. 281: Praenetus in Bithynia). The habit of naming baths and suchlike is both pleasant and practical, as anyone who has ever tried to find an address in Venice will confirm![23] Apart from the Zeuippus, there were baths called Love (*AP* 9. 626), Horse (9. 628), and Agamemnon (9. 631); also gardens called Love (9. 666, 668–9), and the Olympias fountain (9. 699). No name, however, is affixed to the restaurant halfway between the Zeuxippus and the Hippodrome celebrated by Leontius Scholasticus (*AP* 9. 650) in what is perhaps the most distinctive testimony to Byzantine notions of the perfect day out.

More mundane things could on occasion lend themselves to poetic treatment. A bridge over the Sangarius river provided Agathias with a convenient tribute to Justinian.[24] And, speaking of conveniences, there are his latrine poems (*AP* 9. 642–4, 662), an unpromising theme to some tastes, dowright shocking to others.[25] Agathias, however, cleverly combines linguistic parody with moral lesson,[26] as do two similar poems painted on the walls of a latrine in Ephesus,[27] affording perhaps a distinctive and welcome twist on the adoxographical prose exercises of the Second Sophistic.[28]

Yet literary frivolity and day-to-day practicality converge here. Agathias appears to have been a *curator civitatis*, as such in charge of public buildings. The provision of latrines, a very Roman benefit,[29] was a great blessing in the unhygienic conditions of antiquity. The aforementioned baths at Praenetus were built on waste land which the natives had been using as a privy. They were erected at the private expense of the scholar-bishop Alexander of Nicaea, a benefaction in the spirit of the affluent professors of the Second Sophistic. The Byzantine definition of what constituted a civilised city was essentially a classical one, with churches substituting for temples and with the addition of that greatest of Byzantine gifts to the world, the charitable institution.[30] In the hey-day of the Roman empire, Pausanias regarded government offices, a gymnasium, a theatre, a marketplace, an aqueduct, and a fountain as minimum requirements.[31] His list is almost identical with that contained in the Procopian account (*Aed.* 2. 10. 22) of Justinian's rebuilding of Antioch.[32]

As with Christodorus' poem, the *Buildings* of Procopius is another tedious-looking document ("Dull and monotonous" was the verdict of Dewing, the Loeb editor) that is full of important information about Byzantine policies and priorities. The first book is quite naturally devoted to the capital, beginning with an account of St. Sophia and the other churches (1. 1–1. 9. 18). It is good to see that more than affluent and empty piety was at stake. As Gibbon remarked about the library and harem of the Roman emperor Gordian II, some of these buildings were for use as well as ostentation. Thus, one shrine was intended for socialising in (1. 6. 4), another (1. 6. 5–8) for the incurably sick. With these to his credit, it is easy to forgive the emperor the one-upmanship evinced in his renovation of a small and gloomy shrine of the Archangel Michael put up by a private benefactor (1. 3. 14–8).[33] Other imperial works singled out by Procopius are cisterns for public drinking-water (1. 11. 10–11), a seaside promenade (1. 11. 1–10), a hostel for visitors to the city (1. 11. 23–7), and above all the Metanoia convent for reformed prostitutes, a project in which Theodora (given her own past, the irony is obvious) interested herself as much as her husband. The notoriously irreconcilable pair of verdicts on this scheme offered by Procopius in the *Buildings* (1. 9. 5–10) and the *Secret History* (17. 5–6) probably reflects in part the controversy the policy caused.[34] Justinian was no more or less successful than anyone else in eliminating prostitution; his solution, however, was emulated by Michael IV,[35] and has been tried in modern times by the communist governments of China and Vietnam.

Unlike the *Res Gestae* of Augustus, which enumerates only that emperor's metropolitan buildings and rebuildings,[36] the greater part of Procopius' account is given over to the benefits conferred on the provinces. Apart from the provision of military defences, the commonest item is concern for supplies of public drinking-water (2. 2. 1–2, and *passim*). Like any well-intentioned modern government, he sometimes had to reckon with human cussedness. Those who think that ecology is a modern worry will be shaken to find (2. 9. 12–17) the natives of Hierapolis polluting their chief source of water by laundering and throwing rubbish in it.

The overall impression is of a policy of considerable pragmatism and imagination, with no expense shared. Justinian was as willing to fortify Anchialus (3. 7. 19–25) to protect those who went there for its therapeutic warm waters as to develop roads for the territory of the Tzani in order to keep the newly-converted Christians there "pious" through intercourse with their neighbours (3. 6. 1–14). Local needs and capabilities were taken into account. The long register of projects in Jerusalem and the East (5. 9. 1–38) is unique in the *Buildings* in that it contains churches and social works, not forts as in all other lists. Nor were the provinces necessarily fobbed off with second-best; the Church of the Apostles near Ephesus is expressly stated (5. 1. 4–6) to have been a rival to the one in Constantinople, and the Church in Jerusalem (5. 6. 1–26) is "incomparable". Finally, it is worth noting that when he felt he could trust them, the emperor gave money to the locals and left the rest to them (3. 4. 8).

As we have seen, Byzantine definitions of the good life extended well beyond defence walls and reservoirs. From time to time in the *Buildings*, Justinian can be seen furnishing baths, theatres, and the like. But relatively sparingly, and after a definite pattern. He is most lavish with cities where he had a distinguished Roman predecessor to live up to, or which he is founding in someone's honour. Thus, Circessium has its public baths restored (2. 6. 10–11) since they had been built by Diocletian; likewise Zenobia (2. 8. 24), whose baths and stoas had been the work of *the* Zenobia, and the great cities of Carthage (6. 5. 8–11) where Romans and Vandals had to be surpassed and Leptis Magna (6. 4. 1–5) where emulation of Septimius Severus was called for. The new city in honour of Helena, mother of Constantine, was predictably lavish (5. 2. 1–5). Even less surprisingly so was Justiniana Prima, built to commemorate the emperor's own birthplace of Taurisium (4. 1. 17–27), a model classical-cum-Byzantine foundation. Yet the best example of all is the virtual rebuilding of Antioch (2. 10. 19–25) as a deutero-Constantinople, with all the classical and Christian amenities. Here,

above all, Justinian shows himself to be both a Roman and a Christian emperor.[37]
In North American terms, the policies of Justinian are a mixture of aid and local initiative grants. To Procopius they are a theme for both praise and damnation. For when we turn from the eulogies of the *Buildings* to the diatribes of the *Secret History*, the emperor is found under attack for destroying the basis of civilised life, in the provinces as well as the capital (*Anecd.* 26. 1–11). He is said to have removed state support from rhetors, school teachers, and doctors; to have confiscated local revenues earmarked for these and for practicalities such as street lighting;[38] and to have closed the theatres, hippodromes, and circuses.

There is no mention of schools or premises for higher education in the *Buildings*. As with education itself, their provision will have been largely the responsibility of private individuals and local communities. We do not know much about the minutiae of elementary Byzantine education.[39] But schools there clearly were, since the record shows beyond any doubt that it was possible to acquire an education at all levels of society, in the provinces as well as the capital. Just how many Byzantines were literate at any one period is a matter of continuing debate.[40] In general, a distinction needs to be made between functional literacy and higher education. Most of the saints (not all) could read and write,[41] and this seems taken for granted in both their urban and rural provincial worlds. Good evidence of this is furnished by the *Pratum Spirituale* of John Moschus, a document of particular interest and relevance thanks to the wide geographical area encompassed by its adventures.[42] Whilst Moschus and Sophronius are waiting for an audience with the sophist Stephen in Alexandria (77), they sit in the Tetrapylon reading the books they have with them, presumably bibles. There is also the old man whose remarkable piety permits him to keep his eyes glued to his bible whilst three young men disport with a whore in a lodging house in Tarsus (31). Other typical characters include the erudite eunuch abbot Cosmas (40) and a pair of heroes, Theodore the philosopher and the calligrapher Zoilus (171). Further pertinent anecdotes involve the pious destruction of two volumes of Nestorian heresy (46), and (modern scholars will relish this!) a miraculous textual emendation (147). Literacy at this level tends to the utilitarian, its main purpose being the conversion or refutation of pagans and heretics. A simple old man rebukes two quibbling intellectuals for being φιλόλογοι rather than true φιλόσοφοι (156; cf. 195) Cosmas the Studite (172) had the biggest private library in Alexandria, from which he freely lent books to all comers. Unhappily, to modern taste, the exclusive use to which this collection and munificence was put was refutation of the Jews.

Education was not confined to the three R's. Surprising specialisms were sometimes available. In his *Lives of the Eastern Saints*,[43] John of Ephesus alludes to a poor widow who lived from art and who gave art lessons for money to young girls. We cannot say how typical this sort of thing was. It is a tidbit of information both precious and frustrating. Does a woman teaching girls betoken artistic apartheid? Or may it have led to a distinctive "feminist" school?

This is not the place for an essay on women in Byzantium. But a further word on the subject is apposite. Eudocia, Cassia, Anna Comnena are all familiar names. All imperial ones, too. It is hardly surprising that royal ladies should enjoy particular access to literacy. Apart from Anna's well-known account of her own education, there is an interesting snippet in the *Suda* concerning one Dioscorius, a grammarian who rose to hold both the urban and praetorian prefectures:[44] he was retained to give instruction to the daughters of Leo I.

Not all were royal women. Hypatia comes immediately to mind. There is also a certain Theosebeia, author of a single epigram (*A P* 7. 559) on the subject of great doctors of the past. She could, partly in light of her poem's theme, be the sister of Zosimus the alchemist, the probable dedicatee of his work.[45] The Camerons,[46] without dwelling on the consequences, include her in the *Cycle* of Agathias. This would make Theosebeia the only female member of that group; her presence might be connected to Agathias' own sister Eugenia, commemorated by her brother as skilled in poetry and law.[47]

At the elementary level, the pupil's point of view is rarely heard. The boy whose prize-day poem survives in a small fragment of papyrus[48] clearly enjoyed his education, looking forward as he does to many more years as a student. However, this form "swot" is probably no more typical of his class than the young Euaristus the Studite[49] who worked right through his lunch hours! The average school almost certainly was not, and need not have been, more than minimal in size and facilities. There must have been many Byzantine equivalents to the little red school house.

There is much better information about premises for higher education. In a recent paper[50] on academic instruction in Constantinople, A.J.M. Davids opined that "Where exactly a Libanius or a Themistius could have delivered their lectures is still a mystery." In fact, no mystery at all. The professors could do what they did in other cities. According to Eunapius (*VS* 483), all the sophists in Athens lectured in their private houses out of fear of town-gown riots. He instances the case of Julian of Cappadocia, whose house (bequeathed to him by Prohaeresius), albeit μικραν μεν και ευτελῆ, had a lecture theatre attached.[51] Libanius gave lectures at the baths in Nicomedia (*Or.* 1. 55), whilst at Antioch he could be heard in the temples, the museum, and the bouleuterion (*Or.* 1. 102–4). All of this was possible in other cities, including Constantinople.[52] There is ample evidence of the use by Themistius of one of the two senate houses in the capital for oratorical displays.[53] The Zeuxippus with its profusion of statues as backdrop would have made an admirably atmospheric venue. The most privileged will sometimes have performed in the palace itself; the least might be heard, as was the tub-thumper Uranius in Agathias, amidst the bookstalls of the Royal Stoa.[54]

There are two very good reasons why the cultural history of early Byzantium was richer and more diverse than is often recognised or admitted. As in imperial Rome, from the time of Augustus, men of letters continued to receive both legal and fiscal privileges.[55] These are spelled out in the prolix enactments of various emperors preserved in the Theodosian Code.[56] A logical consequence, also hallowed by Roman tradition, was the granting of preference to literary men for high positions in the imperial service. This principle is continually formulated in the literature of the period, not least by those who benefited from it. Symmachus is perhaps the snappiest: *vetus sententia est artes honore nutriri.*[57]

Alan Cameron has shown in a characteristically brilliant paper[58] how successful in material and political terms were many of the poets in early Byzantine Egypt. Only one of his arguments calls for comment. The reconstruction of some of the (in Cameron's words) journalistic warfare between the poets turns on the alleged rule that in titles of books and poems εις is used of a work written to honour someone, προς of a piece intended to refute or discredit. If this rule genuinely does hold, then a good deal of literary history will have to be rewritten. Zosimus the alchemist, for easy instance, would then have written his book against his own sister rather than dedicate it to her.[59] But in point of fact, there are notices in the *Suda* where προς cannot conform to Cameron's law: it is inconceivable that Paul the Silentiary intended his *Description of St. Sophia* against Justinian or Oribasius his books against Julian.[60]

Egypt had for long been hospitable to poets. A late third-century papyrus[61] from Oxyrhynchus lists, over the period 261/2-288/9, the names of prize-winners in competitions entitled to tax exemptions. There are three categories: heralds, trumpeteers, poets. That is something of a turn up for the bookish! Why? Some have inferred that Upper Egypt was relatively prosperous. Given the state of the Roman world, and the normal condition of Egypt, this does not seem very likely. Remembering the typically irascible comment of Eunapius[62] to the effect that Egyptians are mad about poetry but care for nothing serious, it may be permissible to see this policy as a quixotic one, comparable to the tax exemptions granted nowadays to *bona fide* artists by that not notably rich country, the Irish Republic.

Not that the phenomenon was restricted to Egypt. Take the case of Icarius, said by Libanius (*Or.* 1. 225) to have been appointed *comes Orientis* because of his poetic talents. Libanius numbered about twenty poets amongst his correspondents, some of whom had good careers.[63] Nor is it only poets who do well. Papyri[64] commemorate men such as the literary philanthropist Theon and the Tyrian orator-diplomat-general Maximus, both of whom could have walked out of the pages of Bowersock's *Greek Sophists in the Roman Empire.*

The other great thing about early Byzantine culture was that it was not monopolised by the natives and tastes of just one city. In this, it is comparable to the United States, where New York, Los Angeles, and Washington each lead in different areas of life, unlike Britain and most European countries where a single metropolis enjoys unhealthy domination. True, the Queen City[65] soon became a lure for men of letters, on the evidence of the unsympathetic Libanius (*Or.* 1. 30) who goes on to contrast unfavourably its neophilia with the "true" culture of Nicomedia (1. 52) and to brand its senate as a bunch of hard-drinking philistines (1. 75–6). But it is important to remember that these comments of a parochial and biased observer are at least partly literary *topoi.*[66] Important, because similar dispraise of Byzantine Athens on the part of Synesius, Aeneas of Gaza, and Michael Acominatos has been taken too seriously by some scholars as indicative of the intellectual decline of that city.[67] One can no more take these comments at face value than believe an Oxonian on the subject of Cambridge or a Harvard man on Yale.

Obviously, the capital was a magnet for many people. Procopius (*Aed.* 1. 11. 23–7) observes that there was such an influx of hopefuls from all walks of life that Justinian had to build a large hostel especially for them. The Constantinople "Y"? The same historian also gives us the rather moving (albeit not so intended) account of the future emperor Justin I, an illiterate peasant from the backwoods, setting out with only toasted bread in his bag to seek his fortune in the big city (*Anecd.* 6. 2–3). The same story is later told of Basil I.[68] One thinks of Dick Whittington, or the young Samuel Johnson riding on horseback from Derby to London to make good in Grub Street. Another who came was Amalasuntha, who thought (rightly, but not, alas, how she had hoped) to change her life by leaving the Goths for Constantinople (*Anecd.* 16. 1–5).

Just as it is notoriously hard to find a Roman writer actually born in the city of Rome, so provincial immigrants bulk very large in the literary history of early Byzantium. Prejudice they must on occasion have encountered; but it should be remembered that prejudice is not simply a matter of master and subject, or rivalry between metropolis and province. A glance at one such career will be a convenient way of pulling many threads together.

John Lydus[69] left his native city of Philadelphia for Constantinople at the age of twenty-one. He employs the emotional language of the standard rags-to-riches autobiography: from a home town "below Mount Tmolus" to "this Blessed City". The plan from the beginning was to get into the civil service. As with all civil services, one had to be patient. While he waited, John kicked his heels profitably by enrolling in the philosophy courses of Agapius, a successor of Proclus. Here he may have met another provincial place-seeker of the reign of Anastasius, the poet Christodorus.[70] In his choice of courses, John was shrewdly cautious. Agapius was a pagan, but the lectures John attended emphasized not so much Plato as Aristotle, a classic thought by the Christian authorities to be somewhat less subversive.[71]

Philosophy, however, promptly took a back seat when John obtained a position as a shorthand writer, a breed (it is worth remembering) detested by Libanius, thanks to Zoticus, a fellow-citizen just promoted to praetorian prefect. Zoticus, though quite naturally a hero of John, was in reality not all that more admirable than the great villain of the *De Magistratibus*, John the Cappadocian. His tips on how to make extra money from the job enabled Lydus, on his own coy admission, to come into possession (σωφρόνως, *he* claims) of a thousand gold pieces.[72] Graft regularly abets and is abetted by nepotism: the partnership of Zoticus and John will not have been impeded by another fellow-official, Ammianus, who happened to be a nephew of John's father.[73] One thousand gold pieces a year compared all too well with John's official salary of twenty-four. To show his gratitude, he produced a panegyric on Zoticus. Pleased by what he heard, and no doubt influenced by the fact that it was only a short poem, the prefect rewarded John with a gold piece for every line. This was no unique transaction; the poet Oppian had once got the same rate from Marcus Aurelius.[74]

Another source of money for John was his wife, procured for him by Zoticus at the promptings of Ammianus. Though he duly praises her quality, John openly regards the lady as preeminently a financial and political boon.[75] Subsequently, Justinian invited him to deliver a panegyric before a distinguished audience, which task John performed so well that the emperor then commissioned a history of the imperial wars. Shrewdly, Justinian does not put more cash into the Lydian's ever-receptive palm. Instead, a literary contract and permission to moonlight from the service as a teacher. John was clearly disappointed, but could hardly argue. He goes on to vegetate ever more bookishly at his desk until retirement with the rank of *cornicularius* after a total career of forty years and four months.

Depending on circumstances, John could take the smooth with the smooth or the rough with the rough. A provincial himself, he is vicious on the accents and characteristics of Syrians and Cappadocians, classical prejudices found elsewhere at this time.[76] Above all, John is eloquent on the subject of Latin, constantly lamenting its decline, in complete contrast to a Libanius who regretted its vogue in his day. For John and others, Latin was an emotional issue tearing them between passion and reason. The large number of sometimes surprising Latin authors paraded by John may or may not truly reflect his personal knowledge of that language.[77] Though John himself is inclined to put the blame on Cyrus of Panopolis (*De Mag.* 2. 12. 2; 3. 42. 2) for discontinuing the issuance of decrees in Latin, blame should more properly go to Cyrus' emperor, Theodosius II, whose arrangements for the new University of Constantinople in 425 had given Greek two more professorial chairs than Latin. That there was still an audience for Roman poetry in John's lifetime is evidenced by the panegyrics of Priscian and Corippus; there is no point in writing, of all things, encomia if no one can read them. Sadly, however, the true state of affairs is belied by an official admission[78] on the part of Justinian, himself the last Latin-speaking emperor, that Greek had almost ousted Latin for practical purposes. John nourished his disappointments, but he had a good career. So no doubt did Agathias (to take a complementary example), though it may be a trifle naive to take his claim of a heavy workload at face value: such protestations were commonplace.[79] Neither man came from an important centre, albeit Agathias had plans to write on the *patria* of his (*Hist., praef.* 15). The popularity of this genre constitutes a tribute to the continuing spirit of civic pride,[80] another legacy of classical Greek particularism and the Roman municipal *civitas* ethos. This spirit comes out in other ways. At their very different levels, Libanius and Malalas are equally biased in favour of their native Antioch. And while it did not normally take very much to provoke an epigram from the atrabilious Palladas of Alexandria, his rejoinder (*AP* 11. 291) to a certain Nicander for lampooning his native city is worth remarking.

Throughout the period of the Second Sophistic, there were many centres of literary training and practice.[81] The number is reduced by the late fifth and early sixth centuries, and some different names have come into the picture. Juxtaposition of old and new provides instructive balance. As earlier seen, Egypt dominates, if she does not monopolise, one aspect of literary history down to the reign of Anastasius. Cameron rightly emphasises the plethora of poets coming from the Thebaid rather than Alexandria. But this again is nothing new. Alexandria had lagged curiously in the production of sophists in the first and second centuries, even though the dearth is not quite so bad as Bowersock,[82] misled by too narrow a reliance on Philostratus, implies. There were Egyptians and Egyptians. It is a common spectator sport to ridicule the versifications of Dioscorus of Aphrodito in the later sixth century; Page could not even bring himself to print them![83] And indeed, unless we take the charitable view that what we have are rough drafts only (very rough!), it can be assumed (or hoped) that he was a small fish in a small pond. Yet one's humanity should not slumber under the spell of literary criticism. There is something very poignant about his writing a poem to honour the arrival of a statue of Justin II in Egypt, one of several echoes of a provincial sense of remoteness.[84]

Athens holds a special interest in the context of this paper, thanks to the celebrated issue of precisely what, if anything, happened to the Academy in 529. Here again, Alan Cameron has settled the issue, although not to universal satisfaction.[85] Additional support for his thesis is provided by a much-neglected source, the Autobiography of Ananias of Shirak.[86] Written in the mid-seventh century by a Christian Armenian, this one man's intellectual odyssey gives a fascinating picture of the cultural geography of the time. Wishing to improve his mathematics, Ananias automatically set out for Greece. His first port of call was Theodoupolis, where a Christian scholar Eliazar referred him to a mathematician by the name of Christodotus[87] in Fourth Armenia. Ananias duly went there, but after six months had exhausted that savant's knowledge, and so went on to Constantinople. There he was met by friends who redirected him to the expatriate Byzantine sophist Tychicus, whom they billed as an influential polymath, skilled in Armenian and numbering princes amongst his students.

Tychicus must have been approved by the authorities, since Ananias found himself in the company of the deacon Philagrius who was chaperoning a flock of Christian youth to Trebizond for instruction under him. He did not disappoint Ananias who spent eight years with him, learning mathematics and much else. Tychicus had a large and fascinating library: "secret books and open, sacred and secular, scientific and historical, medical and chronological." He also had an intriguing autobiography of his own to relate. In his youth he had served in the army in Armenia, with some sort of furlough during the reign of Maurice which he devoted to the study of literature. Returning to the colours, he fled to Antioch after sustaining a wound in a battle against the Persians. His wound healed, Tychicus set off on a scholarly pilgrimage that took him to Jerusalem, Alexandria, Rome, Constantinople, and (*the* point, as far as Cameron's thesis is concerned) Athens, which he calls the city of philosophy[88] and where he found an unnamed philosopher to instruct him. Clearly, Athens is still very much in the business of philosophy. And Tychicus remained very much the Hellene, undeterred by his long pedagogic intercourse with Armenians from calling them "lazy and stupid."

Equally absorbing for the light it sheds on the intellectual cross-currents of the sixth and seventh centuries is Ananias' Tract on Easter. Extensive research on the niceties of the Christian calendar in the reign of Justinian was conducted at Alexandria, still the "metropolis of all the sciences," despite the suppression of its law school in 533, by a stuningly international conference of scholars: Aeas of Alexandria supported by a coterie of local experts, the Jewish Phineas of Tiberias, Gabriel of Syria, John the Arab, Abdiah from the Ethiopians, Sergius the Macedonian, Eulogius from the Greeks, Gigas the Roman, and unnamed others to a grand total of thirty-six. Excluded was the Byzantine court physician Iron, thanks to some unspecified scholarly squabble; he promptly came up with a rival calendar of which Ananias thought very little.

On a more mundane level, but none the less interesting for that, is the cultural fusion attested to by Procopius in a passage (*Aed.* 3. 3. 9–11) describing the border zone of Chorzone where Byzantine and Persian subjects lived together in peace, sharing intermarriage and common markets, refusing to fight each other when ordered.

Gaza produced a cluster of writers in the early sixth century. It is going too far, however, to represent them as a school distinctively different in anything. Even the number of savants is not all that impressive when one considers that a single family in Tralles gave birth to five distinguished brothers: Anthemius, the celebrated engineer and architect; the mathematician Metrodorus; Olympius a lawyer; and two doctors, Dioscorus and Alexander.[89] The interests and productions of the Gaza scholars were by and large typical. The only unusual item (omitted by Downey![90]) was the play written by Timotheus as part of a campaign against the chrysargyron tax.[91] Any sort of secular drama in this period is unusual enough; one written for agit-prop purposes may have been unique.[92]

Timotheus was a man of characteristically wide learning, writing also about animals and birds. His play, whatever its precise nature, serves to illustrate a feature of Byzantine literature not always appreciated. This literature is often envisaged as the worst sort of ivory tower unreality, archaism for archaism's sake, and so forth. Gibbon, of course, must take a good share of the blame for such stereotypes. The truth is frequently very different. As Cameron showed, poetry for the Egyptian adventurers of the early Byzantine period was a profession, something to be exploited or not according to circumstance. An attitude not uniquely Egyptian: Agathias (*Hist., praef.* 8, 11–13) and Menander Protector (fr. 1) are blatantly honest about art for art's sake versus writing that brings tangible reward. It is notable how many of the *Cycle* poets were lawyers or otherwise career men. Their epigrams were the fruits of their spare time. The old Roman notion that senators did not write poetry seriously was still alive.[93] This central feature serves to bring many aspects of early Byzantine life and literature into clearer focus. The practical element is manifest in morality and miracle: witness the dominant themes in the *Pratum Spirituale* of Moschus,[94] also many of the activities of the Stylites, a worthier side of

their "aerial penance".[95] One of Agathias' objections to Uranius (*Hist.*
2. 29. 6) was that he held no firm (i.e. practically useful) view of God.
Basil's approach to pagan literature emphasized the practical value to
be had from a selective reading of it.[96] This approach is visible at many
levels. Churchgoers and members of literary circles from the age of
Gregory of Nazianzus to that of Photius copied down fine phrases and
flosculi for their own use.[97] Byzantine historians are justly criticised for
many faults: archaism, affectation, distortion of facts for the sake of
literacy pastiche. Yet it is no perversity to suggest that in one way they
were superior to their classical avatars. The provision of a formal
bibliography by Evagrius,[98] the punctiliousness of Agathias and others
in citing texts and sources *in extenso*,[99] the willingness to acknowledge
openly and honestly the work of others (Agathias' referral of his readers to Paul's *Description of St. Sophia* is arguably one of the first
scientific footnotes in historiography),[100] all of this puts many of the
big names of the past to shame.

An early opponent of Libanius competed against him in a battle of
declamations with a prose ecphrasis of the Great Church in Antioch,
built by Constantius in 341 (*Or.* 1. 39–41). A microcosm of the pagan-
Christian conflict of that age. By the time of Justinian, this was more
or less over, though we should remember that the converted Syrian
Jew Romanus the Melode with his punning attacks (33, str. 17) on the
old culture (a piquant opposite to Palladas of Alexandria and his
punning attacks on the new) was as much as a feature of Justinianic
literary life as the classicising epigrammatists.[101] This co-existence is a
tribute to the healthy diversity of the literary life of the period. The
adoption and adaption of classical forms to the new order was continued and perfected. The famous enterprise of the brothers Apollina-
ris, who responded to Julian's ban on Christian teachers by rewriting
the gospels and so on in classical forms, had shown the way. Homeric
verses as church dedications[102] and the poems in the first book of the
Anthology[103] mark a completion of the process. By their practical
streak, the Byzantines provided the answer to Tertullian: Athens had a
lot to do with Jerusalem. The Romans had absorbed one culture, that
of Greece; the Byzantines amalgamated two, to create a third: their
own.

Notes

1. For the ideology of this question, cf. N. G. Wilson, *An Anthology of
Byzantine Prose* (Berlin, 1971), 1–2.

2. 'The Hellenistic Origins of Byzantine Literature,' *DOP* 17 (1963), 39–52.

3. For some valuable generalisations, cf. W. T. Treadgold, 'The Revival of Byzantine Learning and the Revival of the Byzantine State,' *AHR* 84 (1979), 1245–66.

4. E. Stein, *Histoire du Bas-Empire 2* (Paris, 1949), 692.

5. C. Mango, 'Antique Statuary and the Byzantine Beholder,' *DOP* 17 (1963), 55–75.

6. An epigram by Ablabius *illustrius* (*A P* 9. 762) seems to speak of an art collector, and Ablabius has been assigned to the *Cycle* of Agathias by Averil and Alan Cameron, 'The Cycle of Agathias,' *JHS* 86 (1966), 6–25. Despite their confidence, this is quite uncertain, as is their subsequent ('Further Thoughts on the *Cycle* of Agathias,' *JHS* 87 (1967), 131) removal of Eutolmius *illustrius* from the *Sylloge* of Palladas to the *Cycle*. Apparently on the strength of his title, an argument, employed in the first volume of *PLRE* (Cambridge, 1971) to deny authorship of the epigram in question to any of the earlier Ablabii. But an *illustrius* in the fourth century is feasible; cf. the account of this title in *PW* 9 cols. 1071–4. It is also worth noting that, apart from Ablabius and Eutolmius, no other *illustres* occur in the Camerons' register of *Cycle* poets. The epigram itself could imply a single find, perhaps not premeditated, rather than (as, e.g., Paton, the Loeb editor) a regular collector.

7. Cf. Mango, *art. cit.*, 58.

8. Ed. Preger (Leipzig, 1901–7), 2, 221, 24; 2. 278, 200.

9. For some archaeological confirmation or at least hint of this, see Mango, *art. cit.*, 58 and the excavation report cited therein.

10. Cedrenus, p. 648 (Bonn); Migne, *PG* 121. 708A.

11. *HA, AS* 29. 2, citing a contemporary source which, if genuine, might have been an ecphrasis.

12. On this time-honoured issue, see now B. Baldwin, 'Photius and Poetry,' *BMGS* 4 (1978), 9–14.

13. The absence of Polybius may support the suspicions of Byzantine neglect voiced by Momigliano, 'Polybius' Reappearance in Western Europe,' *Entretiens Hardt* 20 (1973), 348 (= *Essays in Ancient and Modern Historiography* (London, 1977), 80–1). Plutarch and some representatives of the Second Sophistic are commemorated in Byzantine epigram; cf. *AP* 16. 315 (Thomas Scholasticus compares Aristides to Demosthenes and Thucydides), 331 (Agathias on a painting of Plutarch).

14. That the statue of Caesar is physically close to that of Chryses is guaranteed by the word εγγυς (92).

15. A howler perpetrated in the Commentaries on Bede by Thomas Anglicus (Migne, *PL* 63, 752).

16. According to the *Suda* X 525 (Adler).

17. Cf. B. Baldwin, 'Virgilius Graecus,' *AJP* 97 (1976), 361–8.

18. Creusa was a uniquely Virgilian character; see Austin's long note on *Aen.* 2. 795.

19. *De Mag.* 3. 64. 5: *De Mens.* 4. 116. 2. In the first of these passages, John refers to the *Erotica* of Apuleius. This may be his own predilection showing: he also adduces the Suetonian biographies of famous whores. Apuleius is also paraded as a philosopher by Cassiodorus, *Inst. Div.* 3. 12.

20. See, for notable instance, the elaborate account of the statue of an unnamed wrestler (228-40).

21. Cf. R. Browning, 'Homer in Byzantium,' *Viator* 8 (1975), 15-33. Needless to say, Homer (like Shakespeare) will sometimes have been more admired than read.

22. *Suda* M 194 (Adler).

23. A difficulty immortalised in the following exchange from Shakespeare's *Merchant of Venice* (Act 2. 2. 41-7): *Gobbo*: Master young gentleman, I pray you which is the way to Master Jew's? *Launcelot*: Turn up on your right hand at the next turning, but at the next turning of all, on your left: marry, but at the very next turning, turn of no hand, but turn down indirectly to the Jew's house. *Gobbo*: By God's sonties, 'twill be a hard way to hit.

24. It is known from other sources that this was an inscriptional poem: cf. Averil Cameron, *Agathias* (Oxford, 1970), 24.

25. Agathian authorship was denied simply on the grounds of taste by A. Mattsson, *Untersuchungen zur Epigrammsammlung des Agathias* (Lund, 1942), 88.

26. See the admirable analysis of R. C. McCail, 'The Erotic and Ascetic Poetry of Agathias Scholasticus,' *Byzantion* 41 (1971), 227-32.

27. One of which is a largely Homeric parody, the other almost identical to *AP* 10. 87 (Palladas): cf. E. Kalinka, 'Das Palladas-Epigramm in Ephesos,' *Wiener Studien* 24 (1902), 292-5.

28. For these variously amusing and wearisome exercises, somewhat comparable to the zeal for trivia in modern "Camp", see A. S. Pease, 'Things without Honor,' *CPhil* 4 (1909), 27-42. Interest in them persisted into later Byzantium and mediaeval Europe. Eugenius of Palermo, for instance, manufactured an iambic poem in refutation of Lucian's *Muscae Encomium;* cf. the edition of M. Gigante *(Palermo, 1964)*.

29. See Appendix 51 to Friedlaender's *Sittengeschichte Roms.*

30. Which compliment does not overlook the philanthropic capacity of Greece and Rome, on which see A. R. Hands, *Charities and Social Aid in Greece and Rome* (London, 1968). But as even the emperor Julian had to admit, they were outdone by the Christians in practical charity.

31. Pausanias 10. 4. 1, a judgement no doubt influenced by his own extensive travels.

32. Similar Byzantine definitions of the good life can be found in the historians Olympiodorus of Thebes (fr. 43) and Priscus of Panium (fr. 22).

33. For the text and interpretation of this passage, cf. B. Baldwin, 'senator or Senator?' *Glotta* 57 (1979), 227-8.

34. A notion perhaps enhanced by Procopius' statement (*Aed.* 1. 8. 20) that this was the long-awaited part of his narrative.

35. Psellus, *Chron.* 4. 36.

36. *RG* 19–21, a section of the document that must have aroused envy amongst at least some provincial readers.

37. In this context, it is worth comparing *Anon. Vales.* 2. 71 on the building programmes of that other would-be Roman, Theodoric the Goth.

38. According to Priscus (fr. 3a), Cyrus of Panopolis earned the applause of the Hippodrome factions for supplying lighting for the city's workshops both in the evening and the night. C. D. Gordon, *The Age of Attila* (Ann Arbor, 1960), 69, translated the passage but was at a loss to understand it. In fact, it can easily be explained. We know from Libanius (*Or.* 11. 267; 2. 6; 33. 35–7) that the famous street lighting at Antioch was achieved largely at private expense. Shopkeepers had to maintain oil lamps outside their premises. The same will have been true of Constantinople. Cyrus earned his popularity by subsidising or assuming the expense, thereby setting an enduring precedent.

39. There are good general accounts by G. Buckler in Baynes-Moss, *Byzantium* (repr. Oxford, 1961), 200–20; S. Runciman, *Byzantine Civilisation* (repr. Oxford, 1961), 223–39.

40. See above all P. Lemerle, *Le premier humanisme byzantin* (Paris, 1971), 255–7; R. Browning, 'Literacy in the Byzantine World,' *BMGS* 4 (1978), 39–54.

41. A matter thoroughly investigated by A. Moffatt, 'Schooling in the Iconoclast Centuries,' *Iconoclasm* (Birmingham, 1977), 85–92.

42. A point rightly emphasised by A. J. Butler, *The Arab Conquest of Egypt* (rev. ed., Oxford, 1978), 97–8. For Moschus in general, see H. Chadwick, 'John Moschus and his Friend Sophonius the Sophist,' *JTS* N.S. 25 (1974), 41–74.

43. *PO,* 1, 15–6; cf. H. J. Magoulias, 'Trades and Crafts in the Sixth and Seventh Centuries as viewed in the Lives of the Saints,' *Byzantinoslavica* 37 (1976), 11–35.

44. *Suda* D 1208 (Adler); like Cyrus of Panopolis before him, he may have held these offices simultaneously.

45. See later for a possible problem, with wider ramifications, about this.

46. *Art. cit.,* 8; see also the notice on Zosimus' sister in *PLRE* 1.

47. *AP* 7. 593, accepting the lemmatist's word on this, and making due discount for a filial exaggeration.

48. No. 100 in Page's collection of literary papyri (Loeb *Select Papyri,* 3).

49. His life is contained in *Anecd. Boll.* 41 (1923).

50. 'A Note on Academic Instruction in the Capitol of Constantinople,' *Studia Byzantina et Neohellenica Neerlandica* (Leiden, 1972), 235–40.

51. Cf. A. Frantz, 'From Paganism to Christianity in the Temples of Athens,' *DOP* 19 (1965), 187–205.

52. A full account is provided by J. W. Walden, *The Universities of Ancient Greece* (London, 1912), 267–9).

53. Demonstrated by Alan Cameron, 'Some Prefects called Julian,' *Byzantion* 47 (1977), 52.

54. Agathias, *Hist.* 2. 29. 2; cf. Aulus Gellius, *NA* 5. 4, for Roman debates in bookshops. Habitués of Blackwell's will recognise the phenomenon.

55. Fully documented and analysed in two admirable studies by G. W. Bowersock: *Augustus and the Greek World* (Oxford, 1965); *Greek Sophists in the Roman Empire* (Oxford, 1969).

56. See especially 6. 21; 13. 3 f; 14. 1; 14. 9; *Nov. Theod.* II. 11.

57. *EP.* 1. 43. Libanius, *Or.* 18. 158, is (predictably) eloquent on the subject of Julian's preferment of poets and historians; cf. W. E. Kaegi, 'The Emperor Julian's Assessment of the Significance and Function of History,' *Proc. Amer. Philos. Soc.* 108 (1964), 33. Anastasius, on the evidence of John Lydus, *De Mag.* 3. 50. 3, deemed only literary men suitable for the praetorian prefecture. John himself is a perfect example of the system: vain about his own learning, he regularly evaluates other officials on the basis of their education. For many other texts, and criticism of the principle, cf. A. Alföldi, *A Conflict of Ideas in the Late Roman Empire* (Oxford, 1952), 106 f. In his novel *The Masters* (Penguin ed., 28), C. P. Snow (himself a product of the system) quips nicely on the survival of the principle in Britain: "He's thought to stand a chance of the colonial service if he can scrape a third. Of course, I'm totally ignorant of these matters, but I can't see why our colonies should need third class men with some capacity for organised sports."

58. 'Wandering Poets: a Literary Movement in Byzantine Egypt,' *Historia* 14 (1965), 470–509.

59. *Suda* Z 168 (Adler); the notices of both Zosimus and Theosebeia in *PLRE* I regard the latter as dedicatee.

60. H 478, 0 543 (Adler).

61. *P. Ox.* 2338.

62. *VS* 493, making due allowance for the traditional nature of such generalising condemnations of Egyptians; cf. Tacitus, *Hist.* 1. 11; *HA, Quad. Tyr.* 7. 4; 8. 5; Ammianus 22. 6. 1; 22. 7. 4.

63. As listed by O. Seeck, *Briefe des Libanius* (Leipzig, 1906), 480, with the comments and additions of T. Viljamaa, *Studies in Greek Encomiastic Poetry of the Early Byzantine Period* (Helsinki, 1968), 26.

64. Texts in Page, *op. cit.*, nos. 130, 132; both characters are omitted from *PLRE* I.

65. This expression began to be applied to Constantinople in fourth-century oratory, when it was replacing Rome. The phrase is also used of Rome herself, and sometimes Antioch; the emperor Julian (*Or.* 1. 4) was being both passionate and rhetorical when he insisted that Rome was the queen of all cities. The phrase is ubiquitous in Menander Protector (frs. 9, 28, 43, 47, 49, 54, 63, 64), almost invariably in the context of people visiting or returning to

the capital: Byzantium is *the* place to which one comes. It also designates the capital in officialese: e.g. *P. Cairo Masp.* 67032; *P. Genev.* Inv. 210; *Cod. Just.* 1. 1. 7; 1. 11. 9.

66. See, for instance, Philostratus, *VS* 492, on the sophist Favorinus and the Roman senate; cf. Norman's note on Libanius, *Or.* 1. 75–6.

67. Synesius, *Ep.* 136; cf. H. I. Marrou, 'Synesius of Cyrene and Alexandrian Neoplatonism,' in *Paganism and Christianity in the Fourth Century*, ed. Momigliano (Oxford, 1963), 126–50. Aeneas of Gaza, *PG* 95. 877A; Michael Acominatos, ed. S. Lampros 2, 44. For the general issue, see the sensible remarks of Alan Cameron, 'The Last Days of the Academy at Athens,' *Proc. Cambr. Phil. Soc.* N.S. 15 (1969), 25–6, against the exaggerated view of Gaza put forward by G. Downey, *Gaza in the Early Sixth Century* (Oklahoma, 1963).

68. Cf. G. Ostrogorsky, *History of the Byzantine State* (Oxford, 1968), 232.

69. John tells his story in *De Mag.* 3. 26. 1 f; for some useful commentary, cf. T. F. Carney, *Bureaucracy in Traditional Society* (Lawrence, 1971).

70. At all events, John is the unique testimony here to Christodorus' poem *On the Pupils of the Great Proclus*, and the reference may have been intended as a courtesy.

71. Cf. Cameron, 'Last Days of the Academy,' 9.

72. Just as Cicero made an "honest profit" of 2,200,000 sesterces as a provincial governor in the late Roman Republic.

73. One cannot help noticing that Ammianus does not seem, overtly at least, to have helped John into the service. But he did assist him to find a wife, and may have put in a word; at any rate, John speaks highly of his character.

74. *Suda* 0 452 (Adler); Oppian got far more, since he was thus rewarded for all of his extensive poems.

75. Of many classical precedents, that of Agricola is perhaps best: *Hinc ad capessendos magistratus in urbem degressus Domitiam Decidianam, splendidis natalibus ortam, sibi iunxit; idque matrimonium ad maiora nitenti decus ac robur fuit* (Tacitus, *Agr.* 6. 1.).

76. Classicial attitudes are too familiar to require documentation. As is so often the case in any age, it is impossible to determine to what extent the racial and personal elements are interdependent. Had Marinus not been a Syrian, would John have disliked that breed so intensely? For some very British-looking views on the importance of accent, see Quintilian 1. 1. 13; *HA, Hadrian* 3. 1; Galen, *De ordine suorum librorum* 5; Philostratus, *VS* 553, 563. Cf. Procopius, *Anecd.* 14. 2–3; 20. 17, for some offensive comments in John's vein on other people's accents.

77. Opinions range between Wachsmuth's contemptuous dismissal (Teubner edition of the *De Ostentis*, 39) of John as *homine Latini sermonis misere gnaro* and the belief of B. Rubin, *Das Zeitalter Justinians* (Berlin, 1960), 427, that his knowledge was sound. When John can be seen translating

Latin, as in *De Mag.* 3. 3. 1, mistakes do occur. But he clearly knew some. The
parade of authors includes Apuleius, Petronius, and the (to us) obscure satirist
Turnus. For tables and commentary, cf. Carney, *op. cit.*, 47–76, who is, however, misleading on several counts. For instance, John's knowledge of Virgil is
not restricted to the *Aeneid; De Mens.* 4. 73 alludes to *Eclogues* 1. 30, fascinat-
ingly in that it imports the fashionable modern theory of political allegory in
Virgil's pastoral. Carney also misses references to Ovid (*De Mens.* 4. 2) and
Seneca (*De Mens.* 4. 107). In the wider context, of course, the precise amount
of John's own Latin expertise is irrelevant: the dropping of all these names
presupposes an audience which would be impressed by them.

78. *Novel.* 7 (near the beginning).
79. Agathias, *Hist.* 3. 1. 4, a claim by Averil Cameron, *Agathias*, 3, and
supportable by the statement of John of Epiphaneia (fr. 1) that Agathias was
one of the capital's most eminent lawyers. For the commonplace nature of the
overworked man of law, cf. Horace, *Serm.* 1. 1. 10 (with Palmer's note).
80. Cf. Agathias, *Hist.* 5. 21. 2, where Justinian's adornment of the imperial birthplace if commended as the proper thing to do. For a good general
treatment, see A.H.M. Jones, *The Later Roman Empire* (Oxford, 1964), 721.
81. Conveniently tabulated at the end of K. Gerth's often unreliable article
on the Second Sophistic in *PW*, Suppl. 8, cols. 719–82. Cf. Bowersock, *Greek
Sophists in the Roman Empire*, 17–29; Walden, *op. cit.*, 116.
82. *Op. cit.*, 20–1, to which may be added Archibios (*Suda* A 4106), Dio-
dorus Valerius (*Suda* D 1150), Pollio Valerius (*Suda* P 2166), and Ptolemy
Chennos (*Suda* P 3037). Records of other cities can similarly be amplified.
83. *Op. cit.*, pref. xiii: "No useful purpose would be served by republishing
the fragments of Dioscorus of Aphrodito." Most of Dioscorus' work is in E.
Heitsch, *Die Griechischen Dichterfragmente Der Römischen Kaiserzeit* (Göt-
tingen, 1963). For the man and his work, see J. Maspero, 'Un dernier poète
grec d'Égypte,' *REG* 24 (1911), 426–81; H. I. Bell, 'An Egyptian Village in the
Age of Justinian,' *JHS* 66 (1944), 21–36; A. Calderini, 'Piccola Letteratura di
Provincia nei Papiri.' *Aegyptus* 2 (1921), 151–3; R. Keydell in *PW*, Suppl. 6,
cols. 27–9; Cameron, 'Wandering Poets,' *passim;* Viljamaa, *op. cit.*, 32–3,
86–91, 122–9.
84. Justinian allegedly exacerbated provincial feelings of isolation by cur-
tailing the postal service: Procopius, *Anecd.* 30. 1–11. In an earlier age, Eunapius (fr. 74) complained that residence in Sardis cut him off from western
happenings.
85. 'The Last Days of the Academy at Athens,' *Proc. Cambr. Phil. Soc.*
N.S. 15 (1969), 25–6. Alison Frantz, 'Pagan philosophers in Christian Athens,'
Proc. Amer. Philos. Soc. 119 (1975), 129–38, remained unconvinced on
archaeological grounds. As a supporter of Cameron's basic thesis, I find three
of his arguments vulnerable. First, I think that R. C. McCail, 'Κυαματρῶξ
᾽Αττικος in Paulus Silentiarius, *Descriptio* 125,' *Proc. Cambr. Phil. Soc.* N.S.
16 (1970), 79–82, has cogently demonstrated that there is no allusion to Sim-

plicius in this line. To McCail's thesis one can add the fact that the line is cited (unnoticed by Adler) in the *Suda* K 2578 as illustration of the ancient Athenians. Second, the wealth of texts that Simplicius clearly had at his disposal need not imply that he was working in Athens. In spite of Cameron's doubts, Alexandria, dubbed the city of all the sciences by Ananias of Shirak (on whom, see below), could have supplied all the books Simplicius needed. The large private libraries of the day should not be overlooked. Apart from that of Cosmas the Studite (cf. above), the Syrian bishop of Amida, Moro Bar Kustant, formed a large collection whilst in Alexandria in the early sixth century, according to Zachariah of Mitylene, *Chron.*, p. 209. So in Ananias' day did the sophist Tychicus in Trebizond. Finally, there is no need to suppose with Cameron that participles of the verb κρατεῖν are to be understood as neoplatonist code-phrases for the Christian authorities. They are used by secular historians such as Priscus (frs. 21, 24, 29, 42) to denote both Byzantine emperors and barbarian chieftains.

86. Translated into English by F. C. Conybeare, *BZ* 6 (1897), 572–84, along with his Tract on Easter.

87. Christodotus clearly had Christian parents but, as Cameron, 'Wandering Poets,' 475, n. 33, sensibly observes, a man need not be presumed as Christian as his name.

88. When all due allowance has been made for literary flourishes, this constant habit of extolling particular cities as the centre of a discipline may be taken to reflect the continuance of local pride and provincial activity, sometimes perhaps with a conscious effort to rival the Queen City affectation of Constantinople itself. Thus Beirut is the "School of Greek Learning" in Eusebius, *De Mart. Pal.* 4. 3; the "Nurse of Tranquil Life", Nonnus, *Dionys.* 41. 396; the "Pride of Phoenicia", Agathias, *Hist.* 2. 15. 2.

89. Agathias, *Hist.* 5. 6. 4–6. The subsequent careers of this remarkable quintet serve to illustrate the theme of cultural geography. Justinian, hearing of their fame, summoned Anthemius and Metrodorus to the capital, where their practical talents were harnessed to imperial use; Olympius also seems to have come to Constantinople (Agathias is not explicit, but his admiring reference betokens personal acquaintance); Dioscorus stayed in Tralles; Alexander, intriguingly, accepted a distinguished offer from Rome.

90. *Op. cit.*, 112.

91. *Suda* T 621 (Adler); Cedrenus, p. 627 (Bonn); *PG* 121. 684A.

92. According to Photius (*Bibl.*, cod. 279), the fourth-century poet Andronicus included drama in his repertoire. Back in the age of Trajan and Hadrian, the Alexandrian grammarian Ptolemy Chennos produced what the *Suda* (P 3037) calls an historical drama entitled *Sphinx*.

93. See on this G. Williams, *Change and Decline: Roman Literature in the Early Empire* (Berkeley & Los Angeles, 1978), 53. The caustic Eunapian distinction between poetry and usefulness will be recalled.

94. The commonest miracles reported by Moschus represent wish-fulfilment at the personal and society level: preservation of a vow of male chastity: 14, 39, 60, 152, 205, 217; calming of wild beasts: 2, 18—cf. Theodoret, *HR* 1375D, for a hermit keeping tame lions, with an obvious classical precedent in Androcles; suppression of bandits: 15, 143, 155, 165, 212; conversion or at least refutation of pagans, heretics, or other sinners: 32, 47, 156, 195. Christ himself, of course, preferred miracles giving practical benefits to gratuitous conjuring.

95. As Gibbon so nicely called it; cf. the superb article of P. Brown, 'The Rise and Function of the Holy Man in Late Antiquity,' *JRS* 61 (1971), 80–101.

96. For Basil on Greek Literature, cf. the excellent edition of N. G. Wilson (London, 1975).

97. See the detailed study of this whole question by H. Hunger, 'On the Imitation (Mimesis) of Antiquity in Byzantine Literature,' *DOP* 23 4 (1969 70), 15–38.

98. *HE* 6. 24.

99. E.g., Agathias, 2. 17. 6–9; Menander Protector, fr. 12; John Lydus, *De Mag.* 3, 46, 4.

100. *Hist.* 5. 9. 6–8, an act of considerable self-restraint, given the marvellous opportunity for ecphrasis thus surrendered. Olympiodorus of Thebes was no doubt the true pioneer in these practical virtues; cf. E. A. Thompson, 'Olympiodorus of Thebes,' *CQ* 38 (1944), 43–52.

101. Assuming the correctness of Romanus' location in this period by Papadopoulos-Kerameus and Maas. For discussion and full bibliography, see P. Maas & C. A. Trypanis, introd., xv–xvi, to their edition of the *Cantica Genuina* (Oxford, 1963).

102. *SEG* 8. 119, 243; cf. R. Browning, 'Homer in Byzantium', 21.

103. Observe the triumphant lemma to this collection: "Let the pious and holy Christian epigrams take precedence, even if the pagans do not like it." For some features of them, cf. P. Waltz, 'Notes sur les épigrammes chrétiennes de l'Anthologie Grecque,' *Byzantion* 2 (1925), 317–28.

2

CITY AND COUNTRYSIDE
IN LATE ROMAN PANNONIA:
THE *REGIO SIRMIENSIS*

John W. Eadie
(University of Michigan)

When Attila and the Huns captured Sirmium and Bassiana in A.D.
441, the *regio Sirmiensis*—the rich grain-producing sector of Pannonia
between the Save and the Danube—passed irretrievably into barbarian
hands.[1] No longer able to call upon regular Roman troops for assistance and afraid to rely on the meagre protection their delapidated
defensive walls afforded, the inhabitants of the towns were forced to
choose between exile or collaboration. Not even the presence of the
praetorian prefect Apraemius, the last representative of Roman
authority in Pannonia, offered any guarantee of eventual rescue. And
when Apraemius decided to save his own skin by fleeing to Thessalonica, whatever resistance the local militia had mounted collapsed.[2]
Unlike previous barbarian groups that had passed through the *regio*
en route to Italy, and had lingered only to seize the necessary provi-
sions for the journey, the Huns occupied Sirmium and established
themselves as *possessores* in the adjacent countryside. For the next few
years the only contact between the *regio* and the central government
was through embassies sent out to recover imperial property or to
reassert imperial claims.[3] These missions may have maintained the

25

lines of communication between the capital and Barbaricum but they could not reestablish Roman authority in the regio.

If it is clear that the 'invasion' of Attila marks the end of Roman administration, it is equally clear that it was not the decisive factor in the Roman withdrawal from this sector of Pannonia. Decades of barbarian raids migrations had already destroyed the integrity of the regio and undermined the Roman resolve to defend this frontier zone. Here I do not intend to put forward an alternative date for the "end" of Roman occupation or to identify the invasion that ultimately persuaded the Roman government to withdraw. Rather, I propose to examine developments between 375 and 441 that may have accelerated the Roman decision and to assess the ways in which demilitarization may have affected the civilian population of the *regio Sirmiensis*. In the course of this investigation, I shall also explore the indigenous conditions that shaped the relationship between city and countryside and attempt to trace the elements of Romanitas that survived the barbarian assaults and the Roman withdrawal.

The last quarter of the fourth century was a tumultuous period in the region: no less than three major incursions are recorded in the literary sources. The first of these, the Quadi Sarmatian raid of 374 5, was not decisive but it served to demonstrate that the security of the *regio* was now seriously threatened by tribal movements in the Hungarian Plain. Disturbed by Valentinian's efforts to refortify the Pannonian frontier, the Quadi launched a major attack on the Roman garrisons in Valeria and cooperated with the Sarmatians further downstream in raids on the Sirmium sector.[4] According to Ammianus Marcellinus (29 .6 .7), a group of Quadi and Sarmatians almost succeeded in capturing the daughter of the emperor Constantius while she was having lunch "*in publica villa quam appellant Pristensem,*" situated some 26 miles from Sirmium. She was rescued by Messala, the governor of Pannonia II, who personally drove her to Sirmium in the state carriage (*iudicialis carpentum*).[5]

His timely intervention, of course, did not halt the raids. The Quadi and Sarmatians continued to ravage the countryside around Sirmium—driving off cattle, burning farmhouses, massacring the inhabitants—and even threatened the city itself. Probus, the praetorian prefect who was then residing in Sirmium, prepared for an attack by rebuilding the walls—"*pacis diuturnitate contemptam et subversam*"— and by summoning a "*sagittariorum cohortem e statione proxima.*"[6] But the barbarians, unaccustomed to siege warfare, did not attack the city. Instead, they withdrew to Valeria, where they were defeated by two Roman legions (Pannonica et Moesiaca).[7]

There is no reason to doubt Ammianus' assertion that the fortifications of Sirmium had been neglected or that the city did not have a regular garrison. Sirmium had frequently served as a staging area for armies involved in major Danubian campaigns but it had always relied on the garrisons of nearby *castella* for protection in time of attack. It is not surprising, therefore, that Probus was forced to summon a *cohors sagittariorum* to assist the citizens against the marauding Quadi and Sarmatians. The barbarians evidently were content to raid the countryside around Sirmium and did not challenge the regular troops in the garrison-towns on the Danube. Their hit-and-run attack was not intended to dislodge the Romans or to prepare the way for settlement of their warbands in the *regio*. For the next three years Pannonia was spared further depredations. In 378 Theodosius, who had been recalled from voluntary exile in Spain, was required to put down a new "*bellum Sarmaticum*" (Pacatus *Panegyr*. 10, 2; Themistius *Or*. 15, 198a), but the settlements in the Sirmium sector apparently were not affected. Ammianus (31, 11, 6) certainly does not indicate that the garrison-town of Bononia lay in ruins when Gratian passed through the *regio* later in the year en route to join Valens in the East.

More problematic are the movements of the Goths in 378/9. Following the battle of Adrianople, a coalition of Goths, Huns, and Alans marched from Thrace to Valeria—"*ad usque radices Alpium Juliarum*" (Amm. Marc. 31, 16, 7)—and may have passed through Pannonia II.[8] Pacatus (*Panegyr*, 32, 4) says that the Pannonian provinces were temporarily "lost" to the invaders—the Pannonian cities supposedly were depopulated—but it is not clear how one should interpret this statement. All that we know for certain is that the struggle ended in 380 when Gratian concluded a peace treaty with Alatheus and Saphrax, the leaders of the coalition, and settled their followers as *foederati* in Roman territory. Whether the *foederati* were settled "auf dem Gebiet von Pannonia Secunda (und Savia)" or in Valeria is not important for our purposes.[9] The point is that they were not settled in the *regio Sirmiensis* and therefore did not dislodge its Roman inhabitants. For the *regio* at least, the year 380 was not necessarily a "turning point".[10]

From Ambrose's statement (*ep*. 18, 21 = Migne PL 16, col. 1019ff.) that there were grain surpluses in Pannonia one might infer that the province was prospering at the end of the 4th century.[11] It would be unwise, of course, to read too much into a single inference—based perhaps on the results of an unusually productive harvest—to purchases of *frumentum Pannoniae*. On the other hand, it is clear that the barbarian leaders *believed* that access to the Pannonian fields and granaries would enable them to meet the nutritional demands of the warbands. Jordanes (*Getica* 141) stresses the importance of *victualia* in his account of the peace treaty that Gratian offered in 380 and Pacatus (*Panegyr.* 32. 5) connects the preservation of the peace, and the loyalty of the *foederati*, with the grain supply. If Pacatus is to be believed, Theodosius I may have had at his disposal large quantities of Pannonian grain, sufficient perhaps to feed both the Romans and their *foederati* for several months.

Whether grain produced in the *regio Sirmiensis* was included in the transaction Ambrose recounts is uncertain. We do know, however, that the decision to settle *foederati* in Savia—a decision that fundamentally altered Roman-barbarian relations in Upper Pannonia—did not directly affect the *regio*. Indeed, the course of development in the *regio* and in Pannonia north of the Drave diverged after 380. The barbarian groups that threatened upper Pannonia in 386 7, for example, did not pass through the *regio*. The inhabitants of Sirmium and the garrison-towns may have suffered the *metus hostilis* that afflicted all frontier populations in this period, but they were not required to experience every assault.[12]

The *regio* may even have avoided the larger-scale invasion of 395, the event that many believe led to the Roman withdrawal from Pannonia. In that year, new groups—Goths according to Claudian (*In Rufinum* 2. 26–27), Huns according to Philostorgius (11. 8) and Sozomen (8. 25. 1)—crossed the Danube and devastated the Roman frontier provinces "*ad usque Dalmatiae fines.*"[13] It should be noted that none of the accounts specifies the point on the Danube where the invading groups crossed or the extent of the purported devastation. Nor do they collectively provide any information concerning the response of the Roman authorities. In short, the effect of these invasions, if any, on the *regio Sirmiensis* is not known. Dušanić has connected the transfer of the imperial textile factory (*gynaecium*) from Bassiana to Salona with this incursion, but this assertion rests on a brief entry in the *Notitia Dignitatum* (Oc. xi. 46) which cannot be securely dated to 395. There is no reason, in fact, to assume that the transfer had anything to do with the incursion; the operations of the *gynaecium* in Sirmium, also listed in the *Notitia*, evidently were not affected.[14]

That the central government was aware of the threat to the *regio*, however, is clear. In 396/7 Stilicho dispatched the senator Flavius Lupus to Pannonia II with instructions to conduct a census that would establish the tax liability of landowners in the province. It was Lupus' responsibility, as *peraequator glebalis*, to assess the sum each landowner owed and to ensure that a portion of the tax collected would be allocated for the restoration of town walls in the province.[15]

Lupus' mission was part of a larger effort by the central government, alarmed by the condition of fortifications in the frontier provinces, to raise new funds for the construction or restoration of town walls. In their letter of 24 March 396 (*CTh* 15.1.34) Arcadius and Honorius had instructed the praetorian prefect of the Orient to order a fresh tax assessment in all the provinces under his jurisdiction and to inform the municipal senates of their responsibility for the collection of taxes assessed.[16] Similar instructions must have been given to the western praetorian prefect as well. Indeed, the mission of Lupus demonstrates that the western government had received the directive and was determined to enforce it in the *regio Sirmiensis*.[17]

All these preparations were abandoned, however, when the emperors withdrew whatever troops remained and ceased to contest the passage of barbarian groups through the *regio*.[18] According to the *Notitia Dignitatum*, during the last half of the 4th century nine garrison-towns defended the Sirmium sector of the Pannonian frontier:

Cornacum:	*equites Dalmatae* (31, 31)
	cuneus equitum scutariorum (32, 22)
Cuccium:	*equites sagittarii* (32, 32)
	cuneus equitum Promotorum (32, 25)
Bononia:	*legio V Iovia, cohors V* (32, 44)
	equites Dalmatae (32, 33)
Onagrinum:	*legio VI Herculia, cohors X* (32, 48)
	auxilia Augustensia (32, 41)
Cusum:	*equites Dalmatae* (32, 34)
Acumincum:	*cuneus equitum Constantium* (32, 26)
	equites sagittarii (32, 25)
Rittium:	*equites Dalmatae* (32, 36)
Burgenae:	*legio V Iovia, cohors V* (32, 46)
	cuneus equitum Constantianorum <sic> (32, 24)
	equites Dalmatae (32, 37)

Taurunum: *cuneus equitum Promotorum* (32, 35)
              auxilia ascarii (32, 43)

If the assignment of a legionary cohort to a town indicates its relative importance in the military defense structure, then it follows that Onagrinum, Bononia, and Burgenae were the principal garrison-towns in this sector. The most striking feature of the list, however, is the surprisingly large number of military units in the sector. Assuming that each of the units was roughly the equivalent of a *cohort* (500 men), a force of some 9,000 *pedites* and *equites* was assigned to the garrison-towns of the *regio* in the late 4th century. Whether one should place much trust in the Pannonian lists, infected as they are by patent anachronisms, is debatable. At the very least, one should not assume that all the units in the list were stationed in the garrison-towns at any one time or that they were maintained at full strength.[19]

Systematic excavation of the most important garrison-towns might shed light on this question, and might also settle some of the larger issues concerning the Roman withdrawl, but to date archaeological activity has been sporadic and largely superficial. To assemble the archaeological data, such as they are, one must rely on inadequately published reports of 'soundings' and on analyses of chance finds housed in regional museums. Only in Bononia (modern Banoštor), situated near the intersection of the N-S road from Sirmium (approximately 30 km to the south) and the E-W road along the Danube, has there been any systematic excavation.

An important military post in the third century, which guaranteed access routes to the interior and monitored Danubian road and river traffic, Bononia was occupied by Romans, or Romanized groups, until the last half of the fourth century. The extent of its port facilities is not known—a *classis* apparently was not stationed there—but because the Danube can be crossed with comparative ease at Bononia it is clear that the town was an important point of disembarkation. It was at Bononia that Julian landed in 361 to begin his campaign against Sirmium, at that time held by Lucillianus, *comes et magister equitum in Illyricum.*[20] And several years later (378) Gratian, en route to join Valens in the East, *"cum expeditore militum manu, permeato Danubio, delatus Bononiam, Sirmium introiit."*[21]

Unfortunately, the 1970-71 excavations in Bononia did not produce new evidence concerning the garrison. There is no trace in the villa and associated structures that were excavated of the units the *Notitia* assigns to Bononia. The only military finds were bricks with the stamp *L(egio) VI H(erculia) C(ohors) X*.[22] This *cohors* was almost certainly quartered in Onagrinum (*contra Bononia*), the forward camp established by Diocletian in barbarian territory across the Danube.[23] Whether the commander of the garrison at Bononia had jurisdiction over all the troops in the immediate neighborhood is not clear. Some have suggested that the small fort at Gradac, 13 km. from the Danube, was attached to Bononia, but nothing indicates that Gradac was still a military post in the 4th century. Certainly the *cohors II Alpinorum*, which in the 2nd century may have been garrisoned at Gradac, was no longer in Pannonia by the end of the 4th century (it is not listed in the *Notitia Dignitatum*).[24]

Until the *castellum* of Bononia has been located and systematically excavated, the fate of the military garrison and the circumstances of destruction will remain problematic. Although there is considerable material evidence of reoccupation in the villa—*inter alia* the compact floors of huts and other irregular buildings erected in the ruins of the Roman structures—it is not possible to identify the "squatters" or to determine the date of their arrival in Bononia. In the 1970-71 excavations we did not find *fibulae* or other jewelry that have been traditionally associated with Gepids, Goths, and other Germanic folk.[25] On the other hand, there is nothing in the archaeological record that would exclude from the list of possible "assassins" the one barbarian group that is known to have passed through the *regio* in 401—viz. the Visigoths.[26]

The central government was sufficiently alarmed by conditions in Illyricum—the diocese that encompassed the Pannonian provinces—to issue at least two emergency decrees during the first decade of the 5th century (*CTh* 11. 17. 4; 15. 1. 49). In these *edicta* the emperors, Honorius and Theodosius I, instructed Herculius, praetorian prefect of Illyricum, to see to the repair of town walls and to arrange for the purchase and transport of supplies (*necessitates Illyricianas*). Whether the emperors were responding to an existing emergency or were preparing the inhabitants to defend themselves against an imminent invasion is not certain. Nor is it possible to determine the year in which the decrees were issued.[27]

Nonetheless, it is tempting to connect these decrees with the Visigothic incursion and to argue that Alaric's warbands had inflicted serious damage on the garrison-towns and urban centers of the *regio Sirmiensis*. That Illyricum was in considerable disarray between 401 and 410 is indisputable. The edict (*CTh* 10. 10. 25, securely dated to 10 December 408) prohibiting the enslavement of fugitives from a barbarian attack testifies to the seriousness of the emergency. And yet, neither in this edict nor in the contemporary decrees cited above is there any reference to the role that military units were expected to play in the defense of the diocese. If the troops were still at their posts, why were they not called upon to assist the civilian authorities? For such questions we have no satisfactory answers. Nor is it likely that we shall ever be in a position to assess all the factors that inspired the decision, whenever it was taken, to demilitarize the *regio*. It may have been the political struggles of the 390's, as Alföldi has suggested, that decided the issue.[28] Alternatively, it may have been the Visigothic incursion that convinced the central government that the costs incurred in the defense of the *regio* were no longer acceptable. This much is certain: although the government continued to claim authority over the *regio*, nothing in the extant evidence indicates that they were also prepared, after 401, to provide troops for its defense.

The decision to withdraw the protective cordon of garrisons exposed the *regio* to the "outer barbarians" as never before, but it did not fundamentally alter the relationship between Romans and natives that had evolved during four centuries of imperial administration. The topography of the region between the Sava and the Danube, bisected as it is by the Fruška gora range, dictated the separation of the Roman population into two strata—the garrison-towns that monitored the activities of the 'outer barbarians' and the indigenous population assigned to *civitates*, and the urban centers in which a mixed population of Romans and Romanized natives conducted the everyday business of provincial management. Reluctant to sponsor the colonization of the *regio* by citizens from the Mediterranean provinces, the Romans had relied from the beginning on their ability to urbanize, and thereby tranquilize, the indigenous population. Sirmium, the first urban center in the *regio*, was an amalgam of Romans (administrators, traders, veterans) and Amantini. A similar amalgam of Romans and Romanized natives (in this instance members of the *civitas Scordiscorum*) comprised the population of the *municipium*, later *colonia*, of Bassiana.[29]

The fundamental change in Roman-native relations occurred in the third century. With Caracalla's extension of the citizenship and the consequent dismantling of the *civitates*, the inhabitants of the countryside migrated in even greater numbers to the garrison-towns and urban centers. The countryside may not have been depopulated at this time, but it is clear that the greater opportunities for advancement offered by Bassiana and Sirmium—especially after the latter became an "administrative capital" in the late third/early fourth century—were increasingly difficult to resist. For their part, the Romans may have welcomed the migration to the towns, not only because it facilitated their administration of the *regio* but also because it confirmed the success, at least from their perspective, of the policy of assimilation the imperial administrators had sponsored.

That civilians would have remained in the garrison-towns after the troops departed seems unlikely. The prudent course was to seek shelter in Bassiana or Sirmium, whose town walls offered some security against the "outer barbarians". But even against barbarian groups with little experience in siege warfare these fortifications, perennially in a state of disrepair, were not impregnable barriers. And they certainly could not prevent the devastation of the countryside on which the townspeople depended.

Unfortunately, the events of this crucial period (401–441) cannot be traced in the archaeological record. Even in Sirmium—where Yugoslav, American, and French archaeological teams have been at work for two decades—it is not possible to measure the effect of a particular barbarian incursion. The cumulative effect, however, can be discerned. The construction of monumental buildings, of the sort commissioned by the fourth-century emperors, ceased altogether in the fifth century. Nor were the citizens of Sirmium in a position to underwrite the costs of new basilicas and other Christian monuments. Indeed, the relative poverty of Sirmium, compared with the towns of similar size in the Mediterranean hinterland, is accurately reflected in its fifth-century architecture.[30] By 441 the once-prosperous administrative capital was little more than a *refugium*, a frontier town in which the dispossessed inhabitants of the *regio* were engaged in a day-to-day struggle for survival.

The gradual disappearance of a money-economy (*Geldwirtschaft*) in the *regio* undoubtedly contributed to the impoverishment of Sirmium and Bassiana. So long as the troops remained in the garrison towns along the Danube, regular shipments of coins from local or extraprovincial mints would have been necessary. There is every reason to believe, in fact, that the pattern of military/monetary development in this frontier zone begun during the 3rd century—when the dramatic increase in the number of troops under the Severi was accompanied by the opening of the mint at Siscia—continued until at least the third quarter of the 4th century. The mint at Siscia, which issued most of the coins found in the garrison-towns of Pannonia II, did not cease operation until 387: the mint at Sirmium, established under Constantine, was in operation until c. 367.[31] While the mints remained in operation the troops probably received the bulk of their salaries in currency rather than through requisitions.[32] During the fourth century, therefore, there was a sufficiently large volume of coinage produced within Pannonia II to support a *Geldwirtschaft* in both the public and private sectors.

The distribution of fourth century coins found during the excavations in Bononia substantiates the conventional view that the circulation of coins dramatically diminished after 378. Of the 23 fourth century bronze coins found, 18 were minted before 378, most of them struck by the mint in Siscia, and only five were issued between 378 and 408 (possibly before 395). That the reign of Arcadius (383–408) marks the end of the circulation of Roman coins in Bononia is confirmed by the collection of chance finds in the Zagreb Museum.[33] The latest coins in the collection are a *Salus Reipublicae* bronze issued by Arcadius - Theodosius I and a *Gloria Romanorum* bronze struck under Honorius.

For the most part, chance finds from other garrison-towns along this section of the Danube conform to this pattern: Cornacum (no coins minted after 395); Rittium and Bassiana (only 1 Byzantine coin after 395); Burgenae (four coins minted between 395 and the Byzantine 'reconquest', five Byzantine coins, two sixth-century German coins).[34] Similarly, no more than a handful (17/2300) of the excavation coins from Sirmium were issued after 395. The fact that a "disproportionate number" of these coins are very worn, however, indicates that some coins may have remained in circulation after the mints closed and the troops departed.[35]

Only at the monastery (*castellum*?) of Rakovac near Čerević, where Brunsmid discovered a deposit of 1186 bronze coins—beginning with the reign of Trajan and ending with Valentinian III—does the pattern differ.[36] The presence of coins of Valentinian III (425–455) in this hoard led Alföldi to conclude that Roman troops continued to operate in the *regio* after 395 and Kent to suggest that the reoccupation of Pannonia in 427—reported by Marcellinus Comes (a. 427, *chron.*

min. ii, 76) and Jordanes (*Getica* 166)—"was effective to the line of the Drave."[37] Neither interpretation is convincing. In the first place, the prominence in the hoard of coins minted by eastern emperors makes it likely that the depositor was an outsider (perhaps an itinerant merchant?) and not a soldier stationed in one of the garrison-towns. Moreover, it is far from certain that the Roman expulsion of the Huns in 427, if this occurred at all, affected the *regio Sirmiensis*. Neither Marcellinus Comes nor Jordanes mentions Sirmium/Bassiana or the garrison-towns of the *regio*. The "Huns" in question are clearly members of the Hun-Goth-Alan coalition that the Romans had settled as *foederati* in Valeria/Savia in 378/9.[38]

Should one conclude that the distribution of coins in the Rakovac hoard, which is not paralleled in any other numismatic collection, reflects the normal pattern of circulation in the *regio* during the early fifth century? I think not. On the contrary, the uniform evidence from the garrison-towns and from Sirmium indicates, as clearly as numismatic evidence can, that very few Roman coins remained in circulation after the reign of Arcadius Honorius.

Demilitarization, and the sharp decline in circulation of coins that resulted from the departure of the troops, undoubtedly disrupted the mercantile network that had enabled local mandarins to rise to prominence. For a time they may have been sustained by the border (or barbarian) markets, but without Roman troops to guarantee access and order these markets must have atrophied.[39] Nor would they have been able to compensate for the lost markets by investing in agriculture. Harvests were imperiled every time a barbarian group passed through the *regio*. The less serious incursions could be contained by agreeing to provide the food and supplies the group needed for the journey, but when a large number of barbarians chose to settle rather than move on, as the Huns did in 441, these conciliatory measures would not have been effective.

Were *metus hostilis* and the erosion of *Geldwirtschaft* sufficiently distressing to convince the local mandarins to flee to safer ground? Not immediately, it seems. All the known fugitives from Pannonia during the first quarter of the fifth century were residents of towns in the valley of the Drave, the region that the Hun-Goth-Alan *foederati* had occupied for several decades.[40] For Roman citizens in these barbarian communities, of course, life may well have been more precarious than in the *regio Sirmiensis*. But it would be wrong to infer from the epi-

taphs of two or three fugitives that a major exodus occurred even in the
Drave valley.

And there is certainly no evidence of emigration from the *regio
Sirmiensis* before 441. The *communis opinio* is that the first émigré
from the *regio* was the abbess Johanna of Sirmium, who "fled" to
Salona sometime during the sixth century. Unfortunately, the epitaph
(from Salona) on which this interpretation is based does not reveal the
circumstances of her flight and cannot be dated to the period of any
particular barbarian incursion.[41] There is no reason to assume, in fact,
that she had been driven out or that she was part of a major migration
of Christians from Sirmium.

Two later epitaphs of émigrés from Sirmium, also found in Salona, are equally ambiguous. Neither can be securely dated and nothing
in the texts points to the conditions in Sirmium that may have forced
them to leave.[42] Not even the statement that Domnica, the child commemorated in one of the epitaphs, had been brought to Salona from
Sirmium (*a Sirmio Salonas adducta est*) offers a firm basis for judgment. The epigraphic evidence from Salona, in short, does not prove
that a substantial number of the Roman (or Romanized) population of
Sirmium fled south along the Sirmium-Salona "escape route" after
441.

Similarly, although the individuals who appear in the epitaphs
were Christians, it should not be assumed that the Christian community in Sirmium went into exile. Between 401 and 441 the bishop of
Sirmium was the preeminent, and quite possibly the only, high church
official in Pannonia. According to Priscus (frag. 8), the bishop (not
named) was still in residence when Attila attacked the city in 441.[43]
Priscus does not record his fate, although he implies that the bishop
perished, nor does he provide any information concerning the subsequent activities of the Christian community in Sirmium. Nonetheless,
the fact that the abbess Johanna resided in Sirmium during the first
half of the sixth century indicates that some Christians remained in the
beleaguered city.

With the Huns firmly in control of the *regio* after 441, of course,
the Romans who remained, whatever their number, had no choice but
to collaborate. The western emperor, in fact, pointed the way by des-
patching an embassy to the *regio* to negotiate the return of church
property that had passed into Attila's hands during the sack of Sirmium. The mission, which Priscus recounts in some detail, was an
instructive failure.[44] The interview with Attila, who was ensconced in a

vicus (ἐν μεγίστῃ κώμῃ) decorated with spoils from the towns of the *regio*, was anything but reassuring. To demonstrate the superiority of his claim, not only to the church but to all of Rome's possessions in the *regio*, Attila instructed Onegisimus, one of his lieutenants, to show the ambassadors the bath building on the "estate" that had been designed by a captive architect from Sirmium and constructed with material looted from Pannonian sites. The point cannot have been lost on his guests.

The transition from Roman to barbarian management, set in motion when the central government disclaimed responsibility for the *regio* and withdrew its military shield, was now complete. But more was involved here than simple political or military dominance. The "outer barbarians" introduced an entirely different perspective. They did not share the cultural prejudices of their predecessors, and had not been conditioned by decades of clientage to accept without question the superiority of the Roman way.

In one sense, the *regio* under the Huns and their successors returned to its natural, pre-conquest state. But the Roman retreat did not rekindle Celtic or Illyrian nationalism or reveal sub-Roman groups strong enough to endure without the protection of Roman town walls. The indigenous Celts and Illyrians had lost their separate identities two centuries earlier when they accepted Roman citizenship and took up residence in the urban centers. This pattern of acculturation did not appeal to the barbarian groups that governed the *regio* after 441. They may have reconstructed baths on their country estates and preserved for decorative purposes the plundered artifacts of the towns, but they could not appreciate the *Romanitas* that had inspired these creations and were not prepared to resuscitate the towns they had looted. For the new rulers of the *regio* the distinction between city and countryside, cultivated for more than four centuries by successive Roman administrators, had little meaning.

Notes

1. Jordanes *Getica* 292: Procopius *Aed.* 4. 5. 6–7. On the date see M. Mirković, "Sirmium—its History from the I century A.D. to 582 A.D.," *Sirmium* I (Belgrade, 1971) 47ff.; A. Mócsy, *Pannonia and Upper Moesia* (London, 1974) 350.

2. *CJ Novellae* xi; cf. Mirković *op cit.* 43.

3. The decision to settle the Huns in Savia in 427 (Mócsy *op cit.* 350; cf. L. Várády, *Das Letzte Jahrhundert Pannoniens, 376–476* [Amsterdam, 1969] 278ff.) effectively separated the regio from the western government in Italy. Valentinian III confirmed this separation in 437 when he agreed to transfer responsibility for the regio to the eastern emperor Theodosius II (for the evidence see Mirković *op cit.* 42ff.). The western emperor, however, attempted to reassert his authority after 441 and occasionally despatched embassies to negotiate with Attila (see p. 36).

4. According to Ammianus Marcellinus 30. 6. 2 the construction of a *"munimentum"(palisade? fossatum?)* had stimulated the attacks. Whether this structure was connected with the *"praesidiaria castra"* Valentinian constructed across the Danube, in Quadi territory, is not clear (Amm. Marc. 29. 6. 2); cf. Mócsy *op cit.* 292ff.; S. Soproni, "Eine spätrömische militärstation im sarmatischen Gebiet," *Roman Frontier Studies 1969,* ed. E. Birley et al (Cardiff, 1974) 197ff., who discusses the burgus of Valentinianic type situated in Sarmatian territory.

5. Messala is the last governor of Pannonia II (c. 373) mentioned in any source.

6. If *"e statione proxima"* is taken literally, the *cohors sagittariorum* could have been summoned from Cuccium (*Not. Dign* 32. 33) or Acumincum (*Not. Dign.* 32. 25).

7. Amm. Marc. 29. 6. 8–14. In 375 Valentinian crossed the Danube to punish the Quadi, but he did not live to complete the restoration of the frontier in Valeria (he died of apoplexy in Brigetio).

8. The invasion route is confirmed by Ambrose (*De fide* 2. 140), who was residing at the time in Sirmium, but he does not specifically mention Pannonia II. T. Nagy ("The Last Century of Pannonia in the Judgment of a New Monograph," *AA* 3–4 (Budapest 1971) 315ff.) speculates that Ambrose, who wanted to interpret the invasion as God's judgment on the Arians, decided "to spare" Pannonia II because he had recently succeeded in re-catholicizing the province. An alternative interpretation has been offered by J. Otto Maenchen-Helfen, *The World of the Huns* (Berkeley, 1973) 32ff. Arguing that Gratian returned to Sirmium *before* the battle of Adrianople, he concludes that the invaders avoided Pannonia II because it was guarded by Gratian's army.

9. L. Várády, *op cit.* 14. 168ff.; cf. Mócsy, *op cit.* 341ff.; T. Nagy, *op. cit.* 319. The treaty is reported in Jordanes *Getica* 141; according to Pacatus *Panegyr.* 32. 4, the coalition later supplied troops to Theodosius.

10. *pace* S. Dusanić, "Bassianae and its Territory," *Archaeologia Jugoslavica* 8 (1967) 73.

11. *De Gallis quid loquar solito ditionibus, frumentum Pannoniae, quod non severant, vendiderunt; et secunda Rhetia fertilitatis suae novit invidiam.*

12. There may have been two incursions in 386. The first (*CTh* 1. 32. 5, 29 July 386) evidently was directed against Macedonia, Dacia mediterranea, and Moesia (seu Dardania); the second, reported by Zosimus (4. 42. 5; 4. 45. 4),

seems to have penetrated upper Pannonia. As J. F. Matthews (*Western Aristocracies and Imperial Court, A. D. 364–425* [Oxford, 1975] 181, n. 1) has suggested, Jerome's home town of Stridon located at the "*Dalmatiae.* . . *Pannoniaeque confinium*" may have been destroyed in the course of this incursion.

13. At first glance, Marcellinus Comes (a. 427, *chron. min.* 2. 76) and Jordanes (*Getica* 166) seem to confirm Philostorgius and Sozomen. *Pannoniae, quae per quinquaginta annos ab Hunnis retinebantur, a Romanis receptae sunt* (Marcellinus); *nam duodecimo anno regni Valiae, quando et Hunni post pene quinquaginta annorum invasam Pannoniam a Romanis et Gothis expulsi sunt* (Jordanes). Since this expulsion occurred around 427, however, the invasion of the Huns fifty years earlier clearly refers to the events of 378 9, when the Hun-Goth-Alan coalition became *foederati.* Mirković (*op. cit.* 46) and others believe that Jordanes borrowed the passage from Marcellinus Comes, but T. Nagy ("Reoccupation of Pannonia from the Huns in 427," *AA* 15 [Budapest, 1967] 159ff.) argues that Jordanes may simply have reproduced the entry in Cassiodorus' *Chronicon.* Less persuasive is Nagy's suggestion (independently put forward by Maenchen-Helfen, *op. cit.* 79) that the ultimate source was Symmachus' lost *Historia romana.*

14. S. Dusanić, *op. cit.* 74. The evidence does not support his conclusion that the barbarian invaders of 395 "were joined by the colonists of 380 and the poorest among the provincials, so that there began an almost continuous series of tumults, which practically, though not yet formally, marked the end of the Roman government."

15. Text from Teano: *pera [equator propter] muro cincten [das urbes iudicio] sac (ro) glebalis ce [nsus per secun] dam Pannoni [am].* For an interpretation and discussion of the date of Lupus' mission see A. Chastagnol, *Epigraphica* 29 (1967) 105ff; L. Várády, *AArch Hung* 24 (1972) 262ff.

16. An earlier law (*CTh* 5. 15. 35, 6 August 395) permitted the allocation of 1 3 of the regular tax (but not *vectigalia*) for the construction restoration of town walls. This evidently was the fraction Valentinian had also authorized (cf. *CTh* 15. 1. 33, 5 July 395).

17. Whether Lupus was later *procurator saltus per provincias Valeriam et P (icenum et Campa)niam*—as Chastagnol, *op. cit.* 114ff. believes—or *P(rimam Panno)niam*—as Várády, *op. cit.* 263 has proposed—is not important for our immediate purposes. But even if one accepts Várády's expansion, it does not follow that Lupus conducted his tax assessment in *Pannonia prima* as well as *secunda.*

18. After 400 the garrison-towns, the backbone of the frontier defense, disappear altogether from the literary record. Procopius (*Aed.* 4. 5. 6ff.) unfortunately terminated his survey of the Danubian fortresses at the border of *Moesia-Pannonia secunda* (at Singidunum). Nor is there much to be learned from Jordanes' references (*Getica* 264) to the Pannonian cities: *ornata patria civitatibus plurimis, quarum prima Syrmis, extrema Vindomina.*

40 EARLY BYZANTINE ERA

19. For a discussion of the Pannonia lists see D. Hoffmann, *Das spätrömische Bewegunghsheer und die Notitia Dignitatum*, I, *Epigraphische Studien* 7. 1 (Düsseldorf, 1969) 516, *passim;* cf. S. Dusanić, "Roman Army in Eastern Srem," *Zbornik Filosofskog Fakulteta Universiteta u Beogradu* 10 (1968) 112 (in Serbian with English summary).

20. Amm. Marc. 21. 9. 6–7

21. Amm. Marc. 31. 11. 6

22. Brick stamps *L VI HR CX* from Bononia: CIL 3. 10665, b-c; during the 1970 season another stamped brick was found which corresponds to type IV of the Sirmium collection (see A. Milosević, *Sirmium* I [1971] 101).

23. Onagrinum was established in 294: *Fasti Hydatii a.* 294 (*MGH, AA* ix, *chron. min.* i. 230); cf. S. Soproni, "Contra Acinco et Bononia: Bemerkungen zu den Fasti des Hydatius," *Studien zu den Militärgrenzen Roms II; Vörtrage des 10. Internationalen Limeskongresses in der Germania Inferior, Bonner Jahrbücher* Beih. 38 (Bonn, 1977), 393ff. Although the site has not been systematically excavated, the cemetery and general outline of the *castellum* have been identified. The *cohors* is attested by bricks with the stamp *L VI HRC X* (*CIL* 3. 10665 d; P. Velenrajter, "Castellum Onagrinum," *Rad Vojvodanskih Muzeja* 7 [1958] pls. 1–7). Bricks manufactured by cohors X have also been found in the cemetery at Cerević (CIL 3. 10665 a), in the nearby monastery of Rakovac (J. Szilágyi, *Inscriptiones Tegularum Pannonicarum, Dissertationes Pannonicae*, ser. 2 [1933] pl. xi, 42), and in Sirmium (A. Milosević, *op. cit.* 101).

24. O. Brukner partially unearthed foundations of buildings and walls of the fortress at Gradac: *Arheoloski Pregled* 5 (1963) 109ff. (in Serbian with French summary).

25. For an attempt to associate objects of this sort found over the years in some of the frontier settlements in the *regio*—Taurunum, Burgenae, Rakovac, Cuccium—with successive barbarian incursions see J. Kovacević, *Varvarska Kolonizacija Juznoslovenskih Oblasti* (Novi Sad, 1960), with French summary pp. 61–67. Precisely because these objects are chance finds—i.e. they were not recovered through controlled excavations—their value for historical reconstruction is slight.

26. Jordanes *Getica* 147: [Alaric] *sumpto exercitu per Pannonias Stilichone et Aureliano consulibus* [A.D. 400] *et per Sirmium dextroque latera quasi viris vacuam intravit Italiam. . .;* cf. Mócsy, *op cit.* 347. There may well have been little resistance to Alaric, but this passage ("*quasi. . . Italiam*") does not prove that Pannonia II was now "devoid of any Roman troops" (*contra* J. Wilkes, "A Pannonian Refugee of Quality at Salona," *Phoenix* 26 [1972] 385).

27. For both decrees the editors of the *Codex Theodosianus* offer a choice between 407, 408, and 412.

28. A. Alföldi, *Die Untergang der Römerherrschaft in Pannonien*, II (Berlin and Leipzig, 1926) 74ff.

29. On the Scordisci in Bassiana see S. Dusanić (*supra* n. 10)

30. For a discussion of the archaeological evidence available in 1970 see V. Popović, *Sirmium* I (1971) 130ff.

31. For the closing dates see Mócsy, *op cit.*, 343 (Siscia) and the discussion by C.E.V. Nixon in his (as yet unpublished) catalogue of the excavation coins from Sirmium; cf. the less satisfactory discussion by I. A. Mirnik, *Coin Hoards in Yugloslavia* (*BAR International Series* 95, 1981) 8ff.

32. The *annona* had been introduced in the third century but troops and administrators continued to receive "at least part of their wages in the form of a cash *stipendium*. . . natural products served both government and subjects as an additional form of currency" (C.E.V. Nixon, *loc. cit.*)

33. A Alföldi, *op. cit.* 25–26

34. Alföldi, *idem*, 26–27 (Cornacum), 24 (Rittium), 27 (Bassianae), 21–24 (Burgenae).

35. C.E.V. Nixon, *loc. cit.*; cf. R. Reece ("Roman Coinage in the Western Empire," *Britannia* 4 [1973] 249) who cautions that "coins lost on any site give information on the supply of money to the province in question during the period of issue of each coin, and information on the state of the site one or two periods after each coin was minted."

36. Alföldi, *op. cit.* 25

37. Alföldi, *idem*; J.P.C. Kent, "Coin Evidence for the Abandonment of a Frontier Province," *Carnuntina, Römische Forschungen in Niederösterreich* (ed. E. Swoboda), II (1956) 89.

38. For the evidence see *supra* n. 13.

39. Traffic on the Danube apparently continued into the early 5th century (Rutilius Namatianus 485)

40. E. Tóth, "La survivance de la population romaine en Pannonie," *Alba Regia* 15 (1977) 107ff.; J. Wilkes, *op. cit.* 377ff.; Mócsy, *op. cit.* 354ff.

41. *ILJug* 1653 (=*CIL 3. 9551): A. and J. Sasel, "Inscriptiones Latinae quae in Iugoslavia. . . repertae et editae sunt,"* Situla 5 (1963). Based on the date given in the text—*IIII idus Maias indictione qu*[*ar*]*ta decima*—the epitaph was inscribed in 506 or 551. This rules out Tóth's suggestion (*op. cit.* 109) that Johanna fled during the Avar attack in 582.

42. *ILJug* 118 = *CIL* 3. 1987: *Fl. Fidentius ex/comitibus Sirmesis/hic est depositus/vixit an xx; ILJug* 4455 = *CIL* 3. 9576: [*depo*]*setio infantis/*[*Do*]*mnicae viii kaled/Octobres, quae a Sirmi/o Salonas adducta est.*

43. Between 401 and 417 Laurentius, the bishop of Sirmium, was still under the authority of Pope Innocent (*Innocenti ep.* 41, Migne PL 20, 607); cf. V. Popović, "Le dernier évêque de Sirmium," *Revue des études Augustiniennes* 21 (1975) 91ff.

44. Priscus, frag. 8 (Müller *FHG* iv. 84ff.); cf. Mirković, *op. cit.* 47.

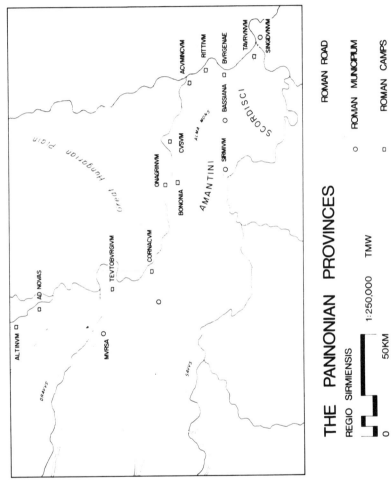

THE PANNONIAN PROVINCES

REGIO SIRMIENSIS

0   50KM

1:250,000   TMW

——— ROMAN ROAD

○   ROMAN MUNICIPIUM

□   ROMAN CAMPS

Figure 1

3

FORTIFICATION AND URBAN DESIGN IN EARLY BYZANTINE GREECE

Timothy E. Gregory

(Ohio State University)

It has long been commonplace to point to the essential connection between cities and the development and maintenance of classical civilization.[1] In recent years, however, we have come to view this issue in much more sophisticated terms, no longer content merely to observe the identity of civilization and urban life, but determined to explore the phenomenon and to inquire into the dynamic factors involved in this relationship.[2] Naturally enough, much attention has been focused on the formative period: the rise of cities and their attendant institutions.[3] This is a reasonable place to start, for if we understand the formation of the earliest cities (at least in the Mediterranean area), we will perceive a great deal more about the civilization that they nurtured. The same can be said, however, about the cities at the other end of the chronological scale, those of the late Roman and early Byzantine period.[4] Clearly, an understanding of early Byzantine urbanism is essential for any analysis of the "fall of the Roman empire" in the East (if the concept has any validity in that area) and the transformation of the classical world into that of medieval Byzantium.

As is generally known, during late antiquity the cities of the Mediterranean basin experienced serious upheavals, including barbarian invasions, institutional dislocation and collapse, and probable population loss. These changes were reflected in the shape and physical

43

appearance of cities which, while they may not have become "medieval" in character, began to depart significantly from their classical form. One aspect of this change was the construction of monumental fortification walls. For years previously, most of the great cities of the Mediterranean had stood open and unwalled, sprawling in luxurious confusion around their monumentally adorned centers; this was a period of prosperity and growth and the Roman government naturally viewed with suspicion any attempt to construct interior defenses.[5] The legions guarded the frontier and city walls could be interpreted only as a sign of rebellion.

Beginning in the third century, however, all this changed and the needs of defense led to the construction of new walls.[6] These walls were important in their own right and an examination of their chronology, military considerations, and building techniques is naturally significant. The present study, however, will investigate not these, but the more "functional" aspect of the walls and their relationship to urban design in the early Byzantine period. For practical reasons it will confine itself to a single geographic area: the Roman province of Achaia, which included all of Greece south of Thermopylae.

The best documented example of early Byzantine fortification not surprisingly comes from Athens.[7] There, in the middle of the third century the citizens rebuilt the Walls of Themistokles and apparently even enlarged them to incorporate the area of the city added by the emperor Hadrian. This is the course of the wall indicated by the dotted line on Figure 1. Also perhaps at this time the akropolis was once again fortified by the construction of the so-called Beulé Gate at its western entrance.[8] Despite these precautions, the city was taken and brutally sacked by the Goths and Heruli in A.D. 267 and thick layers of ash and debris encountered in the excavation of the ancient Agora testify to the violence of the destruction. The probable reason for the failure of the defense of the city was, ironically, the very length of the newly-restored walls, which could not be properly defended by the small forces at the disposal of the Athenians.

Rising from the devastation of the Herulian sack, the people of Athens once again turned their thoughts to the necessity of defense, and they constructed a new line of fortifications to the north of the akropolis.[9] The new wall, known generally as the Late Roman Fortification, joined the akropolis ramparts at the Beulé Gate and ran down the north slope of the hill, leaving the ancient Panathenaic Way just outside the circuit. Using the foundations of several buildings and the

whole front wall of the Stoa of Attalos, the wall ran along the eastern
boundary of the ancient Agora and then turned eastward at the end of
the Stoa. It continued in that direction for about 450 m., using the
south wall of the Library of Hadrian (which was thus incorporated
into the defenses) and the north wall of a large Hadrianic basilica.
From that point the Late Roman Fortification turned south once
again and ascended the hill of the akropolis, joining its walls near the
eastern end. (See Fig. 1).

The area enclosed within the third-century wall was vastly smaller
than that of its classical predecessor. It included the akropolis, but
hardly any of the famous buildings and areas in the lower city. The
ancient Agora was the greatest exclusion, but the Hephaistaion, the
Areopagus, the Odeion of Herodes Atticus, the Theatre of Dionysus,
and the Olympieion were all outside the new defenses. A great street,
running between the Roman agora and the Agora of the classical
period, still functioned and it may have been the main east-west thoroughfare in the shrunken urban area. Its course was fixed by long
years of use and by the buildings on either side of it, and the architects
of the new wall had to alter its course slightly to take account of the
street's exit between the ruins of the Stoa of Attalos and the Library of
Pantainos.[10] Other important streets, however, lay outside the wall
and two of these actually bounded the fortified area on two of its three
lower sides: perhaps the streets provided the open space that was desirable on the exterior of the wall. Thus, we have already mentioned that
the Panathenaic Way ran along the outside of the wall through nearly
the whole of its western side. On the north another road passed just
under the outside of the wall, apparently for its entire length.[11]

Archaeological investigation has suggested that the Athenians hesitated to construct new buildings on the site of the ancient Agora in the
years immediately following the Herulian raid.[12] Obviously they were
afraid of yet another invasion and they were unwilling to tempt fate by
building outside the fortified area. Thus, in this sense at least, the
construction of the Late Roman Fortification had an important
immediate effect on the shape of Athens in the later third and fourth
centuries.

A more fundamental question involves the course of the early
Byzantine wall and its exclusion of the ancient Agora, especially the
buildings along its western edge which had served as the center of
Athenian government for centuries.[13] Surely, important considerations must have caused the virtual abandonment of the ancient civic

center. In part, the reason for this decision may have been strategic and economic: to extend the line of the walls westward to enclose, say, the Bouleterion and the Metroon would have made them considerably longer and thus much more difficult to defend. Perhaps the Athenians had learned the liability of expansive fortifications at the time of the Herulian invasion. There is, however, no compelling reason why the wall ever had to extend as far as it did to the east. It could easily have included the Agora by rising up the hill of the Areopagos and descending to that of Kolonos Agoraios before turning eastward. This would have provided an eminently defensible line and it would have deprived an enemy of the advantage that these heights afforded. The decision to exclude the ancient Agora, then, must have been made for other reasons having little to do with strategy or defense.

One approach to this problem is to suggest that the governmental offices of the Athenian state had been transferred from the ancient Agora long before the construction of the Late Roman Fortification. In such a case the new wall would merely have reflected a change that had taken place at some earlier time. Crucial in this regard was the construction of the forum of Caesar and Augustus (the Roman agora) in the area to the east of the more ancient Agora of the Greek period.[14] This had an effect on the old civic center, including the construction of the Odeion of Agrippa in the center of the formerly open expense and the building (or rebuilding) of several temples in the Agora area. All of this emphasized the monumentality of the Agora, while rendering it less useful as a place of congregation. One might note the parallel with the Forum Romanum in Rome, which from this same time onward became primarily a showplace for the monuments of the emperors rather than a place of political assembly.

It would not be unreasonable, then, to suggest that the functions of the Athenian government might have been slowly transferred to the increasingly more important center in the area of the Roman agora. The construction of the Library of Hadrian might have given further impetus to such a move if the suggestion is correct that the Library was used as a repository for the records of the province of Achaia.[15]

Against this argument, however, is a substantial body of evidence to suggest that the buildings along the western side of the Agora continued to serve as the center of civic government until the time of the Herulian attack. Thus, for example, in the middle of the second century Pausanias noted (1.5.1) that the Prytaneis "sacrifice" (θύουσι— present tense) in the Tholos, while an inscription of A.D. 183 4 (IG II²

1799) also refers to the same building in the context of official activity. Remember here that the issue is not simply whether this buildings survived into the third century, but whether they continued to fulfill the same function they had in previous centuries.

In A.D. 203 a statue of the praetorian prefect C. Fulvius Plautianus was apparently erected near the Stoa of Zeus, suggesting that this area was still of political importance at that time.[16] One hears suspiciously little about the Bouleterion, although Pausanias' identification of it (1.3.5) suggests that it was in use at least through his time. The importance of these civic buildings, especially the Metroon, in the Athenian ephebic program further makes the transfer of their functions unlikely at a time when the ephebate was receiving renewed emphasis and when the number of ephebes was dramatically increasing.[17]

The archaeological evidence is generally in support of the conclusion that the west side of the Agora continued to serve as the civic center of Athens until at least the middle of the third century. Thus, the construction of the West Annex of the Tholos and the mosaic repair of its marble floor are both dated to the early years of the third century, while the wells in the area appear to have been in use continuously right up to the destruction in the 260's.[18] Even more instructive is the construction of a series of small offices, sometime in the second century A.D., on the west end of the terrace in front of the Middle Stoa.[19] These offices, then, were in very close proximity to the Tholos and the Bouleterion and they appear to have shared some of the same official functions with those buildings. Thus, two fragments of marble representations of Lakonian roof tiles were found in connection with these offices and they were probably set up as official standards for the manufacture of large roof tiles, parallel to the other standards of weights and measures which had been kept for centuries in the Tholos. The construction of this official complex in the western part of the ancient Agora is further testimony that the Athenians did not contemplate the transfer of the governmental center from its traditional location, even after the construction of the Roman agora and the Library of Hadrian.[20]

To return, then, to the original question: if the civic offices had not migrated out of the ancient Agora before A.D. 267, why did the new wall not include this region and why, presumably, were these finally forced to take shelter behind the new fortification? The reason seems to be, simply, that these buildings had suffered so greatly as a result of the Herulian sack that the Athenians could not contemplate their rebuilding given the weakened state of the community. But there is more. Let us consider for a moment the buildings which are known to have existed in the area around the Roman agora and which would have been enclosed by the new Athenian fortification wall.[21] In the first place there is the Library of Hadrian which, as we have seen, has been suggested as an archive for the province of Achaia from the time of its construction. Following the suggestion of Homer Thompson, perhaps this building replaced the Metroon as the repository for the city of Athens in the years after A.D. 267[22] The building was apparently damaged by the Heruli, but its massive exterior walls remained firm and served as an important stretch of the new fortification. Just to the east of the Library of Hadrian lie the remains of an enormous basilica of Hadrianic date, tentatively identified as the Pantheon.[23] This building apears to have escaped most of the Herulian destruction and its northern wall survived to a considerable height and served as the outer face of the Late Roman Fortification in this stretch. In the present state of preservation it is impossible to be certain about this, but it is likely that the interior walls of this basilica were also intact after 267 and the building was probably fully usable during those years.

We know so much about the buildings in the ancient Agora in part because of the breadth of the excavations in that area, but also because so many architectural fragments of those buildings were used in the construction of the Late Roman Fortification. The destruction or dismantling of the buildings in the third century ironically preserved many important pieces and saved them from later dispersal or destruction in the Byzantine and later lime kilns. For the buildings around the Roman agora the situation is far different, in part because few excavations have been carried out there, but also because the buildings as a whole seem to have survived the third century disaster in relatively better shape and thus their architectural pieces did not find their way so readily into the "museum" of the Late Roman Fortification. In some cases this has meant the better preservation of these buildings— compare the state of the forum of Caesar and Augustus to anything from a similar period in the ancient Agora—but it has also resulted in the loss of much information forever.

As we have suggested, the forum of Caesar and Augustus obviously escaped serious destruction at the hands of the Heruli. The so-called Tower of the Winds was likewise spared devastation and a recent study even suggests that it was converted into a baptistry during the early Christian period.[24] Just south of the Tower of the Winds is a large building, dedicated as was the Roman agora itself, to Athena Archegetis and the divine Augusti.[25] This was undoubtedly a public building connected with the commercial agora, and it survives in a very good condition. Further to the west, beyond the entrance to the market, stood the Agoranomeion in an area where its identifying inscription (IG II² 3391) was found.[26] The famous relief of the Athenian state calendar, containing the only surviving representation of the Panathenaic ship, undoubtedly came from another official building in this part of the city.[27] Its good condition and availability to be built into the Little Metropolis in the late 12th century suggests that the building in which it stood remained in good repair after A.D. 267. The crosses carved into the relief might even date to a period when the stone was in its original position, rather than to its re-use in the Middle Byzantine church. The gymnasium of Diogenes was also in this area somewhere, probably farther up the slope, and this played a large role in Athenian ephebic training. There is no reliable evidence one way or another about its possible survival into the later third century.

John Travlos has suggested the presence of a large Hellenistic stoa in this part of the city, of a type similar to the Stoa of Attalos.[28] Columns from this stoa, he argues, were used in the reconstruction of the interior of the Parthenon, which he dates to the reign of the emperor Julian (A.D. 361–63). In considering this same reconstruction W. B. Dinsmoor, Jr., has proposed a date in the early part of the fifth century after Christ, since some of the fragments of the original Parthenon were found built into late Roman walls of approximately that time.[29] Some of the entablature blocks used in this rebuilding had already been set up elsewhere (perhaps as many as four times), but the availability of such a large number of columns suggests that the building from which they came had survived the Herulian raid in reasonably good condition.

Finally, the colonnaded street and the structures behind the Library of Pantainos were obviously in the area enclosed by the new fortification; the street was that mentioned above as requiring special consideration in the building of the wall.[30] To the surprise of the excavators, this area presented the same situation as that encountered in the Agora proper: destruction at the time of the Herulian raid and desolation for more than a century afterward. Perhaps the area had not contained any strong monumental buildings (such as the Hadrianic constructions) and its proximity to the wall may have required the utilization of surviving buildings in its construction.

This exception aside, it may be suggested that the buildings in the area surrounded by the Late Roman Fortification had been less seriously damaged by the Heruli than those in the Agora to the west. This may explain why the line of the new fortification was placed where it was: the buildings in this area were in relatively good condition, and in the years after A.D. 267 (and not before) they came to house the important functions of civic government. If such a hypothesis is correct, the construction of the Late Roman Fortification did not cause the transfer of the governmental offices; the wall was built, after all, at least ten years after the invasion of the Heruli and the government, however battered, must have functioned somewhere. Instead, the wall followed the recent movement of the civic center to the east and carefully threw its protection around it.

As is generally known, Athens experienced a considerable recovery in the early years of the fifth century, and an ambitious building program was undertaken in the ancient Agora and other areas throughout the city and as far afield as the former Academy of Plato.[31] Such building in the area outside the Late Roman Fortification has suggested that the larger Themistoklean circuit was repaired and put back into operation. That may well have been the case, but one should bear in mind that we have very little direct information as to how early Byzantine fortifications were supposed to operate and what their strategic importance actually was. From the most simplistic point of view, we should note the assumptions of J. C. Russell, who argued that such fortifications should be taken as the geographic limits of the cities and that one can deduce absolute population figures from them.[32] Such an idea is ridiculous and fails to take into account any consideration of the function these walls were meant to serve. In Athens, for example, the excavators noted that even the Agora was inhabited during the fourth century, if only by squatters living amid the ruins. Thus, the wall was not meant to enclose the entire inhabited area, even at the time of its construction. Instead, the wall was apparently designed to serve a dual purpose: to protect the civic center and to act as a bastion or a place of refuge, to which the inhabitants could flee in a time of danger. In this respect it is noteworthy that Athens already had a natural citadel in the akropolis, and this had recently been fortified. Obviously, this was not felt to be sufficient and a fortification around part of the lower city was built. This must have been done to protect the center of the government and the commercial agora, perhaps also to safeguard the houses of the wealthy individuals who underwrote its construction.

Considerable archaeological evidence testifies to the upkeep and consistent repair of both sets of fortifications (plus those of the akropolis) at least to the period of the Frankish occupation in the thirteenth century. It is this combination that gave to Athens its unique spatial characteristics during the Middle Ages: the government and the market apparently continued to exist in the area protected by the Late Roman Fortification, while the medieval town spilled around the northern side of the akropolis as far as the ancient walls of Themistokles. Most of the houses and churches of Byzantine Athens lay in this area outside the Late Roman Fortification, but the center of the city was always within, either on the akropolis or the land directly below. "It is a striking fact that from this time [the third century] until the middle of the nineteenth century, the market place of Athens was located in precisely the same place and the life of the city continued to be concentrated there."[33]

From Athens let us turn our attention to Corinth, which was the capital of the Roman province and probably the largest city of Greece in the early Byzantine period. The classical walls of Corinth were among the most extensive of the ancient world; they enclosed an area so vast that much of it must have been agricultural land even at the height of the city's prosperity (Fig. 2).[34] The Romans methodically levelled sections of the wall when they took the city in 146 B.C. and no attempt was made to restore it or to build another until the barbarian invasions were well under way. In fact, unlike at Athens, the classical walls of Corinth were never rebuilt, except on Akrokorinth, and a new line of fortifications was undertaken only a century later, after the devastation of the city by Alaric and the Visigoths in A.D. 396. Then, with nearly all of the monumental buildings of the city in ruin, a new wall was constructed, and recent study has made it possible to trace its course around most of the city.[35]

What is most striking about this wall is its extent and location (Fig. 2). Although it is noticeably smaller than the enormous classical circuit, it is considerably larger than the Late Roman Fortification at Athens. Moreover, while the latter included the akropolis and a small section of the lower city, the early Byzantine wall at Corinth enclosed all of the central area of the ancient city, including the forum, and it left the heights of Akrokorinth outside the circuit. Akrokorinth itself had, of course, been fortified from an early date and it had formed an integral part of the classical defenses. At some point in the Byzantine period the citadel was again fortified, but it is unlikely that this was contemporary with the wall-building in the lower town. In any case, throughout the Byzantine period Akrokorinth operated as a separate citadel, a place of refuge for the inhabitants below or even the main dwelling-place in a time of difficulty, and it was not directly connected to the city with circuit walls.[36]

The early Byzantine city wall at Corinth was constructed as part of a larger plan to restore the shattered city after the Visigothic devastation. The most significant feature of this program, besides the wall itself, was the transformation of the central area.[37] In the years previous to the Attack of Alaric, the forum had been divided into two parts by the so-called Central Shops. After the departure of the barbarians the debris from these buildings was cleared away and a monumental stair-case, running the length of the forum, was constructed. At the center of this staircase the Bema was flanked by two decorative fountains, and for the first time in its history the upper and the lower parts of the forum were joined together in one monumental whole. This is a clear sign that Corinth continued to exist as a city and that its market place still served the public functions it had fulfilled in the centuries imme-diately preceeding. It is thus not mere chance that the fortification of the city included this urban complex.

Nevertheless, we should not assume that all of the inhabited area of Corinth was included within the new walls. For example, there is ceramic evidence of considerable habitation outside the fortified area, particularly to the east. In this regard, one can argue that relative to the classical walls and the placement of the central area within that circuit, the early Byzantine wall had "drifted" slightly to the east, something which is probably connected with changes in the urban settlement pattern during that period. The same phenomenon is suggested by changes in the forum itself, where activity seems to have decreased in the western area, while that around the Lechaion road—to the south and east of the old center—appears to have become the primary com-mercial area of the city. This development is paralleled at many other cities in this period, where shops along colonnaded streets were pre-ferred to the older squares for commercial exploitation.[38] It is also interesting to note that this area is today occupied by the *plateia* of the modern village of Ancient Corinth; it is possible that, as at Athens, the medieval and early modern urban development of the site took form in the period we are considering.[39]

Along its eastern side the early Byzantine wall at Corinth excluded the amphitheatre, which had apparently been built as late as the third or fourth century after Christ. Perhaps the amphitheatre was seriously damaged by the Visigoths or, more probably, it was considered less vital to the city's interests than the central area. At the western edge of the city recent excavation has discovered a Roman villa which was destroyed in the later years of the fourth century, again probably as a result of the Visigothic invasion.[40] The early Byzantine walls were built leaving the ruins of the house unprotected—and the villa was never rebuilt. In the western area, then, the wall may have represented the limit of the heavily populated urban area.

Another topographic feature apparently connected with the wall at Corinth is the location of cemeteries.[41] Despite statements to the contrary, in the classical and Roman periods the Corinthians had no hesitation about burying the dead within the walls of the city. It is probably not mere chance, however, that with one or two exceptions that can be explained on other grounds, there are no burials within the early Byzantine walls before the late sixth or seventh century. Furthermore, all of the important cemeteries known from this period were located immediately outside the walls, probably near important gates: these were the cemeteries at the Kraneion Basilica, Hadji Mustafa, Anaploga, Lerna Hollow, and the Stikas Basilica. It could be argued that these cemeteries were mostly near the great early Christian basilicas of Corinth and that their location had nothing to do with the walls. The cemeteries, however, seem generally to pre-date the churches and probably even the wall itself, and it appears that the architects who designed the wall consciously did so to exclude the cemeteries from the defensive circuit. It has been noted that the Late Roman Fortification at Athens enclosed few if any early Christian churches;[42] the same can be said of Corinth. Thus, of the some seven or eight early Christian basilicas identified at Corinth, only one—the newly-discovered church on Temple Hill[43]—lay within the new circuit. Whether or not this represents the division of the communities along religious lines is difficult to say: in Athens it is a distinct possibility, but the fortified area in Corinth seems to be too large to think that only pagans lived within it as late as the early fifth century.

The fortifications at Epidauros (the city, not the more famous sanctuary of Asklepios) on the western coast of the Saronic Gulf present a type that is very different from those of Athens and Corinth. Here the walls of the classical period ran around the two hills of the peninsula, on the northwest corner of which was, presumably, the agora.[44] Hence, even in the classical period the fortifications of Epidauros were different from those of the cities we have examined in that they enclosed only a small territory and left out many structures on the plain below. As we have seen, early Byzantine fortifications are normally much smaller than their classical predecessors, and Epidauros was no exception in this regard.

Probably in the early fifth century a wall was built at Epidauros using masonry technique identical to that used in Corinth. This wall, however, did not encircle the whole of the peninsula, but only the westernmost of its two hills, reducing the classical circuit by as much as two-thirds. Ceramic evidence and aerial photography, however, show that, as in the earlier period, settlement extended well beyond the fortified area.[45] Thus, there is considerable evidence for early Byzantine habitation along the coast, both north and south of the peninsula, but, interestingly enough, nothing from the eastern end of the peninsula, which lay outside the fortified area. Here again, the fortification wall did not mark the limit of habitation, but it serves as an indication of the direction of settlement. The early Byzantine settlement at Epidauros has received almost no scholarly attention and the wall has been noted only because it contains many inscribed blocks from the earlier theatre. It does, however, deserve thorough exploration and study.

The wall at Epidauros, then, seems to have enclosed the akropolis of the city, or perhaps even only a portion of that. A similar situation appears to have characterized the early Byzantine fortifications at Sparta where the walls had contracted radically and enclosed only the area of the ancient akropolis.[46] (Fig. 3) Why this should have been the case at Sparta is far from clear; certainly it was not because Sparta had sunk into insignificance in this period. All indications, including much evidence from the lower town, suggest that Sparta was a thriving community in the fourth through the sixth century.[47] Perhaps the explanation lies in the geographical situation of the akropolis, which is neither very high nor very steep on any side, but which occupies a considerable expanse of reasonably flat land. In fact, an examination of the plans of the two cities will show that the area enclosed within the early Byzantine walls of Sparta is roughly the same as that within the fortifications at Athens. The walls at Corinth are clearly much larger, but Corinth was the capital of the province and it was also probably larger than either Athens or Sparta at this time.

The topography of ancient Sparta is very poorly known, but it is likely that the agora was located just south of the akropolis, on the flat ground now occupied by the football stadium.[48] If that is correct, the early Byzantine walls at Sparta, like those at Athens, will have excluded the ancient civic center. Presumably, as at Athens, the functions of government at Sparta were transferred to quarters within the new fortifications. Again, topographic evidence is all too sketchy, but Sparta was clearly a flourishing city under the Roman empire and, if we are to believe Pausanias, its monuments must have been spectacular. Archaeologists have been put off by the statement of Thucydides and do not expect impressive buildings at Sparta—and indeed they do not find them. The same situation that biases the evidence at Athens, however, may be at work in Sparta. Thus, the buildings on the akropolis may have fared better than the lower city at the time of Alaric's invasion of Lakonia. In any case, the early Byzantine wall was constructed shortly after that event, cannibalizing many near-by buildings, including the whole of the theatre, which served as a bastion anchoring the southwestern corner of the fortification. Subsequently the fortified area became the center of activity and thus it remained at least until the migration of the Lakedaimonians to Mystra in the thirteenth century. Meanwhile, the ancient monuments of the city were buried beneath the debris of centuries.

The ruins of two churches have been identified within the walls at Sparta.[49] One of these has never been explored, but it has the ground plan of a typical early Christian basilica. The other is the church of St. Nikon which has traditionally been closely connected with the saint and dated to the late tenth or early eleventh century. Recent investigation, however, has suggested a date in the sixth century.[50] If this is correct Sparta will stand out as (perhaps with Epidauros) the only one of these cities which had significant ecclesiastical representation within its walls in the early Byzantine period. Perhaps the church of Sparta was in some way stronger or paganism weaker.

Thus, to summarize some of the observations noted in this brief survey. First, there were at least three separate types of city fortification from this period in Greece: the fortress, where only the akropolis was defended by circuit walls (Epidauros, Sparta); the composite type, where lower city and akropolis were fortified and joined together by city walls (Athens); and the extended type, where only the lower city was fortified or the akropolis formed a separate citadel of its own (Corinth). The latter two types were obviously required only when there was a substantial urban settlement to protect, but one must be very careful in using the size of fortifications as a guide to population size or urban vitality. As we have repeatedly seen, settlement frequently occurred outside the fortified area and walls were meant to serve different functions at different sites. Epidauros was certainly smaller than Athens or Corinth, but we hardly need an examination of fortification walls to tell us that. Whether Athens was larger than Sparta or Corinth is a more important question, but a comparison of the areas included within their early Byzantine fortifications would, I think, do little toward an answer.

What seems clear is that the fortification of cities both reflected contemporary situations and helped to determine future urban development. In the end, the form of the walls by themselves probably tells us little about the survival of cities in the Byzantine period, but it provides valuable information toward the history of events at individual sites. Certainly, the urban fortifications of late antiquity bore no simple relationship to the survival of urban forms, and one should similarly abandon the idea that a fortified city was *ipso facto* in decline. In fact, the construction of defensive walls is probably evidence of a certain degree of civic vitality, enough at least to respond to a crisis with organized and appropriate action.

As a footnote to this study we might mention yet another aspect of the early Byzantine city wall: it was designed not only for military purposes but also to express aesthetic monumentality. This may be difficult to imagine for anyone who has seen the beauty of a well-made classical wall, with its precise edges and tight mortarless joins, but walls of the Byzantine period were made in a different technique, and tastes had changed—as any comparison of a Byzantine church with a classical temple will clearly show. Therefore, instead of pointing to these structures as decadent examples of post-classical building technique, we should examine them for what their architects intended them to be. This will, first, require the abandonment of the idea that early Byzantine walls were hurried constructions built only for the needs of the moment.

For example, we may briefly return to the wall at Corinth, where one of the towers presents a strange triangular projection.[51] At first the excavators thought that the overlapping stones were the result of careless building, but a closer examination shows that the stones were carefully and deliberately cut to produce a kind of rustication when seen from outside. Virtually all surviving examples of early Byzantine walls in Greece demonstrate a similar concern for appearance: stone courses are normally levelled (even though most of the material is re-used from earlier structures), there is concern for the harmony of stone color and texture, and columns and other cut blocks are frequently integrated in a carefully thought out manner. The best example of this is from the southern side of the wall at Sparta.[52] Here the builders constructed an imitation Doric frieze, utilizing plain slabs and column drums in place of metopes and trigylphs.

In the instances where dating evidence is available, the cities of Greece appear to have been fortified either in the middle of the third century (at the time of the initial barbarian raids) or in the first years of the fifth century (after the invasion of Alaric). These fortifications were not "medieval" in the sense of later castles, since even the smallest of them allowed room for the inclusion of considerable habitable area and the institutions of civic life. None were situated on high and inaccessible hilltops, since this would have turned the cities into mere citadels and precluded organized urban life of any kind.

On the other hand, the fortifications were unlike their classical predecessors in that they were all much smaller and did not enclose any agricultural land or even all of the urban territory: in this way they served, like later medieval castles, as a place of refuge and a last line of defense. (And it should be remembered that classical walls frequently served the same purpose.) To be sure, the limits of the early Byzantine fortifications were tightly drawn and, as Lewis Mumford has pointed out, the function of a wall is not only to keep the invader out, but also to keep the inhabitants in and under the control of the government. In examining the effect of the fortification of the cities of Greece, we should not ignore the possibility that this contributed to the growing regimentation that was a general feature of the period throughout the empire.

Too much should not be made of this negative aspect, however, nor of the picture of the inhabitants of the cities huddling behind their walls for several centuries. We have already seen that most of the cities of Greece were unwalled until the beginning of the fifth century, and there is considerable evidence that the fortifications were already in disrepair by the middle or end of the century. It was fortunate for the cities of Greece that no serious invasion occurred during the fifth and early sixth centuries; had this occurred the disaster might have been on a scale of the invasion of Alaric.[53]

Toward the middle of the sixth century Justinian made some attempt to restore the fortifications of Greece, as part of an empire-wide program of defense.[54] Archaeological evidence of his work comes from Athens and a few other sites, but we now know much less about the nature of the Justinianic program than we once thought we did, when it was possible to assign every late wall to that emperor. In fact, it appears that Justinian's fortification of Greece was limited to restoration and it concentrated heavily on such "long walls" as those at the Isthmus of Corinth.[55] Indeed, Procopius himself tells us that Justinian hesitated to restore the walls throughout the Peloponnesos because the effort was simply too great. In other words, the building activity which was carried out in the early fifth century was no longer possible for an emperor in the middle of the sixth century.

Perhaps for these reasons—or perhaps because Justinian placed his hopes in imperial rather than local troops, or perhaps because social and economic collapse had exhausted the cities of Greece—they all, one by one, fell victim to the Slavic invaders in the late sixth and early seventh century. The walls, apparently, had failed to do their job. The Slavs, however, do not seem to have occupied the cities this far south in the Balkan Peninsula, and the fortifications remained, at least partially intact, to serve as the foundations for Middle Byzantine rebuilding and urbanization.

Notes

1. On the ancient city in general see first the classic work of Numa D. Fustel de Coulanges, *The Ancient City* (London 1873); also W. W. Fowler, *The City State of the Greeks and Romans* (London 1893), and Mason Hammond, *The City in the Ancient World* (Cambridge, Mass. 1972).

2. Ernst Kirsten, *Die griechische Polis als historisch-geographisches Problem des Mittlemeerraumes* (Bonn 1956) and Roland Martin, *L'Urbanisme dans la Grèce antique*[2] (Paris 1974).

3. Carl H. Kraeling and Robert M. Adams, eds., *City Invincible. A Symposium on Urbanization and Cultural Development in the Ancient Near East* (Chicago 1958), Charles Higham, *The Earliest Farmers and the First Cities* (Cambridge 1974), C. Renfrew, *The Emergence of Civilization. The Cyclades and the Aegean in the Third Millenium B.C.* (London 1972), and A. M. Snodgrass, *Archaeology and the Rise of the Greek State* (Cambridge 1977).

4. F. Dölger, "Die frühbyzantinische und byzantinisch beeinflusste Stadt," *Atti del 3° Congresso internazionale di studi sull'alto medioevo* (Spoleto 1958) 66–100. E. Kirsten, "Die byzantinische Stadt," *Berichte zum XI. Internationalen Byzantinisten-Kongress* (Munich 1958), George Ostrogorsky, "Byzantine Cities in the Early Middle Ages," *DOP* 13 (1959) 47–66, Dietrich Claude, *Die byzantinische Stadt im 6. Jahrhundert.* Byzantinisches Archiv 13 (Munich 1969), Clive Foss, "Archaeology and the 'Twenty Cities' of Byzantine Asia," *AJA* 81 (1977) 469–86.

5. A.H.M. Jones, *The Greek City* (Oxford 1940) 256.

6. For the construction of early Byzantine walls in general see Lloyd W. Daly, "Echinos and Justinian's Fortifications in Greece," *AJA* 46 (1942) 500–08, Michael Vickers, "The Late Roman Walls of Thessalonica," *Transactions of the 8th International Congress of Roman Frontier Studies* (Cardiff/Birmingham 1974) 249–55, and Clive Foss, "Atticus Philippus and the Walls of Side," *ZPE* 26 (1977) 172–80.

7. Much of what follows is based on Homer A. Thompson, "Athenian Twilight: A.D. 267–600," *JRS* 49 (1959) 61–72, John Travlos, Πολεοδομικη Έξελεξις των 'Αθηνων (Athens 1960), and *Idem, Pictoral Dictionary of Ancient Athens* (New York 1971).

8. Travlos, *Pictorial Dictionary (supra* n. 7) 161, 323, 483.

9. Travlos, Πολεοδομικη Έξελεξις *(supra* n. 7) 126–28 with the bibliography listed here.

10. Homer A. Thompson, *Hesperia* 28 (1959) 95–96.

11. Travlos, *Pictorial Dictionary (supra* n. 7) 439.

12. Thompson *(supra* n. 7) 65–66.

13. *Ibid.,* Travlos. Πολεοδομικη Έξελεξις *(supra* n. 7) 129–30. According to Travlos, the new wall enclosed an area of 160,000 m², approximately one-fourteenth of the ancient walled area. Note also that the Areopagus, which was presumably the site of the meeting of the Council of the Areopagus (which had increased in importance in Roman times) was outside the wall. Thompson, *The Tholos of Athens and its Predecessors.* Hesperia Supplement 4 (Cambridge, Mass. 1940) 137, suggests that the Metroon may have been used again for official purposes, but the evidence for this is slim.

14. Travlos, *Pictorial Dictionary (supra* n. 7) 28–29.

15. M. A. Sisson, "The Stoa of Hadrian at Athens," *BSR* 11 (1929) 50–72, P. Graindor, *Athèns sous Hadrien* (Cairo 1934) 241ff.

16. J. H. Oliver, *Hesperia* 10 (1941) 85.

17. J.A.O. Larsen, in Tenney Frank, ed. *An Economic Survey of Ancient Rome* 4 (Baltimore 1938) 492–96, Daniel J. Geagan, in *Aufsteig und Niedergang* II.7.1 (Berlin 1979) 408–10.

18. Thompson, *Tholos (supra* n. 13) 64 (mosaic repair), 84 (West Annex), 100 (well).

19. Homer A. Thompson and R. E. Wycherly, *The Athenian Agora* 14. *The Agora of Athens* (Princeton 1972) 79–80.

20. *Ibid*. 208–10: "The old administrative buildings, i.e. the Bouleterion, Tholos, Metroon and various civic offices, now went out of use, and as yet we have no idea what took their place."

21. Travlos, Πολεοδομικη Ἐξελεξις (*supra* n. 7) 100–03.

22. Thompson, *Hesperia* 6 (1937) 217–18, n. 5.

23. Travlos, *Pictorial Dictionary* (*supra* n. 7) 439–43.

24. David B. Small, "A Proposal for the Reuse of the Tower of the Winds," *AJA* 84 (1980) 97–99.

25. Travlos, *Pictorial Dictionary* (*supra* n. 7) 37.

26. *Ibid*.

27. L. Deubner, *Attische Feste* (Berlin 1932) 248–54, plates 34–40. Hans Gundel *RE* 2nd series, 10 (1972) 623. The date of the building from which the relief came is still very much in question.

28. Travlos, *Pictorial Dictionary* (*supra* n. 7) 281, *idem*, Ἡ πυρπόληοις τοῦ Παρθενωτος ὑπὸ τῶν Ἐρούλων καί ἡ ἐπιδκευή τοῦ κατὰ τοῦ χρόνου τοῦ αὐτοκράτορο Ἰουλιανοῦ, *AE* 1973, 218–36.

29. W. B. Dinsmoor, Jr., "New Fragments of the Parthenon in the Athenian Agora," *Hesperia* 43 (1974) 132–55. Alison Frantz, "Did Julian the Apostate Rebuild the Parthenon?" *AJA* 83 (1979) 395–401.

30. Thompson, *Hesperia* 28 (1959) 95–96, T. Leslie Shear, Jr., *Hesperia* 42 (1973) 391–92.

31. Thompson (*supra* n. 7) 66–70.

32. *Late Ancient and Medieval Populations* (Philadelphia 1958) 7–8, 71–88.

33. Travlos, *Pictorial Dictionary* (*supra*. n. 7) 29.

34. Rhys Carpenter and Antoine Bon, *Corinth* 3.2. *The Defenses of Acrocorinth and the Lower Town* (Cambridge, Mass. 1936).

35. T. E. Gregory, "The Late Roman Wall at Corinth," *Hesperia* 48 (1979) 264–80.

36. Carpenter and Bon (*supra* n. 34) 128–130, 272–74, Gregory (*supra* n. 35) 378–79.

37. Robert L. Scranton, *Corinth* 1.3. *Monuments in the Lower Agora and North of the Archaic Temple* (Princeton 1951) 131–32: "It may give some indication of the vitality of the city and the scope of architectural imagination at the time, to consider the magnitude of the scale on which [the forum] was laid out again after the disaster." Also, *idem*, *Corinth* 16. *Mediaeval Architecture* (Princeton 1957) 12–14.

38. Clive Foss, *Ephesus after Antiquity* (Cambridge 1979) 66–67.

39. Scranton, *Mediaeval Architecture* (*supra* n. 37) 49, 53, and *passim*, D. M. Metcalf, "Corinth in the Ninth Century: The Numismatic Evidence," *Hesperia* 14 (1973) 180–251, who argues, among other things, an expansion of the city eastwards in the ninth century.

40. Stella Grobel Miller, *Hesperia* 41 (1972) 333 and n. 6.

41. Gregory (*supra* n. 35) 279.

EARLY BYZANTINE GREECE   61

42. But see the following for suggestions of churches in this area: *Deltion* 19
(1964) Chr. Bl, 96, 20 (1965) Chr. Bl, 22 [church in the Roman agora],
Praktika 1950, 56–70 [church in Library of Hadrian; cf. Alison Frantz, *Hesperia* 25 (1966) 377–80, and the new excavations being carried out by Travlos in
1980–81]. Cf. Alison Frantz, *DOP* 19 (1965) 187–205.

43. Henry S. Robinson, *Hesperia* 45 (1976) 221–24; for a convenient survey
of the evidence for early Christian churches in Corinth see T. A. Gritsopoulos, Ἐκκλησιαστικὴ Ἱστορία Κορινθίας. Πελοποννησιακά 9 (Athens 1972)
77–85.

44. E. Protonotariou-Deilaki, *AAA* 5 (1972), Ioannis Papadimitriou, *Praktika* 1951, 204–12.

45. Charalamvos B. Kritsas, *AAA* 5 (1972) 186–99.

46. Ramsay Traquair, *BSA* 12 (1905–06) 415–30.

47. Alan B. Wace, *BSA* 12 (1905–06) 407–14, A. M. Woodward, *BSA* 26
(1923–25) 116–310, 27 (1925–26) 173–254, 28 (1926–27) 1–48. Libanius (*Or.*
1.23) says that he attended the festival of Artimis Orthia when he was a student
in Athens in the mid-fourth century.

48. Pausanias 3.11–14, Nikolaos A. Papahatzis, Παυσανίου Ἑλλάδος
Περιήθησιζ 2–3. Κορινθιακὰ καὶ Λακονι ά (Athens 1976) 337 n. 2, 353 n. 3.

49. G. Dickens, *BSA* 12 (1905–06) 431–39, G. Soteriou, *Praktika* 1939,
107–118.

50. D. I. Pallas, Ἐπετηρὶζ Ἑταιρείαζ Στερεοελλαδικῶν Μελετῶν 6 (1976–77) 1–80.

51. Gregory (*supra* n. 35) 267–68.

52. Traquair (*supra* n. 46) 427.

53. It is true that the Vandals from north Africa may have attacked the
Peloponnesos: Antoine Bon, *Le péloponnèse byzantin* (Paris 1951) 14. And the
Huns posed a serious danger in the middle of the fifth century, reaching
Thermopylae: Robert L. Hohlfelder, "Trans-Isthmian Walls in the Age of
Justinian," *GRBS* 18 (1977) 173–79.

54. Procopius *de aedificiis*, 4.2.23–28.

55. Paul A. Clement, "The Date of the Hexamilion," *Essays in Memory of
Basil Laourdas* (Thessaloniki 1975) 159–64, James Wiseman, *Land of the
Ancient Corinthians* (Götborg 1978) 63–64.

*This study owes much to frequent discussions with Dr. Judith Binder,
Professor Colin N. Edmonson, and Dr. Charles K. Williams II. The plans were
drawn by Suna Güven.

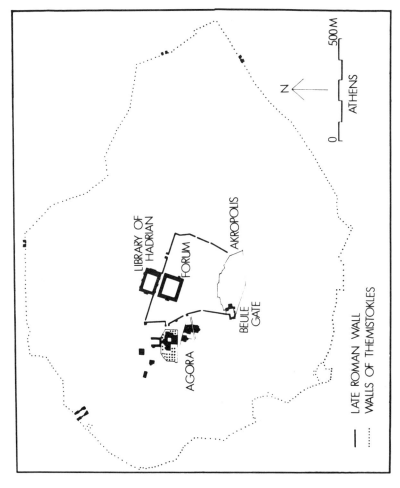

LIBRARY OF HADRIAN

FORUM

AKROPOLIS

BEULE GATE

AGORA

N

0   500 M

ATHENS

——— LATE ROMAN WALL
·········· WALLS OF THEMISTOKLES

Figure 1

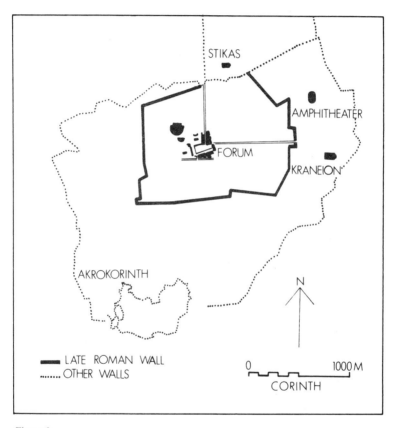

Figure 2

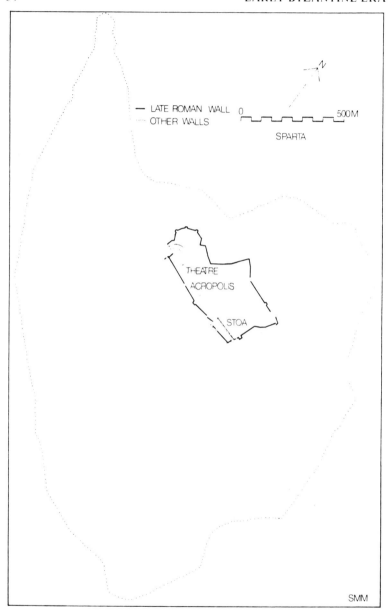

Figure 3

4

CAESAREA AND THE SAMARITANS*

Kenneth G. Holum
(University of Maryland)

The Samaritans, children of Israel who insisted that God's sacred mount was not Zion but Gerizim in Samaria,[1] passed through a distressing age in the later fifth and sixth centuries. Three times, in 484, 529–30, and 556, their distress induced them to rebellion against the Christian Roman Empire. Some time ago M. Avi-Yonah, in an article in *Eretz-Israel*, explored the roots of these revolts, the strength and strategy of the rebels, and the consequences of Samaritan disaffection.[2] He suggested that Samaria fell readily to the Persians and the Arabs in the seventh century in part because the Samaritans actively assisted the invaders. In 1965 Sabine Winkler subjected the second of the revolts (529–30) to a penetrating Marxist analysis.[3] She concluded that the impetus to rebel came from the lowest class of the sect, from Samaritan *coloni* reacting to social and economic oppression. In her view the movement was therefore a genuine popular one (a *Volksbewegung*) and progressive in the Marxist sense (*historisch progressiv*).[4] More recently (in 1971) Hans Gerhard Kippenberg, in his learned work *Garizim und Synagoge*, emphasized instead the eschatological character of the Samaritan uprisings.[5] Much is to be learned from these three scholars, and from others as well who have treated the revolts in more general works.[6] But thus far scholarship has ignored yet another striking feature of Samaritan rebellion, not its progressivism, its eschatological aims, or its contribution to the Persian and Moslem conquests but its Roman character. Unlike other persecuted minorities within the Christian Empire, the Jews for example, the Samaritans did not consider themselves alien to the Roman imperial system. Indeed they exhibited a remarkable level of Romanization, of assimilation to the Roman order.

In the case of the Samaritans this fact is indeed striking. Unlike the Jews, their fellow Israelites, the Samaritans had not enjoyed a measure of official toleration. Diocletian, for example, had freed the Jews from the obligation to perform pagan sacrifice, but not the Samaritans, for he considered them to be gentiles.[7] The Christian Empire, on the other hand, generally grouped the Samaritans with Jews and subjected them to similar legal disabilities. From the beginning of the fifth century, emperors issued constitutions excluding Samaritans from the imperial service, forbidding construction of new synagogues, and interfering with their right of bequest.[8] The Samaritans had the worst of both worlds.

Yet the Samaritans of Palestine flourished. The Samaritans in question were not the pitifully small remnant which survives today in Nablus (Ancient Neapolis) below Mt. Gerizim. They were a large and flourishing community in Samaria and the rest of Palestine, numbering in the hundreds of thousands.[9] Most of them, as Winkler insisted, were peasant farmers or *coloni*.[10] Procopius wrote in his *Anecdota* that decimation of them left the fields surrounding Caesarea Maritima, his native city, desolate.[11] But Samaritans, like Jews, also participated in the urban life of Palestine under the Christian Empire. Substantial numbers pursued the common Jewish occupations in commerce, industry, and the professions, not only in Neapolis, their stronghold, but in Sebaste, Scythopolis, Caesarea, and other urban centers.[12] Some Samaritans became wealthy and acquired land and substance, achieving municipal honors such as *pater* or *defensor civitatis*. Others entered the Roman civil service.[13] A rabbinic source indicates that the *taxis* of Caesarea, the *officium* or staff of the civil governor of the province, was composed mainly of Samaritans.[14] Some also acquired the senatorial dignity of *clarissimus*, Faustinus, for example, a Samaritan who embraced Christianity and advanced to *clarissimus, consularis* (governor) of Palestine, and eventually *epitropos* of the imperial domains there.[15] The notorious Arsenius, a Samaritan of Scythopolis whose adherence to Christianity (Procopius insists) was only nominal, became *clarissimus, illustris*, and a very rich man.[16] These two must represent a much larger group of Samaritans or men of Samaritan origin who had done well within the imperial system.

At the same time their humbler brethren in the countryside and towns of Palestine had apparently entered military service in substantial numbers. Samaritan *banditti* who plagued Christian pilgrims[17] represented a larger rustic stock with obvious military qualities, a welcome source of recruits which the Roman authorities did not neglect. After the Council of Chalcedon (451) a revolt led by the monks against its decisions threatened to detach Palestine from the Empire. Fortunately, the Emperor Marcian could depend not only on "Romans" in the area but also on loyal "Samaritan" troops.[18] The Samaritans in this episode seem to have been undisciplined irregulars, but some of their brethren also enlisted in the cohorts of the *dux Palaestinae*, the local military commander, as regular Roman soldiers.[19] In the fifth century soldiers of Samaritan origin contributed substantially to the security of Roman rule in Palestine.

It appears that at this time the Samaritans had accommodated themselves to the Empire and it to them, despite their religious separatism. This was an accommodation profitable for both parties, but nonetheless it had begun to disintegrate by the end of the fifth century. The government apparently had to look elsewhere for recruits because it began to enforce anti-Samaritan legislation which had been ignored previously. Given the large numbers of rural Samaritans, their military tradition, and their devotion to Mt. Gerizim, the fanaticism of the emperors and of the local Christian populace was bound to provoke disorder.

In 484 the inevitable violence broke out. At Neapolis a Samaritan gang attacked Christians at worship, cut the fingers from their bishop's hand, and insulted the eucharist. This is the account of Procopius of Caesarea, depending on local tradition.[20] John Malalas narrates the course of the broader revolt. According to him the Samaritans selected a "brigand chief" ($\lambda\acute{\eta}\sigma\tau\alpha\rho\chi\sigma$) named Justasas and "crowned him" ($\epsilon\sigma\tau\epsilon\psi\alpha\nu$). Justasas then marched with his Samaritan followers down from the highlands of Samaria and seized Caesarea Maritima, the metropolis of Palestine. There he burned the church of St. Procopius and celebrated chariot races in Caesarea's hippodrome. With assistance from local police cohorts, the *dux Palaestinae* recovered Caesarea, captured and executed Justasas, and dispatched his severed head "with the diadem" ($\mu\epsilon\tau\alpha\ \tau\sigma\upsilon\ \zeta\iota\alpha\zeta\eta\mu\alpha\tau\sigma$) to the emperor Zeno. Zeno punished the rebels in exemplary fashion, depriving them of their sacred mount Gerizim, ordering their synagogue on it destroyed, and consecrating a church to the Virgin Mary *Theotokos* upon the ruins. He also excluded the Samaritans from the imperial service, Malalas relates, and confiscated the estates of the wealthy.[21] Zeno's response guaranteed that this episode would be repeated. In 527 the emperor Justinian issued several edicts confirming the earlier disabilities of Samaritans and Jews and forbidding them in addition to possess real estate. In 529 an edict against the Samaritans alone ordered the destruction of their synagogues.[22] Enforcement of this legislation was the occasion of the second revolt which broke out in 529.[23] Samaritans rose in Neapolis again, this time slaughtering the bishop and seizing back Gerizim. Once again the Samaritans "crowned" a "brigand chief," this one named Julian, and once again this leader celebrated chariot races in the hippodrome, this time in the hippodrome of Neapolis itself.[24] Once again the *dux Palaestinae* was needed to suppress the revolt, and this time not only other Roman generals assisted him but also the federate Ghassanid Arabs under their phylarch Arethas.[25] Once again the Samaritan chief was executed and his head sent to Constantinople "with its diadem." Broader in scope, this revolt resulted in heavier Samaritan casualties. Malalas reports 20,000 dead, Procopius 100,000. Malalas says 50,000 fled to the Persians, and as a reward for his assistance, the Arab phylarch received 20,000 young Samaritan men and women to be sold as slaves. Justinian ordered the rebuilding of damaged Christian sanctuaries on Gerizim and a permanent garrison to forestall further Samaritan attempts to retake their sacred mount.[26]

The third Samaritan revolt, in 556, apparently occurred in Caesarea only and its environs.[27] Sharply reduced in numbers after the rebellion of 529–30, the Samaritans could no longer mount a large-scale revolt in the highlands around Neapolis, which in addition was guarded by the Gerizim garrison. Thus the Samaritans rose against Caesarea and burned its churches. When the provincial governor Stephanus resisted, they slaughtered him in his *praetorium* and put his property to the torch.[28] The Emperor Justinian sent Amantius, the *comes Orientis*, to investigate the affair, and Amantius sentenced the guilty to imprisonment, confiscation, or execution as appropriate in each case. There is no indication that suppression of this third revolt presented major military difficulties.

What is to be made of these rebellions? Sabine Winkler was surely correct in recognizing their popular and ethnic character, although her article reveals some hazards of applying Marxist analysis in an ancient context. It is not necessary to assume that the so-called "brigand chiefs" Justasas and Julian emerged from the proletariate, as she implied, or that the impetus for revolt came from only one social stratum of the Samaritans.[29] Malalas reports specifically (as noted above) that after the revolt of 484 Zeno confiscated the estates of wealthy Samaritans (δημευσας Γαι τους ευπορους αυτων),[30] presumably because these landowning Samaritans had supported the revolt. It is likely that Hans Gerhard Kippenberg was equally correct though one-sided in emphasizing the eschatological hopes of the Samaritans in town and countryside. John of Nikiu relates in regard to the revolt of 529–30 that the rebel leader Julian "seduced many of his people by his lying statement when he declared: 'God hath sent me to re-establish the Samaritan kingdom'; just as (Je)roboam the son of Nebat who, reigning after the wise Solomon the son of David, seduced the people of Israel and made them serve idols."[31] For many among the Samaritans, Julian (and Justasas before him) may well have embodied a Samaritan eschatological figure, the *malkah* ("king") who was to issue from the line of Joseph and restore the Samaritan nation while enforcing its claim to Mt. Gerizim.[32]

It is striking, however, that this eschatological figure appeared in Roman dress. Significantly, the Greek sources perceived not only "brigand chiefs" in Justasas and Julian but also "tyranny."[33] In the Roman world this was the official line not on brigands but on usurpers, on those who laid rebellious claim to the imperial power. The emperor's officials delivered the severed heads of Justasas and Julian to Constantinople—such was the spectacular punishment of "tyrants," and thus it was emphasized to the world that the integrity of the Roman order had been restored.[34] Apparently the emperor's officials also believed that Samaritan "brigand chiefs" had laid claim to the imperial power. With each head came the diadem with which the Samaritans had "crowned" their "brigand chief." Apparently the Samaritans themselves shared the view of the Greek sources and of the emperor's officers, for they had installed their leader in the Roman fashion, by coronation with the diadem.[35] From their point of view he was not a "brigand chief" or "tyrant," of course, or even exclusively *malkah*. He was *basileus*, common parlance for the Roman emperor. Cyril of Scythopolis, a sixth-century author from one of the Palestinian cities implicated in the revolt of 529–30, reports succinctly:

τυραννησαντες εστεψαν εαυτοις βασιλεα 'Ιουλιανον τινα συνεθνον αὐτων

This should mean: "establishing a tyranny, the Samaritans crowned Julian, one of their nation, as their emperor."[36] There is evidence for this interpretation in the course of Samaritan rebellion after coronation of the *basileus*. In both 484 and 529 the newly-crowned *basileus* of the Samaritans celebrated chariot races in the hippodrome, an act which in Roman eyes represented a claim to imperial sovereignty.[37] It is striking, moreover, that during the first revolt Justasas celebrated his coronation as *basileus* in the hippodrome of Caesarea Maritima, the premier imperial city of Palestine.[38] With its hippodrome, *praetorium*, and other imperial furniture, Caesarea would have made an appropriate urban setting for the rule of a separated *basileus*. During the second revolt, that of 529–30, the Samaritans adopted a course more in line with native tradition and cast Neapolis in the same role, for the analogy of Caesarea indicates that Neapolis too was to become capital of a separated *imperium Samaritanum*.

In 556 the Samaritans were left with the means only to lash out in their distress at the power which oppressed them, embodied in Caesarea and the governor's *praetorium* within it. Imperial reprisals after 530 had deprived them of sufficient manpower to inflict heavy damage and of the hope that they could protect their nationhood by constructing their own state independent of the Roman Empire. Paradoxically, the earlier revolts revealed how thoroughly the Samaritans had embraced Roman notions of political order—so thoroughly that in constructing their own state they adopted mainly Roman symbols of rule, coronation with the diadem, the ceremonial of the hippodrome, and the association of emperorship with an imperial city. The revolts therefore place in high relief the malign operation of Roman religious fanaticism and intolerance in preparing the East for the Moslem conquest of the seventh century. Enforcement of imperial legislation had alienated and nearly destroyed the Samaritan people, who earlier, despite their religious sectarianism, had demonstrated themselves to be energetic and devoted supporters of the Roman order.

Notes

*This paper is a slightly revised version of the author's contribution to the 1979 Byzantine Studies Conference. The author acknowledges the encouragement of Robert J. Bull, a member of the conference who is well known for his contributions to our knowledge of both Caesarea and the Samaritans.

1. In general see J. A. Montgomery, *The Samaritans* (Philadelphia, 1907)—outdated but still illuminating; M. Gaster, *The Samaritans: Their History, Doctrines and Literature* (London, 1925); and especially H. G. Kippenberg, *Garizim und Synagoge: traditionsgeschichtliche Untersuchungen zur samaritanischen Religion der aramäischen Periode*, Religionsgeschichtliche Versuche und Vorarbeiten, vol. XXX (Berlin and New York, 1971).

2. M. Avi-Yonah, "The Samaritan Revolts Against the Byzantine Empire," *Eretz-Israel*, 4 (1956), 127–32 (in Hebrew). I thank my colleague David Ruderman for assistance in the interpretation of this article.

3. S. Winkler, "Die Samariter in den Jahren 529/30," *Klio*, 43–45 (1965), 434–57.

4. *Ibid.*, p. 457.

5. Kippenberg, pp. 118–22, cf. *infra*, n. 32.

6. E.g. M. Avi-Yonah, *The Jews of Palestine: A Political History from the Bar Kokhba War to the Arab Conquest* (New York, 1976), pp. 241–43, 251.

7. Jerusalem Talmud *Avodah Zarah* 5. 4–44d; Avi-Yonah, "Samaritan Revolts," p. 128; *idem, Jews*, p. 241.

8. *Cod. Theod.* 16. 8. 16, 9. 28, *Nov. Theod.* 3.

9. Avi-Yonah, "Samaritan Revolts," p. 128, concludes from casualties in the second revolt that the community in Samaria alone numbered about 300,000!

10. Winkler, pp. 454–55; Avi-Yonah, "Samaritan Revolts," p. 129.

11. Procop. *Anec.* 11. 29.

12. Avi-Yonah, "Samaritan Revolts," p. 129; Winkler, pp. 453–54.

13. *Nov. Theod.* 3. 2 and *Cod. Iust.* 1. 5. 12 forbid such advancement for Samaritans and Jews, indicating that it was taking place at the time the legislation was issued.

14. Jerusalem Talmud *Avodah Zarah* 1. 2–39c. For the correct interpretation of this passage see S. Lieberman, "The Martyrs of Caesarea," *Annuaire de l'Institut de Philologie et d'Histoire Orientales et Slaves*, 7 (1939-44), 405-9.

15. Procop. *Anec.* 27. 26–31.

16. *Ibid.* 6–19, also Cyril. Scyth. *V. Sab.*, ed. Schwartz, *TU, XLIX:* 2, 172–73.

17. *Itin. Ant.*, ed. Geyer, *CSEL*, XXXIX, 164; Joh. Mosch. *Prat. sp.* 165, *PG*, LXXXVII: 3, 3032.

18. [Zach. Rhet.] 3. 5. trans. Brooks, *CSCO*, ser. 3, V, 109. According to this text, the local military commander, Count Dorotheus, ordered both "Romans" and "Samaritans" to attack the rebels: "Et Romanis ac Samaritanis mandavit, eosque feriebant et occidebant . . ." Later, renegade monks complained to Emperor Marcian and the Empress Pulcheria that "Samaritans" had plundered churches, and the sovereigns responded by ordering Count Dorotheus to conduct an investigation, restore stolen property, and punish the guilty. See *ACO*, II, 1, 3, 127, 129. Presumably these Samaritans, like the ones

mentioned in [Zach. Rhet.], were irregulars operating on this occasion under the command of Count Dorotheus. For the military organization of Palestine in this period see F.-M. Abel, *Géographie de la Palestine*, II (Paris, 1938), 178–84.

19. Joh. Mal. 15, p. 383 Bonn reports that after the revolt of 484 (*v. infra*) Emperor Zeno excluded Samaritans from imperial service: ποιήσας διάταξιν μὴ στρατεύεσθαι Σαμαρείτην. *Cod. Iust.* 1. 5. 12 forbids Samaritans (and Jews) from receiving the *cingulum militare*. Presumably recruiting among Samaritans had continued despite Zeno's measure.

20. Procop. *De aed.* 5. 7. 5–9.

21. Joh. Mal. 15, pp. 382–83 Bonn. For archaeological evidence of Zeno's church of Mary *Theotokos* and of the fortifications around it see A. M. Schneider, "Römische und byzantinische Bauten auf dem Garizim," *ZDPV*, 68 (1951), 217–34.

22. *Cod. Iust.* 1. 5. 12–14, 17.

23. Procop. *Anec.* 11. 24; Winkler, pp. 449–51.

24. Joh. Mal. 15, p. 446 Bonn. Montgomery, p. 115, n. 116, and Winkler, pp. 442–43, question the authenticity of this report, suggesting that Malalas assimilated this revolt with the one in 484. Cf. J. H. Humphrey, "Prolegomena to the Study of the Hippodrome at Caesarea Maritima," *BASOR*, 213 (1974), 37, also expressing skepticism. This caution is unnecessary. The report of Malalas is too circumstantial to be a doublet. Although archaeologists have not yet uncovered a hippodrome at Neapolis, there is no reason to doubt that one existed there.

25. On this figure cf. I. Kawar, "Arethas, Son of Jabalah," *JAOS*, 75 (1955), 205–16, and *idem*, "The Patriciate of Arethas," *BZ*, 52 (1959), 321–43.

26. Procop. *Anec.* 11. 24–30, *De aed.* 5. 7. 17; Joh. Mal. 15, pp. 445–47 Bonn; also Chor. Gaz. *Laud Ar. et Steph.* 10–19, *Laud. Summ.* 11–15, ed. Foerster and Richtsteig; Cyril. Scyth. *V. Sab.*, ed. Schwartz, *TU*, XLIX: 2, 171–74; cf. Winkler, pp. 435–42, for full discussion of the sources and Schneider, *loc. cit.*, for Justinian's fortress surrounding the *Theotokos* church.

27. Joh. Mal. 15, pp. 487–88 Bonn; Theoph. A. M. 6048, p. 230 de Boor.

28. Remains of part of this *praetorium* have recently been recognized at Caesarea; see R. Wiemken and K. Holum, "The Joint Expedition to Caesarea Maritima, Eighth Season," forthcoming in *BASOR*.

29. Winkler, pp. 453–57.

30. Joh. Mal. 15, p. 383 Bonn.

31. John of Nikiu, trans. Charles, p. 147.

32. Kippenberg, pp. 255–75; also S. J. Isser, *The Dositheans: A Samaritan Sect in Late Antiquity*, Studies in Judaism in Late Antiquity, vol. XVII (Leiden, 1976), pp. 127–31, for positive reaction to Kippenberg and a concise summary of Samaritan eschatological beliefs.

33. Joh. Mal. 15, pp. 382, 446, 447 Bonn; [Zach. Rhet.] 9. 8, trans. Brooks, *CSCO*, ser. 3, VI, 69–70; Cyril. Scyth. quoted *infra*.

34. For parallels see e.g. Amm. 22. 14. 4, 26. 10. 6, 27. 2. 10, and Joh. Mal. 15, p. 389 Bonn. For discussion of severed heads in Roman celebration of victory over tyrants and other threats to the Roman order cf. M. McCormick, "Odoacer, Emperor Zeno and the Rugian Victory Legation," *Byzantion,* 47 (1977), 218, n. 28, and the same author's forthcoming book *Eternal Victory,* a study of the transformation of Roman victory celebrations in Late Antiquity.

35. Cf. K. Holum, *Theodosian Empresses: Women and Imperial Dominion in Late Antiquity* (Berkeley, Los Angeles, and London, 1982), p. 28, n. 84, and literature there cited.

36. *V. Sab.,* ed. Schwartz, *TU,* XLIX: 2, 172.

37. Cf. especially J. Gagé, "ΣΤΑΥΡΟΣ ΝΙΚΟΠΟΙΟΣ: la victoire impériale dans l'Empire chrétien," *Revue d'histoire et de philosophie religieuses,* 13 (1933), 374–79.

38. *Nov. Iust.* 3 *praef.* emphasizes the preeminence of Caesarea among the cities of all three provinces into which Palestine was divided during this period.

A TWILIGHT OF PAGANISM
IN THE HOLY LAND:
NUMISMATIC EVIDENCE FROM THE EXCAVATIONS
AT TELL ER RAS

Robert L. Hohlfelder
(University of Colorado, Boulder)

The Tell er Ras explorations derived from the archaeological efforts at Shechem, the modern city of Nablus, ancient Neapolis, on the west bank of the Jordan River in the region known in antiquity as Samaria.[1] These campaigns were conducted by the Joint Expedition to Tell Balatah and were sponsored by the American Schools of Oriental Research. As part of this larger operation, surveys and excavations were carried out in 1964, 1966, 1968, and 1970 on one of the ridges nearby Mount Gerizim, on a peak known locally as Tell er Ras.[2]

Archaeological interest in Tell er Ras was spawned by a rich literary and numismatic tradition that speaks of the presence of a temple of Zeus Hypsistos on Mount Gerizim above Neapolis.[3] According to the writings of Marinus of Neapolis, a fifth century scholar, this structure had been built during the time of Hadrian. Its most singular feature, mentioned by the Bordeaux Pilgrim, Procopius of Gaza and Epiphanius, was a long stairway leading from the shrine itself down the slope of the mountain to its base. The temple, a secondary structure or altar, and the stairway often appeared as the reverse type on coins struck at the municipal mint of Neapolis from the reign of Antoninus Pius to the cessation of mint operations under Volusianus in the mid third century.[4] The Tell er Ras excavations hoped to document the existence of both the religious precinct and the stairway. Both of these objectives were achieved.

Sondages executed at various locations within the zone of archaeological interest revealed several notable structures, including the foundations of the temple of Zeus Hypsistos, remains of an earlier building beneath this edifice, and a series of cisterns that served the needs of the religious community. It was from the cistern complex that most of the coins were uncovered, although some finds were made in all areas probed. In addition to the 285 coins unearthed, numerous miniscule fragments of late Roman-early Byzantine *minimi* were recovered through a careful screening of archaeological fill. These coin scraps defied easy counting, analysis or cleaning and were not included in this study. A catalogue of all legible finds from the cisterns and elsewhere in the excavations appears as Appendix A.

This modest coin assemblage is of some importance for it provides a glimpse of a twilight of paganism in the Holy Land in the early Byzantine era. As is well-known, one of the major lines of official attack against paganism in the fourth century was an unprecedented barrage of legislation aimed at transforming a society's religious tradition (see *CTh*, xvi, 10, 1-18). The promulgation of a series of restrictive laws, however, in itself provides no gauge with which to judge their effectiveness or jurisdictional purview. In fact, the repetitive character of the surfeit of late fourth century legislation suggests that enforcement was spotty, inconsistent, and dictated more by the persuasion of local officials and religious sentiments of particular communities than by imperial policy.[5] It does seem likely that the hardening intolerance of official attitudes toward paganism was not apparent at the same time or to the same degree throughout the early Byzantine world. Thus, any evidence of a local or regional nature that elucidates progress of Christian suppression of pagan worship is of paramount importance. With sufficient local examples, a better and broader understanding of the translation of this policy to reality may be possible. The archaeological data from Tell er Ras, particularly the coin finds, provide such information. They offer insights into the demise of public pagan worship in one locality in the Holy Land.

The sizeable concentration of coins (nos. 88-192) from the fourth century before the era of Julian suggests that the temple of Zeus Hypsistos had survived the vicissitudes and challenges to paganism authored by the house of Constantine.[6] While the presence of coin finds cannot in any way measure pagan religiosity, the large number of issues does indicate an activity in and around the sanctuary that seems to have been maintained at a considerable level during what should have been difficult times.

The four finds from the reign of Julian (nos. 193–196) offer no clues as to what plans, if any, he may have had for refurbishing or expanding this shrine.[7] Other archaeological data do indicate, however, that portions of the temple were severely damaged by a devastating earthquake that occurred on May 19, A.D. 363 and that no extensive repair efforts were made subsequently.[8] In particular, a significant segment of the cistern complex appears to have been sealed by destruction debris during this disaster and not reopened. Some of the cisterns do appear to have survived the earthquake and continued to function, regardless of any damage suffered, until later in the century. The recovery of 33 fourth century issues (nos. 197–229) with a chronological provenance posterior to the reign of Julian suggests that the site was not abandoned completely or immediately after A.D. 363.

While the death of paganism's last imperial champion in A.D. 363 most probably accounts for the lack of efforts at rehabilitation, it would appear that the temple, regardless of its state of repair, may have continued to serve the religious needs of its pagan constituency in the years that followed. At the very least, the coin finds from after A.D. 363 indicate the continuance of activity in the sacred precinct, although on a reduced level.

It is more appropriate to look for the temple's ultimate moment in the last years of the century in the time of Theodosius I, whose efforts to proscribe paganism are well-known. The coin finds from the late fourth century suggest a gradual abatement, then cessation of use of the sanctuary during the reign of Theodosius or shortly thereafter.[9]

The apparent abandonment of the temple precinct at this time, however, may have had less to do with Theodosius's legislative activities than with the visitation of another natural catastrophe in the year following his death. A serious earthquake struck Antioch and its environs in A.D. 396 and may have caused widespread damage throughout the Levant.[10] Perhaps this disaster, or another one not recorded in surviving texts, was responsible for further damage to the structures on Tell er Ras.

It is also likely that during the end of the fourth century, the temple may have been desecrated and damaged by the wandering bands of Christian holy men who roamed Palestine.[11] Bands of monks were responsible for the commission and agitation of various, widespread acts of terrorism against pagans in the name of their Christian god. Certainly by the reign of Theodosius, the official policies of this ardent supporter of Christianity could only have encouraged the unofficial excesses of zealous, religious fanatics. While no specific evidence exists to link the decline of the temple of Zeus Hypsistos to the acts of Christian brigands, Tell er Ras would not have been immune to the passions sweeping the Holy Land and elsewhere in the early Byzantine empire. Sporadic violence against the temple itself, the physical embodiment of the old order, or any individuals who still held Zeus Hypsistos in reverence must be seen as a distinct possibility.

For whatever reason or combination of factors, by the beginning of the fifth century, the patterns of life surrounding the temple and its related structures appear to have changed dramatically.[12] The total absence of fifth century numismatic material from all excavated area points in this direction. Specifically, the failure of the excavators to find any fifth century coins in the cisterns that had survived the A.D. 363 earthquake suggests a final closing and/or abandonment of all these structures near the end of the fourth century. With their closing/ abandonment, the temple could not easily have functioned. There is every reason to believe public pagan worship of Zeus Hypsistos did not survive beyond the end of the fourth century.

Literary sources suggest that by the end of the fifth century and into the next, the Mount Gerizim region experienced better times. Considerable new construction occurred at that time.[13] The age of Justinian saw significant development as withdrawal from the *Limes Arabicus* to the east and shifting trade routes increased the importance of Neapolis.[14]

The new fortunes of Neapolis did not include the temple precinct. Given the prevailing climate of religious sentiment, it is predictable that no efforts were made to restore the temple. There is even evidence to suggest official cognizance of its looting in the fifth century. The Samaritan Chronicle edited by Adler and Seligsohn states that the doors of the temple of Zeus were removed from the ruined structure for reuse in a synagogue being constructed elsewhere in the Mount Gerizim area.[15]

Tell er Ras does appear to have experienced limited new construction at about this time. Although no fifth or sixth century coins were unearthed, other archaeological data were uncovered to suggest some rebuilding in the area. These new structures, however, were in no way related to the pagan cult once practiced there.[16] Thus, at Tell er Ras, far from the main centers of early Byzantine life, it appears a twilight of paganism ended c. A.D. 400. The uncompromising religious policy of Theodosius had prevailed here, even though it had not been directly responsible for the cessation of public worship of Zeus Hypsistos. Christianity's victory on Mount Gerizim came not by a single official act or mandate but rather by a process of attrition. As elsewhere in the region, paganism yielded grudgingly to the new order.[17]

Notes

1. Preliminary reports on this project appear in Robert J. Bull and G. Ernest Wright. "Newly Discovered Temples on Mt. Gerizim," *HThR* 58 (1965), pp. 234–247; Robert J. Bull and Edward F. Campbell, Jr., "The Sixth Campaign at Balatah (Shechem)," *BASOR* 190 (1968), pp. 2–41; Robert J. Bull, "The Excavation of Tell er-Ras on Mt. Gerizim," *BA* 31 (1968), pp. 58–73; and "A Preliminary Excavation of an Hadrianic Temple at Tell er Ras on Mount Gerizim," *AJA* 71 (1967), pp. 387–93. Also see Robert J. Bull, "A Tripartite Sundial From Tell er Ras on Mt. Gerizim," *BASOR* 219 (1975), pp. 29–37.

2. The Tell er Ras project of the Balatah (Shechem) expedition was directed by Professor Robert J. Bull of Drew University whom I wish to thank for the opportunity to study and publish the 285 coins uncovered during the course of his investigations.

I would also like to extend my gratitude to the Council on Research and Creative Work, University of Colorado and the Center for Byzantine Studies, Dumbarton Oaks, for generous financial support during the course of my research for this article. My preliminary study of the Tell er Ras coins began while I was a visiting fellow at Dumbarton Oaks in AY 1976–77. The final preparation of this material was completed during the tenure of a faculty fellowship from the Council on Research and Creative Work for AY 1981–82, with research conducted at Dumbarton Oaks.

A preliminary report on this topic was presented at the Fifth Annual Byzantine Studies Conference at Dumbarton Oaks, Washington, D.C. October 27, 1979. An abstract was published in *Abstract of Papers* (Washington, D.C., 1979), pp. 34–35.

3. References to pertinent ancient authors appear in works cited in note 1.

4. For the temple precinct and stairway as a local coin type, see *BMC Palestine*, nos. 21 ff., p. 48, *passim*. Also see Y. Meshorer, *SNG: The Collection*

of the American Numismatic Society, Pt. 6, Palestine—South Arabia (New York, 1981), nos. 965, 989, 991, ff. Photographs and line drawings of issues of this coin series also appear in the articles cited in note 1.

5. A point also made by S. Lieberman, "Palestine in the Third and Fourth Centuries," *Jewish Quarterly Review* 36 (1946), p. 344.

6. Robert J. Bull, "Sixth Campaign," p. 6, suggested that the temple was already in ruins by the reign of Julian citing as evidence a Samaritan chronicle edited by E. N. Adler and M. Seligsohn, "Une nouvelle chronique Samaritaine," *REJ* 45 (1902), pp. 82–84 and pp. 232–34. This edition states that it was in the year 4735 in which the huge bronze doors of the temple were taken by the Samaritans for their synagogue. Although the exact reckoning of years in the Samaritan era is controversial, according to the Adler-Seligsohn scheme, the year 4735 A.C. (after creation) would be c. 414 5, clearly not consistent with destruction before Julian. See Aviva Müller-Lancet, "Samaritans," *Encyclopaedia Judaica* 14 (1971), p. 750 for the various Samaritan eras. Hans Gerhard Kippenberg, *Garizim und Synagoge* (Berlin, 1971), p. 111, notes that the building of the Synagogue followed the destruction of the temple but suggests this event occurred slightly earlier than A.D. 415. But regardless of the resolution of this problem, the numismatic evidence clearly indicates extensive use of the cisterns and precinct to and through the reign of Julian.

7. An interesting parallel to the situation at Tell er Ras occurred at Kenchreai (Greece). There a temple of Isis was in use through the fourth century to the time of Julian, when it appears major refurbishing efforts were to have begun. The sudden death of the emperor aborted these plans. Shortly thereafter, in A.D. 365 and A.D. 375, the site was visited by two earthquakes and associated seismic sea waves. During the last years of the century, the temple was finally abandoned. See Robert L. Hohlfelder, "Kenchreai on the Saronic Gulf: Aspects of Its Imperial History," *CJ* 71 (1976), pp. 224–26.

8. Robert J. Bull gives the date of this earthquake as A.D. 362, following D.H.K. Amiran. See "Sixth Campaign," p. 16, *passim*. A new study of this earthquake offers convincing arguments for a slightly later and more specific date. Kenneth W. Russell, "The Earthquake of May 19, A.D. 363," *BASOR* 238 (1980), pp. 47–64. Professor Russell states: "To the author's knowledge, only the mid-4th century destruction evidence at Shechem has been attributed to Amiran's 362 earthquake." (p. 55) The numismatic evidence, which formed the basis of Bull's acceptance of the A.D. 362 date, allows Russell's proposed revision.

9. The latest fourth century coins that can be dated with certainty are nos. 222–228, from a series issued from A.D. 383 to A.D. 395. No. 229, which is in poor condition, may have been struck as late as A.D. 408, but a fourth century issuance seems more probable.

10. D.H.K. Amiran, "A Revised Earthquake-Catalogue of Palestine," *IEJ* 2 (1952), pp. 48–65. Amiran does not indicate that the earthquake of A.D. 396 was particularly severe. Cf. Glanville Downey, *A History of Antioch in Syria*

from Seleucus to the Arab Conquest (Princeton, 1961), p. 438, who suggests this earthquake may "have affected most of the eastern Empire".

11. Peter Brown, *The World of Late Antiquity* (New York, 1971), p. 104.

12. Cf. Bull and Wright, "Newly Discovered Temples," p. 234, who suggest it was certainly not in use by the end of the fifth century.

13. E.g., Proc., *de aed.*, V, 7, 8.

14. M. R. Block, "Salt in Human History," *Interdisciplinary Science Review* 1 (1976), pp. 336–52, suggests that by c. A.D. 600, Neapolis was flourishing owing to its importance as a major station on the salt trading route from the Dead Sea area.

15. See above note 6.

16. Bull, "Excavation of Tell er-Ras," p. 68 and p. 72.

17. On the persistence of paganism see Etienne Chastel, *Historie de la destruction du paganisme dans l'empire d'orient* (Paris, 1850), pp. 207–25 and F. M. Abel, *Histoire de la Palestine*, II (Paris, 1952), pp. 315ff. The survival of paganism in Antioch is discussed by G. Downey, *A History of Antioch*, p. 483 and pp. 491ff. In this same city, it appears a pagan coin type, the tyche of Antioch, may have been struck on local issues until A.D. 528. Dorothy B. Waage, *Antioch-on-the-Orontes* IV, *Pt. 2, Greek, Roman, Byzantine and Crusaders' Coins* (Princeton, 1952), p. 153. At Caesarea Maritima, a building known as the Hadrianeum survived into the sixth century. See Lee Levine, *Caesarea Under Roman Rule* (London, 1975), p. 182, n. 142. The existence of a structure with this name does not prove public pagan worship. In this context, however, Procopius, commenting on his native city of Caesarea, notes the presence of polytheists in the sixth century. Could this be a reference to pagans? *Anecdota*, XI, 26–27. The existence of paganism in Gaza as a vital force even after the reign of Theodosius is noted by Marc the Deacon, *Vita Prophyrii* 41, eds. H. Gregoire and M. A. Kugener, Paris, 1930. Arcadius was reluctant to move against the pagans of Gaza for the city "loyally pays its taxes and contributes a great deal to the treasury." Clearly, religious considerations were not always paramount. His policy for handling the pagan situation was to proceed slowly, undermine the civil positions of the pagan leadership in the community and order the temples closed but not destroyed. This policy of moderation was fought by Eudoxia who did prevail in May, A.D. 402 when the army was sent into the city to ensure the cessation of public pagan worship. Even this act did not bring peace to the city. Pagans continued to quarrel with Christians and civil disturbances continued between the two factions. See Glanville Downey, *Gaza in the Early Sixth Century* (Norman, Okla., 1963), pp. 21ff. Although public pagan worship had been suppressed at Tell er Ras by c. A.D. 400, it would appear that the edict of Honorius and Theodosius of A.D. 423 in which they claim that no more pagans exist (*CTh*, XVI, 10, 22) may have been a bit premature for the Holy Land.

COIN FINDS FROM TELL ER RAS*

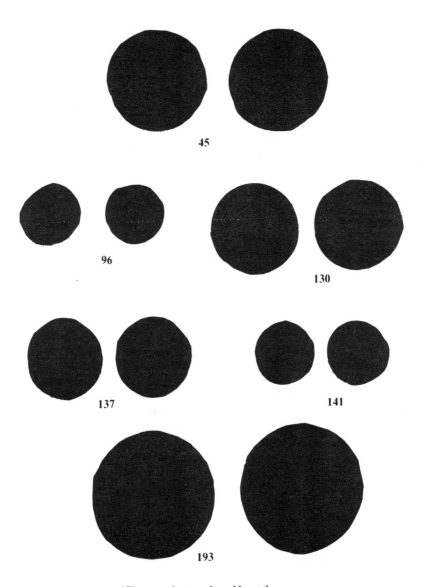

45

96

130

137

141

193

*Photographs to scale and by author

APPENDIX A
COIN LIST

CATALOGUE
NUMBER
(* following number
indicates the coin
was not found in the
cistern excavations;
an underline indi-
cates the coin is il-
lustrated— See Fig.
1.)

ISSUING AUTHORITY, DATE, MINT (if known), DENOMINATION (if known)
REVERSE TYPE
MAXIMUM DIAMETER IN MILLIMETERS
AXIS OF REVERSE DIE
WEIGHT IN GRAMS

(** following the Issuing Authority and Date indicates
that the coin was not available for a confirmation of
the preliminary identification which is here presented)

REFERENCE
FIELD REFERENCE DATA
EXCAVATION/YEAR OF FIND
DATE OF FIND
AREA REFERENCE
LOCUS
REGISTRATION NUMBER
B = Balatah; TR = Tell er-Ras

Pre-Roman Issues

1.* SELEUCUS IV, PHILOPATOR, 187–175 B.C.
ΒΑΣΙΛΕΩΣ ΣΕΛΕΥΚΟΥ; Elephant's head l., below, ˙1
14 / 3.34
cf. BMC Seleucid Kings, no. 29, p. 33
B68 6/29 XII.1.52 L.12135 Reg. 638

2.* ANTIOCHUS VII, SIDETES, 174–183 B.C.
ΒΑΣΙΛΕΩΣ ΑΝΤΙΟΧΟΥ ΕΥΕΡΓΕΤΟΥ; head-dress
of Isis
17 ↑ 4.43
BMC Seleucid Kings, nos. 49–51, p. 73
B68 6/30 XII.15.26 L.121510 Reg. 667

3. ALEXANDER JANNAEUS, 103–76 B.C.**
Meshorer, Jewish Coins, nos. 8–9, pp. 118–119

(APPENDIX A CONTINUED)

B64 - TR 1. F/ P Reg. 695

Star with eight rays
11 - 0.59

4.

AS ABOVE
14 - 1.40

5.*

AS ABOVE
14 - 2.19

6.*

AS ABOVE
15 - 1.92 (frag.)

7.*

AS ABOVE
16 - 2.33

8.*

AS ABOVE
16 - 4.46

9.*

AS ABOVE
16 - 2.15

10.*

AS ABOVE
15 - 2.03

11.*

AS ABOVE
14 - 2.28

12.*

AS ABOVE
15 - 2.65

13.*

AS ABOVE

AS ABOVE
B66 6/14 XII.7.12 1..12708 Reg. 132

AS ABOVE
B68 6 12 XII.2.5. 1.. - Reg. 87

AS ABOVE.
B68 6 11 XII.1.12 1..12138 Reg. 93

AS ABOVE
B68 7 2 XII.12.82 1..123906 Reg. 695

AS ABOVE
B68 7 2 XII.3.82 1..123006 Reg. 697

AS ABOVE
B68 7 2 XII.3.82 1..123006 Reg. 696

AS ABOVE
B68 7 2 XII.3.82 1..123006 Reg. 698

AS ABOVE
B68 7 2 XII.3.82 1..123006 Reg. 699

AS ABOVE
B68 7/2 XII.3.82 1..123006 Reg. 700

Meshorer, *Jewish Coins*, no. 8A, p. 119

Meshorer, *Jewish Coins*, nos. 8–9, pp. 118–119

No.		Reference
	15 - 1.68	B68 7/2 XII.3.82 L.123006 Reg. 701
14.*	AS ABOVE 13 - 1.50	B68 7/2 XII.3.82 L.123006 Reg. 702
15.*	AS ABOVE 15 - 1.95	AS ABOVE B68 7/3 XII.3.85 L.123006 Reg. 723
16.*	AS ABOVE 14 - 1.38	AS ABOVE B68 7/3 XII.3.85 L.123006 Reg. 724
17.*	AS ABOVE 15 - 1.63	AS ABOVE B68 7/6 XII.15.39 L.121509 Reg. 768
18.*	AS ABOVE 15 - 2.03	AS ABOVE B68 7/9 XII.3.92 L.123008 Reg. 849
19.*	AS ABOVE 15 - 1.55	AS ABOVE B68 7/15 XII.2 - Fosse Reg. 965
20.	AS ABOVE** 13 - 1.79	AS ABOVE TR70 XII.7/7.91 L.127007 Reg. 11
21.	AS ABOVE** 16 - 1.80	AS ABOVE TR70 XII.7/7.107 L.127709 Reg. 12
22.	AS ABOVE** 15 - 2.29	AS ABOVE TR70 - XII.7/7.107 L.127709 Reg. 14
23.	AS ABOVE** 11 - 0.61	AS ABOVE TR70 - XII.7/7.107 L.127709 Reg. 16
24.	AS ABOVE** 15 - 1.38	AS ABOVE TR70 - XII.7/7.116 L.127709 Reg. 17

(APPENDIX A CONTINUED)

25. AS ABOVE**   AS ABOVE
    15 - 1.82   TR70 - XII.7/7.119 L..127709 Reg. 18

26. AS ABOVE**   AS ABOVE
    15 - 1.80   TR70 - XII.7/7.119 L..127710 Reg. 19

27. AS ABOVE   AS ABOVE
    13 - 2.07   TR70 - XII.7/7.119 L..127710 Reg. 20

28. AS ABOVE**   AS ABOVE
    15 - 1.26   TR70 - XII.7/7.119 L..127710 Reg. 21

29. AS ABOVE**   AS ABOVE
    14 - 1.73   TR70 - XII.7 7.119 L..127710 Reg. 22

30. AS ABOVE   AS ABOVE
    14 - 1.28   TR70 - XII.7 7.119 L..127710 Reg. 23

31. AS ABOVE   AS ABOVE
    13 - 1.22   TR70 - XII.7 7.119 L..127710 Reg. 24

32. AS ABOVE**   AS ABOVE
    16 - 1.11   TR70 - XII.7 7.119 L..127710 Reg. 25

33. AS ABOVE**   AS ABOVE
    13 - 1.89   TR70 - XII.7 7.110 L..127710 Reg. 26

34. AS ABOVE   AS ABOVE
    16 - 1.86   TR70 - XII.7 7.119 L..127710 Reg. 27

35. AS ABOVE   AS ABOVE
    14 - 1.58   TR70 - XII.7 7.123 L..127710 Reg. 28

36. AS ABOVE**
13 - 0.98

AS ABOVE
TR70 - 7/7.123 L.127710 Reg. 29

37. JOHN HYRCANUS II, 63–40 B.C.
Double cornucopiae with pomegranate between
16 - 1.98

Meshorer, *Jewish Coins*, nos. 18–27, pp. 121–123
B68 6/18 XII.9.29 L.12971 Reg. 458

38. HEROD, 40–4 B.C.
Anchor in wreath
14 - 0.78

Meshorer, *Jewish Coins*, n.51, p. 129
B68 6/29 XII.15.24 L.121509 Reg. 645

39.* HEROD ARCHELAUS, 4 B.C.–A.D. 6
Double cornucopiae
15 \ 1.38

Meshorer, *Jewish Coins*, nos. 56–56A, p. 130
B68 6/15 XII.2.10 L.12265 Reg. 109

ROMAN ISSUES

40.* NERO, AD. 58–59
NEP' in olive wreath tied with X below
ωNO
C
17 ↑ 2.35

BMC Palestine, nos. 1 ff., pp. 266 ff.
B64 - 'TR L. G. Reg. 391

41. ANTONINUS PIUS, A.D. 146–160, Gaza**
. . . ΓΑΖΑ; City goddess r.
16 — —

BMC Palestine, nos. 56 ff., pp. 151 ff.
TR70 - XII.7/7.66 L.127705 Reg. 7

42.* FAUSTINA (the Younger), A.D. 159–160, Neapolis
ΦΑΝΕΑ . . .; Tyche with rudder; to l. E T; to r., IIH
26 ↑ 10.28

BMC Palestine, nos. 53–57, p. 53
B68 7/18 XII.3.114 L.12300.15 Reg. 987

(APPENDIX A CONTINUED)

43.* COMMODUS, A.D. 177–192, Neapolis**
... ΕCTPI. .; Tyche standing l.
18 ↑ 4.42

    BMC Palestine, nos. 80–83, pp. 57–8
B64 TR Locus F Reg. 699

44.* AS ABOVE
Illegible; cult statue of goddess
20 ↑ 8.07

    cf. *BMC Palestine*, nos. 77–78, p. 57
B68 7/9 XII.3.93 L.12300.3 Reg. 814

45. CARACALLA, A.D. 198–217, Smyrna and Pergamum
ΠΕΡΑ-ΜΗΝΩΝ-ZΜΙVΡΝΑΙΩΝ; Asclepius standing
r. and Cybele seated l.; above, ΟΜΟΝΟΙΑ; in ex.,
ΕCΤΕΜΙΝΟ
33 ↓ 18.42

    BMC Ionia, no. 507, p. 306
B68 6 17 XII.9.26. L.12971 Reg. 365

46. ELAGABALUS, A.D. 218–222, Neapolis
Illegible; Mount Gerizim; colonnade at base
20 / 9.42

    BMC Palestine, nos. 95 and 99, pp. 60–61
B66 6 9 XII.7.10 L.12706 Reg. 150

47.* ELAGABALUS, A.D. 218–222, Aelia Capitolina**
... AEL-CAP-CO . . . ; Founder, Hadrian, togate,
ploughing l. with bull
24 ↑ 8.89

    cf. *BMC Palestine*, no. 2, p. 82 for rev.
type issued by Hadrian
(Field reference data not available)

48. ALEXANDER SEVERUS, A.D. 218–222**
PROV-IDENTIA-AVG; Annona standing l; to lower l.,
S; to lower r., C
28 ↑ -

    (Reference not cited with preliminary
identification)
B66 XII.7.28 L. 12717 Reg. 223

49. PHILIP I, A.D. 218–222, Neapolis

    BMC Palestine, no. 117, p. 63

50. Illegible; Mount Gerizim supported by eagle
27 ↑ 18.30

B66 6 20 XII.7.28 I..12717 Reg. 225

AS ABOVE
COL...; Asclepius seated l.; Hygieia standing r.:
between, altar; ex. illegible
27 ↑ 16.95

BMC Palestine, no. 126, p. 66
B66 6 20 XII.7.28 I..12717 Reg. 224

51. TREBONIANUS GALLUS, A.D. 251–253, Tyre
... ETR: Two crowns, illegible inscriptions within;
club and palm branch above; murex shell below
28 ¹² 13.92

BMC Phoenicia, no. 444, p. 285
B66 6/15 XII.7.15 I..12710 Reg. 137

52. VOLUSIANUS, A.D. 251–253, Neapolis
... ΠΟΛΕWC; Mount Gerizim supported by eagle
24 ↑ 10.72

BMC Palestine, nos. 160–162, p. 73
B66 7/6 XII.7.60 I..12717 Reg. 538

53.* AS ABOVE**
27 ↑ 10.72

AS ABOVE:
B68 6/15 XII.12.4 I.-Reg. 113

54. UNCERTAIN, Third Century, Neapolis?
Illegible
25 - 9.00

B66 7/7 XII.7.70 I..12717 Reg. 551

55. GALLIENUS, A.D. 253–260, AkkO Ptolemais
COL-PT-OI.: Diety with shrine
27 ↑ 13.28

Kadman, CAP, no. 266, p. 142
B66 7/6 XII.7.60 I..12717 Reg. 537

56.* GALLIENUS, A.D. 253-268, Siscia, Antoninianus
FORTVNA REDVX; Fortuna standing; to r., S
20 ↓ 2.13

RIC. V, 1, no. 572, p. 181
B68 6/13 XII.2.9 I..12717 Reg. 537

(APPENDIX A CONTINUED)

57.* GALLIENUS: A.D. 259–268**
OPTVMA REIDVX: Felicitas standing
21 ← 2.12
(Reference not cited with preliminary identification.)
B68 - XII.2.9. I..12264 Reg. 103

58. AURELIAN. A.D. 270–275
ORIENS AVG: in ex... XVIIII
22 ↑ -
(Reference not cited with preliminary identification.)
B66 - XII.7.60 I..12717 Reg. 540

59. SEVERINA. A.D. 272–275. Antioch. Antoninianus
CONCORDIAE MILITVM: in ex... XXI; above ex... S
23 ↓ 2.50 (frag.)
RIC. V. 1, no. 20, p. 218
B66/7/6 XII.7.60 I..12717 Reg. 539

60.* CARUS. A.D. 282–283. Antioch. Antoninianus
VIRTVS A-VGG: in ex... XXI; above ex... A
22 ↓ 3.83
RIC. V. 2, no. 124. p. 150
B68/7/6 XII.2.57 I..12292 Reg. 847

61. CARINUS. A.D. 283–285. Cyzicus. Antoninianus
CLEMENTIA TEMP: in ex... XXI; above ex... E
19 ↓ 3.16
RIC. V. 2, no. 324, p. 178
B68/6/17 XII.9.26 I..12971 Reg. 378

62. DIOCLETIAN. A.D. 285–287. Siscia. Antoninianus
CLEMENTIA TEMP: ex. illegible; above ex... A
20 ↓ 2.89 (in frags.)
RIC. V. 2, no. 252, p. 246
B68/6/17 XII.9.26 I..12971 Reg. 383

63. DIOCLETIAN. A.D. 291. Heraclea. Antoninianus
CONCORDIA MILI-TVM: in ex... XII · ; above ex...
E
22 ↑ 2.61
RIC. V. 2, no. 284. p. 249
B68/6/17 XII.9.26 I..12971 Reg. 374

64. DIOCLETIAN. A.D. 292. Heraclea. Antoninianus
AS ABOVE

No.	Description	References
	AS ABOVE; above ex., HA 22 ↑ 3.00 (in frags.)	B66 6/16 XII.7.19 I..12716 Reg. 367
65.	MAXIMIAN, A.D. 293, Cyzicus, Antoninianus AS ABOVE; in ex., XXI·: above ex., Λ 22 ↑ 3.24	cf. RIC, V. 2, nos. 605–606, p. 291 B68 6/17 XII.9.26 I..12971 Reg. 379
66.	DIOCLETIAN, A.D. 295–299, Cyzicus, Follis Fraction CONCORDIA MI-LITVM; below, KΓ 21 ↑ 2.72	RIC, VI, no. 15a, p. 581 B68 6/18 XII.9.29 I..12971 Reg. 457
67.	MAXIMIAN, A.D. 295–299, Cyzicus, Follis Fraction** AS ABOVE; below, KΔ or KA 20 ↓ 2.10	cf. RIC, VI, nos. 15b & 16b, p. 581 B66 - XII.7.19 I..12716 Reg. 370
68.	DIOCLETIAN, A.D. 297, Antioch, Follis Fraction AS ABOVE; in ex., ANT; above, E 20 ↑ 2.18	RIC, VI, no. 62a, p. 621 B66 6/16 XII.7.19 I..12716 Reg. 369
69.	MAXIMIAN, A.D. 305–306, Alexandria, Follis Fraction AS ABOVE; in ex., ALE; above, A or Δ 21 ↑ 2.02	RIC, VI, no. 59b, p. 670 B66 7/7 XII.7.70 I..12719 Reg. 552
70.	MAXIMIAN, A.D. 308, Alexandria, Follis Fraction PROVIDENTIA DEORVM; in ex., ALE; above, Γ 22 ↑ 2.13	RIC, VI, no. 90b, p. 676 B68 6/17 XII.9.26 I..12971 Reg. 375
71.	MAXIMINUS, A.D. 310–311, Nicomedia, Follis GENIO AV-GVSTI CMH; in ex., SMNB 25 ↓ 6.12	RIC, VI, no. 66c, p. 565 B66 7/6 XII.7/60 I..12719 Reg. 546

(APPENDIX A CONTINUED)

72. MAXIMINUS, A.D. 312–313, Alexandria, Follis
AS ABOVE; in ex., ALE; to l., ; to r., Γ
22 ↑ 3.93
RIC. VI, no. 160b, p. 685
B68 6/ 17 XII.9.26 I..12971 Reg. 380

73. MAXIMINUS, A.D. 312, Antioch, Follis
IOVI CONS-ERVATORI; in ex., ANT; to l., *; to r., B
20 ↑ 4.12
RIC. VII, no. 166b, p. 643
B68 6/ 17 XII.9.26 I..12971 Reg. 377

74. LICINIUS, A.D. 313–314, Antioch, Follis
IOVI CONSER-VATORI AVGGG; in ex., ANT; to r., ⅃
20 ↑ 2.71
RIC. VII, no. 8, p. 676
B66 6 18 XII.7.19 I..12716 Reg. 378

75. CONSTANTINE, A.D. 314–315, Rome, Follis
SOLI INV-I-CTO COMITI; in ex., R T; to l., R; to r., X; to r., F
20 ↑ 2.49
RIC. VII, no. 27, p. 299
B66 6 18 XII.7.19 I..12716 Reg. 374

76. AS ABOVE
20 ↑ 2.47
AS ABOVE
B66 7/ 7 XII.7.60 I..12719 Reg. 547

77. AS ABOVE
21 ↑ 2.50
AS ABOVE
B66 7 6 XII.7.60 I..12717 Reg. 541

78. AS ABOVE
20 ↑ 2.61
AS ABOVE
B66 6 18 XII.7.19 I..12716 Reg. 380

79. CONSTANTINE, A.D. 315–316, Rome, Follis
AS ABOVE; in ex., R S; to l., C; to r., S
21 ↑ 2.98
RIC. VII, no. 40, p. 300
B66 6 18 XII.7.19 I..12716 Reg. 379

80. CONSTANTINE, A.D. 317–318, Rome, Follis
AS ABOVE; in ex., R P; to l., wreath
20 ↑ 2.90
RIC, VII, no. 97, p. 309
B66 6/15 XII.7.15 L.12710 Reg. 139

81. CONSTANTINE, A.D. 314–318, Uncertain, Follis
AS ABOVE; field details illegible
19 ↓ 1.73
cf. ABOVE
B68 6/17 XII.9.26 L.12971 Reg. 382

82. LICINIUS, A.D. 318–320, Heraclea, Follis
PROVIDEN-TIAE AVGG; in ex., SMHB; to r., Λ
18 ↑ 1.48 (frag.)
RIC, VII, no. 48, p. 547
B66 7/7 XII.7.70 L.12719 Reg. 548

83. CRISPUS, A.D. 320–321, Aquileia, Follis**
CAESARVM NOSTRORVM; VOT V in wreath; in ex., AQS
19 ↑ 2.68
cf. *RIC*, VII, nos. 68 & 69, p. 402
B66 - XII.7.60 L.12717 Reg. 542

84. CONSTANTINE, A.D. 321, Rome, Follis
DN CONSTANTINI MAX AVG; VOT · XX in wreath; in ex., R Q
20 ↓ 2.21
RIC, VII, no. 237, p. 321
B68 6/17 XII.9.26 L.12971 Reg. 370

85. CONSTANTINE, A.D. 321–323, Antioch, Follis
IOVI CONS-ERVATORI; in ex., SMANTA; to r., X / III'
20 ↑ 2.90
RIC, VII, no. 34, p. 682
B66 6/16 XII.7.19 L.12716 Reg. 371

86.* LICINIUS II, A.D. 321–323, Antioch, Follis
AS ABOVE; in ex., SMANTH; to r., X / III'
18 ↑
RIC, VII, no. 36, p. 682
B68 7/10 XII.2.57 L. - Reg. 848

87. AS ABOVE; (ex., SMANTB)
20 ↑ 2.72
AS ABOVE
B68 6/18 XII.9.3 L.12972 Reg. 460

(APPENDIX A CONTINUED)

Early Byzantine Issues

88. CONSTANTINE, A.D. 324–330, Antioch**
PROVIDEN-TIAE AVGG; in ex., SMANTB
19 ↓ 2.50
I.RBC, no. 1333, p. 30
B66 - XII.7.70 I..12717 Reg. 553

89. AS ABOVE; in ex., SMANTA**
18 ↓ 2.51
I.RBC, no. 1345, p. 30
B66 - XII.7.19 I..12716 Reg. 372

90. CONSTANTINE II, A.D. 324–330, Antioch
PROVIDEN-TIAECAESS; in ex., SMANTS
19 ↓ 2.67
I.RBC, no. 1353, p. 30
B68 6/17 XII.9.26 I..12971 Reg. 371

91. CONSTANTINE, A.D. 330–335, Alexandria
GLOR-IAEXERC-ITVS (2 standards), in ex., SMALA
18 ↓ 1.97
I.RBC, no. 1428, p. 32
B68 6/16 XII.9.22 I..12967 Reg. 320

92. CONSTANTIUS II, A.D. 330–335, Alexandria
AS ABOVE
17 ↑ 1.78
I.RBC, no. 1430, p. 32
B68 6/17 XII.9.26 I..12971 Reg. 398

93. CONSTANTINE, A.D. 330–335, Antioch
AS ABOVE; in ex., SMAN_
17 ↓ 2.10
I.RBC, no. 1356, p. 30
B66 6/15 XII.7.15 I..12710 Reg. 140

94. CONSTANTINE II, A.D. 330–335, Antioch
GLOR-IAEXERC-ITVS (2 standards), in ex., SM_NE
18 ↓ 2.05
I.RBC, no. 1357, p. 30
B66 6/15 XII.7.15 I..12710 Reg. 141

95. AS ABOVE
18 ↓ 2.21
AS ABOVE
B68 6/17 XII.9.26 I..12971 Reg. 396

96.*
AS ABOVE
17 ↓ 2.43
AS ABOVE
B68 6/12 XII.2.7 L.12263 Reg. 88

97.
CONSTANTINE, A.D. 330–335, Constantinople
AS ABOVE; in ex., CONS_
17 ↓ 1.27
LRBC, no. 1005, p. 24
B68 6/17 XII.9.26 L.12971 Reg. 400

98.
CONSTANTINE, A.D. 330–335, Nicomedia
AS ABOVE: in ex., SMNΔ
17 ↓ 1.88
LRBC, no. 1116, p. 26
B68 6/17 XII.9.26 L.12971 Reg. 392

99.
CONSTANTIUS II, A.D. 330–335, Constantinople
AS ABOVE: in ex., CONSI
17 ↓ 2.79
LRBC, no. 1007, p. 24
B66 6/18 XII.7.19 L.12716 Reg. 382

100.
HOUSE OF CONSTANTINE, A.D. 330–335, Siscia
Victory on prow; in ex., BSIS
18 ↓ 2.19
LRBC, no. 746, p. 19
B68 6/17 XII.9.26 L.12971 Reg. 389

101.
AS ABOVE; mint uncertain**
18 ↓ 1.70
cf. ABOVE
B66 - XII.7.19 L.12716 Reg. 373

102.
HOUSE OF CONSTANTINE, A.D. 330–337, Antioch
Wolf and Twins; in ex., SMANT_
17 - 2.27
cf. LRBC, nos. 1359 & 1368, pp. 30–31
B64 - TR Locus   F Reg. 202

103.
CONSTANS, A.D. 335–337, Constantinople
GLOR-IAEXERC-ITVS (1 standard); in ex., CONSIA
16 ↓ 1.31
LRBC, no. 1030, p. 24
B66 7/7 XII.7.70 L.12719 Reg. 549

104.
CONSTANTINE II, A.D. 335–337, Cyzicus
AS ABOVE; in ex., SMKA
15 ↓ 1.32
LRBC, no. 1263, p. 29
B68 6/17 XII.9.25 L.12970 Reg. 348

(APPENDIX A CONTINUED)

105. AS ABOVE; mint uncertain
16 ↑ 1.66
cf. ABOVE
B68 6/17 XII.9.26 L.12971 Reg. 397

106. CONSTANTIUS II, A.D. 335–337, Cyzicus
AS ABOVE; in ex., SMKΓ
16 ↑ 1.49
LRBC, no. 1265, p. 29
B68 6/17 XII.9.26 L.12971 Reg. 393

107. CONSTANTIUS II, A.D. 335–337, Heraclea
AS ABOVE; in ex., SMH_
16 ↓ 1.63
LRBC, no. 937, p. 23
B68 7/16 XII.13.18 L.12306A Reg. 952

108. UNCERTAIN, A.D. 335–341, Mint uncertain
AS ABOVE; in ex., SM_S
coin in frags.
cf. ABOVE
B68 6/17 XII.9.26 L.12971 Reg. 402

109. AS ABOVE
13 ↑ 1.37
AS ABOVE
B68 6/17 XII.9.26 L.12971 Reg. 439

110. AS ABOVE
12 ↓ 1.59
AS ABOVE
B68 6/17 XII.9.26 L.12971 Reg. 410

111.* CONSTANTINE POSTHUMOUS, A.D. 337–341,
Alexandria
Quadriga; in ex., SMALB
16 ↑ 1.53
LRBC, no. 1454, p. 32
B68 6/12 XII.3.20 L.12370 Reg. 98

112. AS ABOVE; Antioch
AS ABOVE; in ex., SMANΓ
LRBC, no. 1374, p. 31
B68 6/17 XII.9.26 L.12971 Reg. 401

113. 15 ↓ 1.29

cf. ABOVE
B68 6/17 XII.9.26 L.12971 Reg. 435

114. AS ABOVE; mint uncertain
AS ABOVE; ex. off flan
15 ↓ 1.39

AS ABOVE
B68 6/17 XII.9.26 L.12971 Reg. 407

115.* AS ABOVE
14 ↑ 1.02

LRBC, no. 1392, p. 31
B68 6/13 XII.3.28 L.12376 Reg. 107

116. CONSTANTIUS II, A.D. 337–341, Antioch
GLOR-IAEXERC-ITVS (1 standard); in ex., SMANE
14 ↑ 1.08

LRBC, no. 1391, p. 31
B68 6/17 XII.9.26 L.12971 Reg. 386

117. AS ABOVE
AS ABOVE; in ex., __AN_
15 ↑ 1.27

cf. ABOVE
B68 6/18 XII.7.19 L.12716 Reg. 383

118. AS ABOVE; mint uncertain
Illegible
15 – 1.52

AS ABOVE
B68 6/17 XII.9.26 L.12971 Reg. 406

119. AS ABOVE
13 – 1.51

LRBC, no. 1476, p. 33
B66 6/18 XII.7.19 L.12716 Reg. 375

120. CONSTANS, A.D. 341–346, Alexandria
VOT XX MVLT XXX; in ex., __ALB
15 ↓ 1.99

AS ABOVE
B68 6/17 XII.9.26 L.12971 Reg. 436

121. AS ABOVE; mint uncertain
16 ↑ 1.02

AS ABOVE

122.
14 ↑ 1.42

B68 6/17 XII.9.26 L.12971 Reg. 432

CONSTANTIUS II. A.D. 341–346. Antioch
AS ABOVE; in ex., SMAN_
14 ↑ 0.99 (badly worn)

I.RBC. no. 1398, p. 31
B68 6/17 XII.9.26 L.12971 Reg. 423

123.
AS ABOVE; in ex., SMANE
14 ↑ 1.39

AS ABOVE
B68 6/17 XII.9.26 L.12971 Reg. 412

124.
AS ABOVE; in ex., _MAN_
15 ↑ 1.39

AS ABOVE
B68 6/17 XII.9.26 L.12971 Reg. 437

125.
CONSTANTIUS II. A.D. 341–346. Nicomedia
AS ABOVE; in ex., _NA·
15 ↑ 0.81 (badly worn)

I.RBC. no. 1156, p. 27
B68 6/17 XII.9.26 L.12971 Reg. 434

126.
CONSTANTIUS II or CONSTANS. A.D. 341–346.
Uncertain
AS ABOVE; mint uncertain
12 ↑ 1.06 (frag.)

cf. ABOVE
B68 6/17 XII.9.26 L.12971 Reg. 426

127.
HOUSE OF CONSTANTINE. A.D. 341–346.
Alexandria
VN MR; in ex., SMALB
15 ↑ 1.34

I.RBC. no. 1473, p. 33
B68 6/17 XII.9.26 L.12971 Reg. 417

128.
AS ABOVE; mint uncertain
12 ↓ 0.63

cf. ABOVE
B68 6/27 XII.9.43 L.12979 Reg. 604

129.*
AS ABOVE

AS ABOVE

130. CONSTANS. A.D. 346–350, Cyzicus, AE 2
FEL TEMP REPA -RATIO (Hut 2); in ex.,_MKS
20 ↓ 3.51
16 ↓ 1.53
B68 6/17 XII.14.1 L.12401 Reg. 487
LRBC, no. 2475, p. 96
B68 6/16 XII.9.26 L.12971 Reg. 366

131. AS ABOVE; Nicomedia
AS ABOVE; in ex., :SMNE
21 ↑ 2.48
cf. LRBC, no. 2291, p. 92
B68 6/17 XII.9.26 L.12971 Reg. 376

132. CONSTANTIUS II. A.D. 346–350. Antioch. AE 2
FEL TEMP RE - PARATIO (FH 4); in ex., ANB; to
l., *
14 ↓ 0.81 (frag.)
LRBC, no. 2620, p. 99
B68 6/16 XII.9.21 L.12965 Reg. 306

133. AS ABOVE; in ex., ANB
25 ↓ 3.20
AS ABOVE
B68 6/17 XII.9.26 L.12971 Reg. 373

134. AS ABOVE
FEL TEMP - REPARATIO: Emperor kneeling with
two captives; in ex., ANB
20 ↓ 3.72
LRBC, no. 2614, p. 99
B68 6/17 XII.9.26 L.12971 Reg. 372

135. AS ABOVE
22 ↑ 3.19
AS ABOVE
B68 6/17 XII.9.26 L.12971 Reg. 369

136. AS ABOVE; in ex., ANE
20 ↑ 3.57
AS ABOVE
B68 6/17 XII.9.26 L.12971 Reg. 367

137. CONSTANTIUS II, A.D. 350, Thessalonica, AE 2
FEL TEMP - REPARTIO Galley (2); in ex., :TSE;
LRBC, no. 1660, p. 78
B68 6/17 XII.9.26 L.12971 Reg. 368

(APPENDIX A CONTINUED)

to l., B; to r., eight point star
24 ↑ 7.19
— LRBC, no. 2632, p. 100
B68 6/17 XII.9.26 L.12971 Reg. 442

138. CONSTANTIUS II. A.D. 351–354, Antioch, AE 3
FEL TEMP - REPARTIO (FH 3); in ex., AN_
16 ↓ 1.38 (frag.)
— AS ABOVE
B68 6/17 XII.9.26 L.12971 Reg. 413

139. AS ABOVE; in ex., ANH
14 ↑ 0.79 (frag.)
— LRBC, no. 2039, p. 87
B68 6/17 XII.9.26 L.12971 Reg. 387

140. AS ABOVE: Constantinople
AS ABOVE; in ex., CONSΓ
18 ↑ 1.89
— cf. ABOVE
B64 - TR Locus G Reg. 387

141.* AS ABOVE: mint uncertain
16 ↓ 2.20
— LRBC, no. 2036, p. 86

142. CONSTANTIUS II. A.D. 351–354. Constantinople AE 2 (?)
FEL TEMP RE - PARATIO (FH 4); in ex., CONSI; to l. E
17 ↑ 2.00
— B68 6/17 XII.9.26 L.12971 Reg. 394

143. GALLUS. A.D. 351–354. Constantinople. AE 2
AS ABOVE; in ex., CONSA; to l., Γ
22 ↑ (frag.)
— LRBC, no. 2029, p. 86
B68 6/17 XII.9.26 L.12971 Reg. 385

144. GALLUS. 351–354. Nicomedia. AE 3
AS ABOVE (FH 3); in ex., _N_
— LRBC, no. 2310, p. 92
B66 6/18 XII.7.19 L.12716 Reg. 381

18 ↓ 2.18

145. AS ABOVE; mint uncertain
19 ↓ 2.09
cf. ABOVE
B68 6/16 XII.9.22 L.12967 Reg. 319

146. CONSTANTIUS II or GALLUS, A.D. 351–354, Antioch, AE 3
AS ABOVE; in ex., ANA
14 ↓ 1.54
LRBC, nos. 2632-3, p. 100
B68 6/16 XII.9.21 L.12965 Reg. 293

147. AS ABOVE
15 ↑ 1.50
AS ABOVE
B68 6/16 XII.9.21 L.12965 Reg. 290

148. AS ABOVE
14 ↓ 1.41 (frag.)
AS ABOVE
B66 6/15 XII.7.15 L.12710 Reg. 143

149. AS ABOVE
12 ↑ 1.21 (clipped?)
AS ABOVE
B68 6/17 XII.9.25 L.12970 Reg. 350

150. AS ABOVE; mint uncertain, AE 2 or 3
17 ↑ 2.28 (frag.)
cf. ABOVE
B68 6/17 XII.9.25 L.12970 Reg. 355

151. CONSTANTIUS II, A.D. 351–361, Alexandria, AE 3
AS ABOVE; in ex., ALEΓ
14 ↑ 0.83 (frag.)
LRBC, nos. 2844 & 2846, p. 103
B68 6/16 XII.9.21 L.12965 Reg. 283

152. AS ABOVE (FH 4); Antioch, in ex., ANA
13 ↑ 2.61
LRBC, nos. 2634-5, p. 100
B68 6/17 XII.9.26 L.12971 Reg. 441

153. AS ABOVE; in ex., ANΓ
14 ↑ 2.09
AS ABOVE
B66 6/18 XII.7.19 L.12716 Reg. 384

154. AS ABOVE; in ex., AN_
AS ABOVE

(APPENDIX A CONTINUED)

13 ↓ 0.96 (frag.) — B68 6/16 XII.9.21 L..12965 Reg. 302

155. AS ABOVE: mint uncertain
14 ↑ 1.31 — cf. ABOVE / B66 7/6 XII.7.60 L..12717 Reg. 544

156. AS ABOVE: mint uncertain
16 ↑ 1.23 — cf. ABOVE / B68 6/17 XII.9.26 L..12971 Reg. 395

157. AS ABOVE (FH 3): AE 2: mint uncertain
18 ↑ 3.31 — cf. ABOVE / B68 6/17 XII.9.26 L..12971 Reg. 388

158. AS ABOVE: AE 3: mint uncertain
12 ↓ 2.32 — cf. ABOVE / B68 6/16 XII.9.21 L..12965 Reg. 276

159. CONSTANTIUS II, GALLUS or JULIAN, A.D. 351–361, mint uncertain, AE 3
AS ABOVE
16 ↓ 1.62 (frag.) — cf. ABOVE / B68 6/16 XII.9.21 L..12965 Reg. 309

160. AS ABOVE: mint and emperor uncertain
15 ↓ 1.16 (frag.) — cf. ABOVE / B68 6/17 XII.9.26 L..12971 Reg. 391

161. AS ABOVE: mint and emperor uncertain
15 ↓ 1.09 — cf. ABOVE / B68 6/17 XII.9.26 L..12971 Reg. 429

162. CONSTANTIUS II, A.D. 352–354, Rome, AE 3
AS ABOVE (FH 3): in ex., R P
18 ↓ 1.64 — LRBC. no. 677. p. 60 / B68 6/16 XII.9.21 L..12965 Reg. 287

163. CONSTANTIUS II, A.D. 355–361, Alexandria, AE 4
SPES REI - PUBLICE; in ex., ALE_ — LRBC. no. 2850. p. 103 / B68 6/17 XII.9.26 L..12971 Reg. 399

16 ↓ 1.58

164. CONSTANTIUS II, A.D. 355–361, Antioch. AE 4
AS ABOVE; in ex., ANA
13 ↓ 1.78
LRBC, no. 2638, p. 100
B68 6/ 16 XII.9.21 L.12965 Reg. 284

165. AS ABOVE; AE 3
FEL TEMP - REPARTIO (FH 4); in ex., A__; to l., M
13 ↓ 1.41
LRBC, no. 2637, p. 100
B66 6/ 15 XII.7.15 L.12710 Reg. 145

166. AS ABOVE; in ex., ANE
15 ↓ 1.20
AS ABOVE
B66 6/ 15 XII.7.15 L.12710 Reg. 142

167. CONSTANTIUS II, A.D. 355–361, Constantinople. AE 3
AS ABOVE; in ex., _ONSI'; to l., ·M·
cf. LRBC, no. 2052, p. 87
B68 6/ 17 XII.9.26 L.12971 Reg. 421

168. CONSTANTIUS II, A.D. 355–361, Cyzicus. AE 3
AS ABOVE (FH 3); in ex., _MKE
18 ↓ 1.83
LRBC, no. 2498, p. 97
B68 6/ 17 XII.9.26 L.12971 Reg. 390

169. AS ABOVE; in ex., SMK_; to l., ·M·
16 ↑ 1.78
LRBC, no. 2502, p. 97
B66 6/ 15 XII.7.15 L.12710 Reg. 144

170. CONSTANTIUS II, A.D. 355–361, Cyzicus. AE 4
SPES REI - PVBLICE; in ex., SMKA
17 ↑ 1.09
LRBC, no. 2504, p. 97
B68 6/ 17 XII.9.25 L.12970 Reg. 347

171. AS ABOVE; in ex., SMKE; to l., Γ
16 ↓ 1.51
cf. LRBC, no. 2506, p. 97
B68 6/ 17 XII.9.26 L.12971 Reg. 408

172. AS ABOVE; mint uncertain
12 ↑ 1.78
cf. ABOVE
B68 6/ 17 XII.9.26 L.12971 Reg. 431

(APPENDIX A CONTINUED)

173. AS ABOVE: mint uncertain
12 ↑ 1.20
cf. ABOVE
B68 6/17 XII.9.26 1..12971 Reg. 418

174. AS ABOVE: mint uncertain
14 ↑ 1.20 (frag.)
cf. ABOVE
B68 6/17 XII.9.26 1..12971 Reg. 427

175.* AS ABOVE
FEL TEMP - REPARTIO (FH 4); ex., off flan: to l..
M
14 ↑ 2.72
cf. ABOVE, no. 165
B68 XII.2.13 1..12268 Reg. 110

176.* JULIAN, A.D. 355–361. Alexandria. AE 3
AS ABOVE (FH 3); in ex., ALEΔ
16 ↓ 1.77
I.RBC, no. 2847, p. 100
B68 6/17 XII.14.1 1..12401 Reg. 486

177. JULIAN, A.D. 355–361. Constantinople. AE 4
SPES REI - PUBLICE; ex. off flan; to l., C
15 ↑ 1.53
I.RBC, no. 2055, p. 87
B68 6/17 XII.9.25 1..12970 Reg. 351

178. AS ABOVE; Cyzicus; in ex., SMK_
18 ↓ 1.82
I.RBC, no. 2505, p. 97
B68 6/27 XII.9.42 1..12958 Reg. 587

179. JULIAN, A.D. 355–361. Nicomedia. AE 3
FEL TEMP RE-PARATIO (FH 3); ex. illegible: to l.. M
14 ↑ 1.44
I.RBC, no. 2314, p. 92
B68 6/17 XII.9.26 1..12971 Reg. 440

180. AS ABOVE (FH 4); mint uncertain
15 ↑ 2.45
cf. ABOVE
B68 - XII.9.26 L.12971 Reg. 430

181.	CONSTANTIUS II or JULIAN, A.D. 355–361, Alexandria, AE 4 SPES REI-REIPVBLICE; in ex., ALEA 13 ↑ 1.88	*LRBC*, nos. 2850–1, p. 103 B68 6/17 XII.9.26 L.12971 Reg. 403
182.	AS ABOVE; Heraclea; in ex., SMHΓ 15 ↑ 1.12 (frag.)	*LRBC*, nos. 1905–6, p. 83 B68 6/17 XII.9.25 L.12970 Reg. 353
183.	AS ABOVE; Nicomedia; in ex., _MN_ 13 ↑ 1.69	*LRBC*, nos. 2315–6, p. 92 B68 6/17 XII.9.26 L.12971 Reg. 414
184.	AS ABOVE; mint uncertain 14 ↑ 1.62	cf. ABOVE B68 6/16 XII.9.21 L.12965 Reg. 298
185.	AS ABOVE; mint uncertain 12 ↓ 1.25	cf. ABOVE B68 6/17 XII.9.25 L.12970 Reg. 356
186.	AS ABOVE; mint uncertain 15 ↑ 1.28	cf. ABOVE B68 6/17 XII.9.25 L.12970 Reg. 354
187.	AS ABOVE; mint uncertain 14 ↓ 1.10 (frag.)	cf. ABOVE B68 6/27 XII.9.42 L.12978 Reg. 590
188.	AS ABOVE; mint uncertain 13 ↓ - (frag.)	cf. ABOVE B68 6/16 XII.9.21 L.12965 Reg. 281
189.	CONSTANTIUS II or JULIAN, A.D. 355–361, Alexandria or Antioch, AE 3 FEL TEMP - REPARATIO (FH 3); in ex., A___ 13 ↑ 1.08	cf. *LRBC*, no. 2637, p. 100 and nos. 2848–8, p. 103 B68 6/17 XII.9.26 L.12971 Reg. 425
190.*	UNCERTAIN, FH type not clear, mint uncertain 18 ↓ 2.91	cf. ABOVE B68 6/12 XII.2.7 L.12263 Reg. 89

(APPENDIX A CONTINUED)

191. AS ABOVE**
14 ↓ -

AS ABOVE
B68 - XII.9.63 L..129797 Reg. 608

192. AS ABOVE
14 - 1.64

AS ABOVE
B68 6/17 XII.9.26 L..12971 Reg. 438

193. JULIAN, A.D. 361–363, Antioch, AE 1
SECVRITAS REIPVB; in ex., ANTΔ (palm fronds to either side)
27 ↓ 8.36

I.RBC, no. 2640, p. 100
B68 6/17 XII.9.25 L..12970 Reg. 346

194. AS ABOVE**
26 ↑ 8.00

AS ABOVE
B66 - XII.7.12 L..12710 Reg. 138

195. AS ABOVE; Siscia; in ex., BSISC· (palm frond proceeds mint mark)
27 ↑ 7.46

cf. I.RBC, no. 1260, p. 71
B68 6/16 XII.9.22 L..12967 Reg. 318

196. JULIAN, A.D. 361–363, Uncertain, AE 4
SPES REI - PVBLICE; ex., off flan
15 ↓ 1.37

cf. I.RBC, no. 2852, p. 103
B68 6/16 XII.9.26 L..12971 Reg. 405

197. VALENTINIAN I, A.D. 364–367, Antioch, AE 3
SECVRITAS - REIPVBLICAE; in ex., _N__
17 ↑ 2.00

I.RBC, no. 2656, p. 100
B68 6/17 XII.9.25 L..12970 Reg. 352

198. VALENTINIAN I, A.D. 364–375, Alexandria, AE 3
AS ABOVE; in ex., _LE_
16 ↑ 0.93 (frag.)

I.RBC, nos. 2860 & 2862, p. 104
B68 6/16 XII.9.21 L..12965 Reg. ?

199. AS ABOVE; in ex., ALEA
13 ↓ 1.68
cf. ABOVE
B68 6/17 XII.9.26 L.12971 Reg. 424

200.* AS ABOVE; in ex.,—EA
15 ↓ 2.63
AS ABOVE
B68 6/8 XII.3.6 L.12363 Reg. 57

201. AS ABOVE; in ex., ALEA
16 ↑ 1.56
AS ABOVE
B68 6/29 XII.9.45

202. VALENS, A.D. 364–375, Uncertain, AE 3
AS ABOVE; ex. illegible
16 ↑ 1.88
cf. LRBC, nos. 2861 & 2863, p. 104
B68 6/27 XII.9.42 L.12978 Reg. 588

203. AS ABOVE
14 ↓ 1.16
AS ABOVE
B68 6/16 XII.9.21 L.12965 Reg. 279

204. AS ABOVE; emperor and mint uncertain
12 - (frags.)
cf. ABOVE
B68 6/17 XII.9.25 L.12970 Reg. 357

205. AS ABOVE
14 ↑ 1.31 (frag.)
AS ABOVE
B68 6/17 XII.9.26 L.12971 Reg. 433

206.* GRATIAN, A.D. 367–375, Uncertain, AE 3
AS ABOVE; ex., illegible
16 ↑ - (frag.)
cf. LRBC, no. 2864, p. 104
B68 6/23 XII.15.6 L.121500 Reg. 489

207. VALENTINIAN I or GRATIAN, A.D. 367–375, Thessalonica, AE 3
AS ABOVE; ex. off flan; to l., A
13 ↓ 2.29 (frag.)
LRBC, nos. 1769–1772, p. 80
B68 6/27 XII.9.43 L.12979 Reg. 605

208. VALENTINIAN I or VALENS, A.D. 367–375, Antioch, AE 3
LRBC, nos. 2658–9, p. 100
B68 6/16 XII.9.21 L.12965 Reg. 285

(APPENDIX A CONTINUED)

209. GLORIA RO - MANORVM (8); in ex., ANTA
15 ↑ 2.92
cf. ABOVE
B68 6/27 XII.9.43 L.12979 Reg. 606

210.* AS ABOVE; emperor uncertain; in ex., ANTA
15 ↓ 0.92 (frag.)
I.RBC, nos. 2738–9, p. 101
B64 - TR 1., G Reg. 385

211. VALENTINIAN II or THEODOSIUS I, A.D. 383, Antioch, AE 4
VOT XX MVLT XXX; in ex., ANE
13 ↓ 1.28
cf. I.RBC, nos. 2881 & 2889, p. 104
B68 6/16 XII.9.21 L.12965 Reg. 303

212. VALENTINIAN II, A.D. 383–392, Unknown, AE 4
VOT X MVLT XX; ex illegible
12 ↑ 1.12
AS ABOVE
B68 6/16 XII.9.21 L.12965 Reg. 294

213.* AS ABOVE
12 ↓ 1.31
cf. ABOVE
B68 6/26 XII.15.21 L.121500 Reg. 575

214. AS ABOVE; emperor and mint uncertain
11 ↑ .79
AS ABOVE
12 - 1.27
AS ABOVE
B68 6/16 XII.9.21 L.12966 Reg. 444

215.* THEODOSIUS I, A.D. 383–387, Aquileia, AE 3
GLORIA RO - MANORVM (6); in ex., SMAQS
- ↓ - (frag.)
I.RBC, no. 1085, p. 68
B66 6/16 XII.1.23 L.12113 Reg. 162

216. UNCERTAIN, A.D. 383–392, Uncertain, AE 3
AS ABOVE; ex illegible
17 ↑ 1.65
cf. ABOVE
B68 6/16 XII.9.23 L.12968 Reg. 328

217. VALENTINIAN II, A.D. 383–392, Antioch, AE 4
SALVS REI - PVBLICAE (2); in ex., ANTA
12 ↓ 1.69
LRBC, no. 2768, p. 102
B68 6/16 XII.8.21 I..12965 Reg. 286

218.* AS ABOVE
12 ↓ 1.05
AS ABOVE
B68 6/25 XII.15.1 I..12500 Reg. 567

219. AS ABOVE; mint uncertain
12 ↑ 1.31
cf. ABOVE
B68 6/27 XII.9.42 I..12978 Reg. 592

220. ARCADIUS, A.D. 383–395, Uncertain, AE 4
AS ABOVE; ex illegible
12 ↑ 1.08
cf. LRBC, no. 2771, p. 102
B68 6/27 XII.9.42 I..12978 Reg. 593

221. THEODOSIUS I, A.D. 383–392, Thessalonica, AE 4
VICTORIA AVG (4); in ex., T___
14 ↑ 1.99
LRBC, no. 1868, p. 82
B68 6/17 XII.9.26 I..12971 Reg. 416

222.* THEODOSIUS I, A.D. 383–395, Antioch, AE 4
SALVS REI - PVBLICAE (2); in ex., ANTB
11 ↑ 1.01
LRBC, nos. 2764, 2767 & 2772, p. 102
B68 6/26 XII.15.21 I..121500 Reg. 573

223. AS ABOVE
14 ↑ 1.12
LRBC, nos. 2769 and 2776, p. 102
B68 6/27 XII.9.42 I..12978 Reg. 591

224.* AS ABOVE; Constantinople; in ex., CONS_
13 ↓ 1.38
LRBC, nos. 2184 & 2192, p. 89
B68 7/1 XII.15.28 I..121502 Reg. 671

225.* AS ABOVE; mint uncertain
12 ↓ 0.83
cf. ABOVE
B68 6/4 XII.1. - L.. - Reg. 16

226.* AS ABOVE
14 ↑ 1.10
AS ABOVE
B68 6/18 XII.13.2 I..121300 Reg. 212

227.	AS AbOVE; emperor and mint uncertain 13 ↑ 1.89	cf. ABOVE B68 6/29 XII.9.46 l..12978 Reg. 650
228.	AS ABOVE 15 ↓ 1.26	AS ABOVE B68 6/16 XII.9.21 l..12965 Reg. 277
229.*	UNCERTAIN. A.D. 383–408, Uncertain. AE 4** VIRTVS - EXERCITI; ex., illegible 14 ↑ 0.91	cf. LRBC, nos. 2205–6, p. 90 B64 - †R l.. F. Reg. 205
230.*	PHOCAS. A.D. 602–608, Alexandria, 12 Nummi IB: between, cross; in ex... _I.E._ 15 - (frag.)	DOC, II, 1, nos. 106.1 ff., pp. 192 ff. B64 †R l.. E Reg. 388
231.	UNCERTAIN. Late Sixth or Early Seventh Century, Alexandria, 12 Nummi AS ABOVE 15 - 1.63	cf. ABOVE B68 6/23 XII.9.36 l..12976 Reg. 473

In addition to the above coins, 52 other specimens from the cistern excavations survived cleaning but were too worn to permit any assignment other than to the Fourth Century. Two post-Classical coins were also uncovered in the cistern probes, an Arab coin of the Eighth Century (too worn for positive identification) and a modern Turkish coin of Abdulmecid struck in 1859.

Notes on the Coins

Most of the coins cited in the catalogue were assigned a preliminary identification by Professor Robert J. Bull. When a coin was not available for examination by the author (indicated by **), his assignment was followed. Special abbreviations used in the catalogue are:

BMC—Catalogue of the Greek Coins in the British Museum.

DOC I, II—Alfred R. Bellinger, *Catalogue of the Byzantine Coins in the Dumbarton Oaks Collection and in the Whittemore Collection, Volume I: Anastasius I to Maurice,* Washington, D.C., 1966; Philip Grierson, *Catalogue of the Byzantine Coins in the Dumbarton Oaks Collection and in the Whittemore Collection, Volume II: Phocas to Theodosius III,* Washington, D.C., 1968.

Kadman, *CAP*—Leo Kadman, *The Coins of Akko Ptolemais,* Tel Aviv, 1961

LRBC—R.A.G. Carson, P. V. Hill and J.P.C. Kent, *Late Roman Bronze Coinage, A.D. 324-498,* London, 1960.

Meshorer, *Jewish Coins*—Ya'akov Meshorer, *Jewish Coins of the Second Temple Period,* trans. I. H. Levine, Chicago, 1967.

RIC—Harold Mattingly, E. A. Sydenham, *et alii, Roman Imperial Coinage,* London, 1923–.

ex.—exergue

frag(s)—fragment(s)

l.—left

r.—right

. . .—impossible to recover exact number of letters

A—reading questionable

1. The reverse mint mark on this coin in the same as on *BMC Seleucid Kings,* no. 23, p. 22. The obverse mint mark, Bl, to l., appears on *BMC Seleucid Kings,* nos. 19-21, p. 22.

3. For all the Alexander Jannaeus issues, unless noted, coins are too worn to discern field details or to permit an exact identification. Most other coin finds are in better condition than one expects for excavation material.

4. This is the earliest issue found in the cistern excavations in 1966. It is not cited by Bull, "Sixth Campaign." It would seem to be an intrusive piece for no other archaeological data suggest such an early date for the opening of the cistern complex.

40. The date for this coin appears at the outset of the obverse inscription, year 5. It would have been issued by the procurator Antoninus Felix (A.D. 52-60).

42. The coins cited in the *BMC Palestine* all feature a Π H to lower r. The first letter on this coin looks more like a V .

46. The bust of the emperor features a countermark by the r. ear. It appears to be a ∧ .

49. The identification of this reverse type is not secure. This specimen would be considerably heavier than similar coins cited in *BMC Palestine*. However, it does appear a wide weight variation was tolerated for what were presumably coins of one denomination. The reverse also has two contiguous circular punch marks.

58. Exergue reading is presented as it was cited in the preliminary field identification.

60. The obverse of this coin features an engraving error. The initial I of IMP of the legend has been omitted.

68–69. The break in the reverse legend is CONCORDIA MIL—ITVM.

79. The obverse legend bears an unusual alteration. The 0 of the emperor's name appears to have been recut in the die above the original, perhaps in an effort to improve the quality of the engraving.

80. The legend breaks on the reverse are uncommon, SOLIIN—VI—CTOCOMITI. See *RIC*, VII, p. 309, n. 97.

85. This series, which features a radiate bust, is the last such obverse type struck at the Antioch mint.

88ff. Full reverse legends are cited for nos. 88–229 for identification purposes only. They are not intended to indicate the legibility of the individual inscriptions.

131. This mint mark, with a dot preceeding the mint designation, is not cited by *LRBC*.

132. *LRBC*, Plate II, where the FH types are illustrated, reverses its examples of FH3 and FH4. No. 2295 is actually no. 2625; no. 2625 is no. 2295.

137. The weight of this coin, 7.19 gr., is high for the AE2 series, almost approximating the theoretical weight of an AE1 issue (7.78 gr.). It must have been lost before it circulated widely. This coin also demonstrates the wide variance of weights accepted for the same denomination.

142. This coin features an unusual rendering of the E in the reverse field. While clearly an FH4 type, it is far too light to be an AE2 issue as cited by *LRBC*, even when one allows for wear.

151–158. The poor condition of these coins does not permit a more specific chronological attribution.

167. *LRBC* does not list this coin (FH4) with · M · in the l. reverse field for Constantius II. Clearly, the series was struck by both the Augustus and his Caesar.

171. *LRBC* does not list a series with a Γ in the reverse field, only with a S. It is possible this field mark is badly rendered, or perhaps the S might be better read as a Γ. Weights for the Tell er Ras SPES REI PVBLICE series seem high for an AE4 series. Perhaps they were intended to be AE3 issues. Allowing for normal wear, it is clear that making distinctions between series in the market stalls of Neapolis and elsewhere would have been difficult.

173. This coin was cut down from AE3 to AE4, or the AE3 die was used on an AE4 blank. Only a small portion of the type fits on the flan.

192. This coin is an extreme example of poor striking, even by 4th century standards. Only a portion of the obverse and reverse types appear on the flan. The reverse was overstruck as well.

193. This coin's superb condition suggests loss before extensive circulation. Its weight, 8.36 gr., also reflects this situation.

195. This series is not cited in *LRBC* with this reverse type.

215. Issues from western mint sites are uncommon at Tell er Ras and elsewhere in the Holy Land.

217. *LRBC* cites this issue as its SALVS REI PVBLICAE (1) type with a christogram in the left reverse field. Elsewhere this particular variant is called SALVS REI PVBLICAE (2). See p. 109 where the two variants are described.

222. *LRBC* cites two coins as their number 2771. This issue is an example of what was intended to be their number 2772 and is so cited.

6

BYZANTINE TOWNS OF THE GALILEE

Eric M. Meyers

(Duke University)

The subject of this monograph is one that is particularly appropriate to Galilean studies at this point in the history of scholarship. The relationship between city and town, between the urban and rural, is one that is extremely complex but certainly central to a reliable understanding of not only all of Syria-Palestine in late antiquity but to the region of Galilee in particular. Cut off from the outer coastal territory on the west and the Sea of Galilee (Kinneret) to the east, central Lower Galilee may be said to be surrounded by a ring of cities on its periphery, constituted of a core of towns, villages and hamlets in its largely agricultural interior.

A recent monograph on the history of Galilee[1] asserts that it is precisely the isolation of central Galilee from the city that accounts for its rural, peasant culture. While in the main such an assertion is correct the picture to be drawn from Galilee is a bit more complicated than this when taking into account regional differences between the Upper and Lower Galilee, a distinction maintained in the ancient literatary tradition.[2] Geographical considerations play a decisive role in determining the character of regions and sub-regions within them[3] and there is no doubt that archaeological evidence has provided the key to refining our understanding of these areas. It is after all the material culture of a region which ultimately defines that area: its coins, its architecture, its art, its artifacts.

Galilee is a rich land of many contrasts. It is both rural and urban, both peasant and agricultural as well as cosmopolitan and urbane. I shall be concerned with four towns of Upper Galilee in the heart of the interior Galilean hinterland, three snuggled alongside the great Meiron massif or Jarmak range (Khirbet Shema', Meiron, Gush Halav) and one alongside the northern slopes of Mt. Canaan in Safed astride the Wadi Dalton (Nabratein). (Fig. 1) All of these towns have been excavated over the past decade by the author and have provided the necessary data by which to reconstruct both the history of these sites and the larger historical setting in which they must be understood.

On the basis of the former three sites, I had previously argued for a high degree of isolation for the Upper Galilean highlands, most of it self-imposed except for the natural protection provided by the mountains.[4] The dominant trading pattern on the basis of coins was clearly northwest to Tyre and the Phoenician coast.[5] City coins of Tyre accounted for the overwhelming majority of city coins from each site except for Nabratein where a new coin profile suggested a different trading pattern if not an entirely different cultural orientation.[6] Fortunately, the selection of a fourth site in a rather restricted area of Upper Galilee prevented any further exaggeration of trends which had come to dominate the material culture of the other sites. Cultural diversity, therefore, is to be found among these sites despite the fact that they are part of a larger homogeneous culture found among these as well as other sites; but each site always speaks with its own unique repertoire of finds and data.

So too for chronological considerations. Although all four sites are occupied in the Byzantine era each one has its own unique stratigraphic history to report, though I will draw some very interesting points of comparisons and contrasts on specific historical issues. Even though the Meiron area is situated in a highly earthquake-prone region which averages two major earthquakes per century and lies within the Safed epicenter, not every site was influenced or disturbed to the same degree when an earthquake struck. All of this suggests that it is only a consideration of the total context, historical and archaeological, that will allow us a complete understanding of the situation of these communities in the Byzantine era.

The religious makeup of this area in the Byzantine era would seem to be predominantly Jewish. Some scholars have maintained that there is also a substantial Christian presence in this period as well[7] but the archaeological record for it is very slim.[8] The discovery of a steady supply of stamped crosses on Late Roman *terra sigillata* wares in all of these excavations however, suggests some sort of Christian presence either in Upper Galilee or on the periphery, or wherever these wares are being produced.[9]

There is no doubt about the extensive Christian remains in the Golan Heights in the Byzantine period,[10] where we know of many communities of Christians living in close proximity to Jewish settlements. Similarly, the Lake Region, with Christian pilgrimage centers at Capernaum and Tabgha at the northwestern corner of Kinneret, or a huge monastery at Kursi on the eastern shore, provide ample testimony to the Christian presence in nearby areas which undoubtedly would have had many contacts with the highland people, Jewish and Christian.

In sum, the four towns to be considered all are to be located in the Upper Galilean highlands, enjoying relative isolation from the Greek cities and municipalities which lie north on the Phoenicia Coast, west on the Coastal Plain of Palestine, south of the major intersections of roads and in the flat plains which criss-cross Lower Galilee, and southeast along the Lake and the Jordan Rift. Only to the north and east, in what is today southern Lebanon and the Golan Heights are major cities not to be found. This geographical reality above all plays a decisive role in the history of this area.

Second, despite relative isolation from the culture of the cities we may point with some clarity to regular contacts with them. Economic realities apparently overshadowed more conservative trends in society which may have urged caution in establishing any close ties with those more Greek and pagan areas.

Third, it is quite certain that the majority of the population was Jewish, adhering to an identifiable outward form of Judaism characterized by a commitment to Aramaic-Hebrew language, and a communal form of village life in which the house of worship and gathering—the synagogue—dominated and influenced the settlement pattern. The architectural and decorative style adopted by the people of the area reflect both their modest ties to the larger world of the Empire and their commitment to the local traditions. The result is reflected in their production of what is known as the "oriental" style.[11]

Chronology

Archaeologically speaking it is not an easy matter at all to determine the end of the Late Roman period and the beginning of the Byzantine period in Syria-Palestine. So it is with transitional periods in most historical eras. Historically, in Palestine at least, it is conventional to date the Byzantine period from the conversion of Constantine the Great until the Arab Conquest (324-640). While there is no gainsaying the significance of the conversion of Constantine and his attempts to Christianize the Empire, there are many forces of continuity which continue to operate at least till mid-century, and possibly as late as Julian. A far better case for discontinuity in material culture can be made for the mid-fourth century than for 324 when speaking about the remains from material culture.

In the Meiron area of the Upper Galilee local Galilean wares continue well on into mid-century and are to be found in the marvelous Patrician House at ancient Meiron, abandoned in the 350's and possibly affected definitively in the earthquake of 363.[12] The persistence of such characteristic local wares as the Galilean bowl with thickened everted lip and vestigial handle, or the Galilean carinated bowl with strip handles both of which originate more than two centuries earlier in the Middle Roman period if not earlier, indicates that cultural continuity is as much influenced by local considerations as international upheavals and major political shifts. The disappearance of our Roman wares occurs only gradually in the fourth century and it is only in the fifth and sixth centuries that the coarser, thicker and darker wares fully replace the more delicate wares of the end of the Roman period.[13]

Similarly, a case can be made for some of the Byzantine wares occurring in context that are in all probability Late Roman contexts. For example, the Byzantine storage jar with reinforcing ridge and painted, dripped decoration does not suddenly appear after Constantine's conversion. It has clearly been isolated to contexts that are early to mid-fourth century in each of the sites here being considered.[14] When it comes to fine wares usually considered to be imported, Late Roman C wares or *terra sigillata*, a similar case for their appearance early to mid-fourth century can now be made.[15]

The argument from ceramic evidence thus indicates the Byzantine period begins to leave its mark only about mid-fourth century and later when one can begin to identify the rooting of a new material culture in both the kitchen wares and in some of the imported wares. An excellent parallel situation is reflected in the building and rebuilding from this period, only some of which can compare favorably with the earlier, Middle-Late Roman style.

It is at this point that we must consider regionalism again. Since there are virtually no decorative mosaic floors from Upper Galilee in the Byzantine period as there are in the Rift and Lake regions, we are perforce required to render judgment on the exteriors and robbed interiors of ancient structures. It is to be expected that the interiors of many of our Byzantine synagogues were far more attractive than their present state of preservation, especially when imagining them with their interiors plastered over in white limestone. But still, there is a kind of debasement at work in both the building techniques and in the decorative style of the Byzantine era.[16]

While the comparative chronological table indicates the complexity of the settlement pattern in the Meiron area of the sites being considered, it cannot adequately describe the diverse circumstances which have given rise to the situation such as we have reconstructed it. Let me begin with Meiron and Nabratein, two sites which apparently come to a long hiatus if not systematic abandonment in the 350's.

Meiron

Without rehearsing the details of the complicated stratigraphic data of ancient Meiron it should be stressed that five seasons of excavations were conducted. The soundings included tombs and cisterns, the upper and lower city, the synagogue and adjoining structures, and at least two agricultural terraces.[17] First and foremost is the fact that characteristic Byzantine wares do not occur in a stratum IV context (Fig. 2). Second, the numismatic data enables us to firm up the data for the end of stratum IV to the 350's but certainly no later than the earthquake of 363 which would literally have rendered the *coup dé grace* to this ancient settlement.[18] The total evidence, however, simply does not comport with the theory that it was the earthquake of 363 alone which caused the demise of Meiron, one of the great upper Galilean villages of late antiquity.

Furthermore, it is quite clear that the causes contributing to abandonment are quite complex. The report on the anatomical remains indicates that disease may have been a genuine factor in the decline of village life.[19] Earlier publications stressed economic decline during the fourth century and the increasing tax pressures levied by the Roman administrative authorities.[20] In particular, the changeover to taxation in kind had a most adverse effect in the large townships such as Meiron which were penalized by virtue of their larger population. Others have pointed to the general decline of agriculture due to natural causes such as famine in the fourth century as reported in the rabbinic literature.[21]

At least two possible historical events may also have played some role in the abandonment of Meiron. The first is the so-called revolt of the Jews under Caesar Gallus in 352/353[22] mentioned in three fourth century sources, Aurelius Victor,[23] Jerome,[24] and John Chrysostum,[25] and less specifically in the rabbinic literature.[26] There seems to be some justification for assuming that the revolt touched much deeper into the heart of the Jewish population than was previously thought. The Greek and Latin sources name the Jews of Diocaesarea as the principal proponents of rebellion but collectively the sources suggest a much wider base. The Jews of Dioceasarea, it is reported, in turn put forward a certain Patricus as head of a new kingdom when Gallus, recently appointed Caesar, was dispatched to the East to crush the revolt, killing thousands and destroying the cities of Diocaesarea, Tiberias and Diosopolis.

The question raised by the evidence from Meiron is simply this: might the repercussions of the revolt have combined with several other reasons for Jews electing to flee or leave Meiron? Or, could the failed attempt to rebuild the Temple under Julian, a second historical event to be considered, have created disappointment among these Galileans who, as a result of that abortive effort and possibly of the earthquake of 363, decided finally to leave their homes?[27]

Nabratein

After two seasons of excavation at ancient en-Nabratein (Naburayya), in 1980 and 1981, it is now possible to argue conclusively for an abandonment and possibly subsequent destruction of a second and final Late Roman phase of occupation in the 350's or in 363. This chronology corresponds precisely with that of Meiron and lends further credence to that history of occupation. This phase of occupation is called Late Roman as at Meiron because of the reasons enumerated above, having mainly to do with ceramic manufacturing style and building style and technology.

Of the two sites Nabratein, situated along the Wadi Dalton only 5 km. from Tell Hazor and the Jordan Rift, would have been the more accessible to the outside world during a period of turmoil. Thus should the Gallus Revolt have touched the Galilean highlands, Nabratein would or could have been among the first to be affected. Because its numismatic profile indicates the presence of so many eastern city mints, there is little doubt that it was heavily involved with trade and traffic with the Rift area. Meiron on the other hand was far more oriented towards Tyre to the northwest and indeed the vast majority of its city coins come from Tyre.

The evidence for abandonment/destruction of Nabratein during this period is both numismatic and ceramic. Our coinage simply breaks off in this decade and resumes in the time of Justinian I.[28] Similarly, the ceramic picture of this phase is dominated by the latest, Late Roman wares without the appearance of the Byzantine coarse wares. Fortuitously, the onset of the Byzantine era can be dated with precision to the 550's or 560's A.D. A dedicatory inscription on the lintel of the rebuilt synagogue has been correctly dated by Avigad to the year 564 in the reign of Justinian I.[29] Also, during the 1980 excavation a gold coin of Justinian I was found just beneath the threshold of the southern portal[30] A resumption of village life, therefore, a little less than two hundred years after the disappearance of the previous phase of occupation is assured.

While the reasons for the resumption of Jewish life in Nabratein are unclear, it is certain on both numismatic and stratigraphic grounds that Byzantine village life functioned, perhaps flourished even, until a generation or so after the Arab Conquest of Palestine, apparently until c. 700.[31] The Byzantine synagogue while less elaborate and less decorated than its Late Roman predecessors is nonetheless an imposing structure, one that had been enlarged from a six column basilica to an eight column basilica.[32]

The question of the resumption of village life in the 550's leads us directly to the question of the chronology of Gush Halav (Gischala), Nabratein's neighbor directly to the west. Thus far our study of the stratigraphy suggests that Gush Halav was destroyed in the earthquake of 551. It is quite possible therefore that settlers from nearby Gush Halav who knew the ruined site of Nabratein decided to start life anew there rather than leave the region altogether. The destruction at Gush Halav was so great that the surviving inhabitants could not face the task of clearing familiar rubble. Rather, a nearby ruin with many cut stones lying about for reuse seemed the least difficult course of action.

Gush Halav

Having suggested the possibility that survivors of the last Byzantine phase of Gush Halav could have resettled at Nabratein, it remains to examine briefly the earlier Byzantine chronology. Due to forces beyond the control of the excavators, a permit to dig could only be secured for the synagogue and several meters around it.[33] Hence the kind of exposure of areas of excavation at Gush Halav was far more limited than at any other site and our conclusions at this point must remain rather tentative. As of this moment, with a final numismatic report still incomplete, there does not seem to be any gap in occupation from 250–551. Despite constant damage from earthquakes and natural causes, constant repairs and excellent maintenance of the synagogue facility enabled the building to survive in basically one basilical form for three centuries. While there are adjustments of the form of the *bema*, the basic type of building remains constant.

The fourth century *bema* or prayer platform is so small and situated in such an awkward position on the south wall that there is little doubt that there was at least one major disturbance in the fourth century which brought about major repairs in the stylobates and the replacement of a much larger *bema* with a much smaller one.[34] It is impossible to say at this time whether this major rebuilding, which coincides with the onset of the Byzantine era, is to be dated to the first half of the fourth century A.D. and possibly related to the 306 earthquake, or to the second half of the century and possibly tied to the events of the 350's and the earthquake of 363. Suffice it to say that from that point to 551 a good measure of continuity is apparent judging from the synagogue remains. On the basis of two tomb complexes excavated in the upper village, the late fourth and fifth centuries are a period of genuine flowering in Gush Halav,[35] surely one of the main centers of Upper Galilean life and culture along with Meiron.

Khirbet Shema'

The flexibility in the dating for the beginning of the Byzantine level at a site is well illustrated at Khirbet Shema'. The chronology of Khirbet Shema' has recently been criticized by R. W. Russell[36] who would separate the Late Roman or Synagogue I phase from the Byzantine or Synagogue II phase on the basis of the 363 earthquake.

This author after giving much consideration to the matter is still of a mind to maintain a stratigraphic separation between Stratum III and IV and assign the collapse of Synagogue I Stratum III to the great earthquake of 306.

In defense of the Khirbet Shema' chronology it must be stressed that none of the declivities sealed in the building phase of Synagogue I or II had any Byzantine pottery. All the coins tend to be earlier because the bulk of filling was done in the third century or Synagogue I phase. Even in the area east of stylobate the fill was homogeneously Late Roman, slightly later than the fill in the other declivities. This can be explained by the fact that this area was the least stable of all in the entire synagogue floor area since it covered over an earlier *miqveh* (ritual bath) and the bedrock dipped off radically here. In any case no Byzantine wares were found in any of the declivities and many destroyed architectural fragments of Synagogue I were found east of stylobate[37] and they suit the Late Roman style far better than the Byzantine.

Perhaps even more definitive, however, is the date assigned the *bema*. By way of self-criticism, the text of the Khirbet Shema' volume while clear on this point[38] is only located at the beginning of the chapter on the synagogue and not in the context of discussion of the *bema* itself.[39] Several coins were found in the rubbly-fill and in the *bema* of Synagogue II including one of Constans (337–341) and one of Alexander Jannaeus (103–76 B.C.).[40] There is no doubt whatsoever, therefore, that the *bema* of Synagogue II can have been completed no later than 341 and hence cannot be part of a post-363 Synagogue II.

In retrospect, several floor repairs in Synagogue II if not the entire floor were doubtlessly undertaken as a result of the earthquake of 363.[41] The fill and accumulation above floor level and not including the declivities all contained Byzantine wares, something quite expected since these fills were not sealed from above and reflect the final stage of use into the fifth century when Synagogue II and the site are abandoned after the 419 earthquake, save for a squatter here and there.

All of this simply adds support to the stratigraphic separation and nomenclature of strata III and IV at Khirbet Shema'. It does not weaken the earlier statement that from the point of view of material culture the Byzantine era really begins later. Stratum IV is called Byzantine because its major occupational history falls within that period, though to be sure its stratigraphic history commences at the very end of the Late Roman period.

The best explanation for the persistence of Khirbet Shema' after the demise of Meiron is that its smaller population meant that it could more easily sustain the shift to taxation in kind. Excavation tends to support the notion that Khirbet Shema', perhaps one tenth the size of Meiron, produced far more olives and olive oil than Meiron and was so recognized in the literature.[42] The impact of the 419 earthquake on Gush Halav is still not fully know, if indeed it had any.

Industry and Trade

It is quite evident that Upper Galilee in the specific Meiron region was best noted for its olive industry and especially the production of premium olive oil whose worth was as good as gold and whose reputation reached legendary proportions already in rabbinic times.[43] Indeed, every one of the sites is specifically mentioned in the literary record in this regard except for Nabratein. Substantial remains of olive seeds have been recovered through flotation and a number of screw presses located, leaving no doubts about the accuracy of such reports. Even to this day olive orchards line the hills of the area and constitute a major industry. A famous first century A.D. resident of Gischala (Gush Halav), a certain John, was known to have traded local olive oil for huge sums of money in nearby Tyre.[44]

There is even indication that transport of olive oil was in barrels as a result of the excavation at Meiron of a large cooperage.[45] Given the terminology for containers in rabbinic literature, however, it is quite possible that oil was transported also in large ceramic amphorae and storage vessels, and leather skins as well.[46] Judging from the huge quantities of storage vessels found at most sites in the area, it is also possible to speculate that fresh dry olives were also transported to areas specializing in olive pressing or simply shipped in brine for eating purposes. Field IV at Nabratein in particular seems to be a kind of processing or storage area for the eastern trade. A very large storage building with facilities for pouring and storerooms suggest that it was a major trading depot.[47]

Galilee is also known for its production of wine which according to at least one rabbinic source was dearer than olive oil.[48] While only one wine press has been recovered in the excavations at Khirbet Shema'[49] at least one site near Nabratein, Acchabaron, just south of Safed, is mentioned as a production center in Upper Galilee. It is quite possible that many of our storage vessels are to be associated with wine storage, though we normally associate amphorae with such storage. Wheat production should also be noted as another prized Galilean commodity which was traded to the Phoenician coast from areas of overproduction.[50]

Gush Halav of the sites being considered is also known for its textiles, and is especially noted for silk.[51] Neutron activation analysis of sherds from each site except Nabratein suggests a local ceramic workshop for the production of kitchen wares and storage vessels.[52] This is hardly surprising though the literature refers to the main centers of production as being at Kefar Hananiyah and Sogane-Sikhnin in Lower Galilee.[53] It has even been conjectured by Dennis Groh, the fine-wares specialist of the Meiron Excavation Project, that by mid-fourth century the local ceramists are imitating imported Late Roman wares.[54] In any event there is no doubt that the local artisans included many fine ceramists. Unfortunately, their manufacturing center and kiln has not yet been precisely located.

Other crafts known from rabbinic sources included scribes, weavers, tanners, cobblers, bakers and smiths.[55] Though several ceramic inkwells have been recovered in these excavations no other indication of scribal activity has been evident, though several rooms adjoining the synagogues could well have functioned as a kind of *scriptorium*.[56] The enormous number of metal objects recovered indicate a rather highly developed metallurgical skill at each site, for it is more than likely that metal fittings were manufactured locally.[57] If this be the case we should also note that carpentry was a highly prized skill and craft in this heavily wooded area.

Recent studies as well as literary sources indicate that glass making was another major industry of Galilee though its center is usually located on the edge of the Coastal Plain near Akko (Ptolemais).[58] While Tiberias is noted for its glass production, the manufacturing source of the considerable glass finds from each site is simply not known. Recent finds in the Golan and at other Galilean sites such as Tell Anafa tend to support the view that there might well have been any number of manufacturing centers and that glass-making was one of the most prized and developed industries of northern Palestine in the Byzantine era and certainly earlier.

Conclusions

It can be said on the basis of considerable evidence now that the Upper Galilee in the Byzantine era is an area which reflects the variety of historical and social changes affecting the broader world of the eastern Mediterranean in late antiquity. While some sites continue to flourish well into the middle or even to the end of the Byzantine period (Gush Halav and Nabratein) others disappears from the landscape of Jewish town life in the same era (Meiron and thenKhirbet Shema'). There seems to have been ample wealth to sustain town life when political circumstances allowed. While witnessing a high inflation rate, Palestine in the fourth century still managed to experience and benefit from a new degree of prosperity brought about by the changeover of the status of the Empire after Constantine. Neither famine nor disease could dislodge pockets of Jewish population here and there, though to be sure there seems to be a general exodus and emigration during this period to the Golan Heights in the East and to both eastern and western Mediterranean areas across the Great Sea. (e.g. Italy and Asia Minor).

From an architectural standpoint the Byzantine synagogues do not compare favourably with their Roman precursors in decorative style and building technique. But still, when possible, as in the case of Capernaum, lavish expenditures and great efforts were invested in a building of unparalleled beauty and elegance.[59] The new wealth which poured into the Holy Land is best reflected in the building of Christian churches and shrines. Christian towns and villages not only in Galilee but in all of Palestine greatly benefitted from this new wealth, inflation and often other negative factors notwithstanding.

There is then a sense in which Jewish town life both peaks and declines in the early Byzantine period, depending upon one's perspective. Since it is precisely at this time (ca. 400) that the Palestine Talmud is completed, it can be said that the incompleteness of the *Gemara* in the Palestinian Talmud, as over against the completed Babylonian version, represents the ambiguity of the situation of Palestinian Jewry in the Byzantine period. What with new studies and excavations, however, there is sure to be further elucidation of towns both Christian and Jewish in this era, one of the most important of periods in western history.[60]

Notes

1. S. Freyne, *Galilee From Alexander the Great to Hadrian*, Notre Dame, 1980.
2. E. M. Meyers and J. F. Strange, *Archaeology, the Rabbis and Early Christianity: The Social and Historical Setting of Palestinian Judaism and Christianity*, Nashville, 1981, pp. 38–40.
3. *Ibid.*, pp. 40–41.
4. E. M. Meyers, "Galilean Regionalism as a Factor in Historical Reconstruction," *Bulletin of the American Schools of Oriental Research* 220/221 (1976), pp. 93–103.
5. R. S. Hanson, *Tyrian Influence in the Upper Galilee*, Cambridge, 1980, Meiron Excavation Project vol. II, ed. E. M. Meyers.
6. See the numismatic report by J. Raynor in "Preliminary Report on the 1980 Excavations at En-Nabratein, Israel," *Bulletin of the American Schools of Oriental Research*, forthcoming.
7. B. Bagatti, *Antichi villaggi cristiani di Galilea*, Jerusalem, 1971.
8. E. Saunders, "Christian Synagogues and Jewish Christianity in Galilee," *Explor* 3 (1977), pp. 70–78.
9. See D. E. Groh, "The Fine-wares from the Patrician and Lintel Houses," in E. M. Meyers, J. F. Strange, C. L. Meyers, *Excavations at Ancient Meiron, Upper Galilee, Israel*, Cambridge, 1981, Meiron Excavation Project, Vol. III, pp. 129–138, for a general consideration of imported wares. The cross as a Christian symbol has been exhaustively treated in a recent Hebrew University Ph.D. dissertation by V. Tzaferis, in which he maintains that only after the period of Constantine does the cross carry specifically Christian meaning.
10. This material is being exhaustively treated in a new study being prepared by R. Gregg and D. Urman. Unfortunately there is not yet any decent publication on the subject. A new museum in the Golan Heights at Qaytsrein houses most of the material.
11. See the author's article, "Ancient Gush Halav (Giscala), Palestinian Synagogues and the Eastern Diaspora," in J. Gutman, ed., *Ancient Synagogues: The State of Research*, Chico, 1981.
12. *Excavations at Ancient Meiron*, MEP vol. III, pp. 123–138.
13. *Ibid.*, pls. 8.10, 8.20–21.
14. *Ibid.*, photos 36–38.
15. See Groh, *op. cit.*
16. This is especially apparent from the sculpture excavated at Nabratein in 1981. The execution of the Roman lions from the *aedicula* far surpasses that of a sculpted lion in a lintel stone. In general the Byzantine style is far less delicate. A catalogue of this sculpture is being prepared by my Duke colleague, John G. Younger.

17. See *Excavations at Ancient Meiron, MEP* vol. III, figure i.1.

18. On the earthquake of 363 see K. W. Russell, "The Earthquake of May 19, A.D. 363," *Bulletin of the American Schools of Oriental Research* 238 (1980), pp. 47–64.

19. See P. Smith *et al,* "The Skeletal Remains," in *Excavations at Ancient Meiron, MEP* vol. II, pp. 110–122.

20. *Ibid., Excavations,* pp. 155ff. and D. Sperber, *Roman Palestine: Money and Prices,* Ramat Gan, 1974.

21. D. Sperber, *Roman Palestine 200–400: The Land,* Ramat Gau, 1978.

22. M. Avi-Yonah, *The Jews of Palestine: A Political History From the Bar Kokhba War to the Arab Conquest,* New York, 1976, pp. 176ff.

23. *De Caesaribus,* 42.9–12. See edition of F. Pichlmayer and B. Greundel, Leipzig, 1970.

24. *Chronicon,* see edition of R. Helm, Berlin, 1956. The *Chronicon* is a continuation of Eusebius' *Ecclesiastical History.*

25. *Adversus Iudaeus.*

26. See Z. Frankel, "Der Aufstand in Palastina zur Zeit des Gallus," *Monatsschrift für Geschichte und Wissenschaft des Judentums* 16 (1867), p. 147.

27. The subject of the so-called Gallus Revolt is the subject of a Duke doctoral dissertation topic of Barbara Geller of Wellesley College and directed by me.

28. See the remarks of Ms. Joyce Raynor, numismatist of the Meiron Excavation Project and curator of the Haifa Maritime Museum, Israel, currently scheduled for *BASOR* 244.

29. N. Avigad, "A Dated Lintel-Inscription from the Ancient Synagogue of Nabratein," L. M. Rabbinowitz Volume III, pp. 49–56.

30. See *BASOR* 244, preliminary report.

31. *Ibid.*

32. See *Israel Exploration Journal,* "Notes and News," forthcoming.

33. "Preliminary Report on the Excavations of Gush Halav," with C. L. Meyers and J. F. Strange, *BASOR* 233 (1979), 31–38.

34. See above, n. 18.

35. See above, n. 8.

36. See above, n. 11.

37. See E. M. Meyers, A. T. Kraabel, J. F. Strange, *Ancient Synagogue Excavations at Khirbet Shema,* Durham, 1976, p. 40, fig. 3.4.

38. *Ibid.,* p. 34.

39. *Ibid.,* pp. 71–73.

40. *Ibid.,* p. 285, area NE1.31, locus 22.

41. *Ibid.,* p. 36.

42. *Ibid.,* p. 13–14.

43. *Ibid.,* pp. 12ff.

44. Josephus *War*, 2.591–594; Hanson, *op. cit.*, and pp. 2–3 of Meyers' introduction.

45. *Meiron* volume III, photo 22.

46. As suggested in private conversations by Professor Saul Lieberman.

47. See forthcoming Nabratein publications.

48. Tal. Bab. Nazir 31b.

49. Khirbet Shema fig. 4.10.

50. M. Avi-Yonah, *The Holy Land: From the Persian to the Arab Conquest*, Grand Rapids, 1977, p. 202 and n. 142.

51. *Ibid.*, see also n. 33.

52. See the neutron activation report in *Meiron* volume III, pp. 139ff.

53. Avi-Yonah, *Holy Land*, p. 205.

54. Groh, *Meiron* volume III, pp. 129ff.

55. Avi-Yonah, *Holy Land*, p. 205.

56. So for example the frescoed room at *Khirbet Shema*, pp. 76ff.

57. The number of metal objects discovered at all the sites is very high, but see individual finds in the publications.

58. Avi-Yonah, *Holy Land*, pp. 204–205.

59. See Meyers and Strange, *Archaeology, the Rabbis and Early Christianity*, pp. 58ff., 128ff. and notes.

60. See above n. 10.

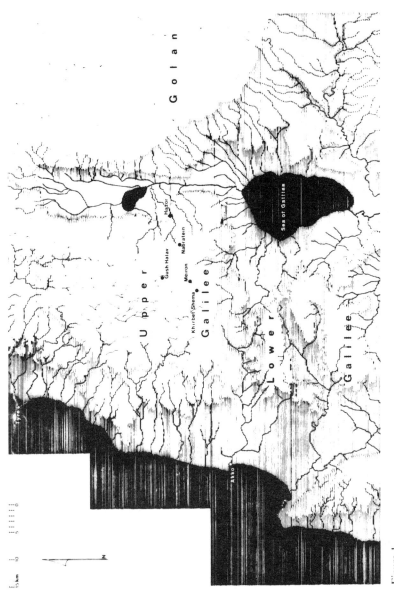

Figure 1

Comparative Chronological Table

Meiron

Stratum I:	200-50 BC,	Hellenistic
Stratum II:	50BC-135 AD,	Early Roman
Stratum III:	135-250 AD,	Middle Roman
Stratum IV:	250-365 AD,	Late Roman
Stratum V:	365-750 AD,	Byzantine Arab
Stratum VI:	750-1000 AD,	Early Arab
Stratum VII:	1000-1399 AD,	Late Arab
phase a.	11th-13th c.	
phase b.	14th c.	

Encyclopedia of Excavations

152-37 BC,	Hellenistic
37 BC-70 AD,	Roman I(Herodian)
70-180 AD,	Roman II
180-324 AD,	Roman III
324-451,	Byzantine I
451-640,	Byzantine II
640-1099,	Early Arab
1099-1291,	Crusader
1291-1516,	Mameluke

Khirbet Shema'

Stratum I:	103-76 BC,	Hasmonean
Stratum II:	130-284 AD,	LR1
Stratum III:	284-306 AD,	LR2
Stratum IV:	306-419 AD,	Byzantine 1
Stratum V:	419-640 AD,	Byzantine 2
Stratum VI:	640-850,	Arab
Stratum VII:	1150-1277,	Medieval

Gush Halav (tentative)

Stratum I:	13th/12th c. BC,	LBII-Iron I
Stratum II:	8th/6th c. BC,	Iron II
Stratum III:	5th/4th c. BC,	Persian
Stratum IV:	2nd/1st c. BC,	Helenistic
Stratum V:	50 BC-135 AD,	Early Roman
Stratum VI:	250-363 AD,	Late Roman
phase a.	250-306 AD,	
phase b.	306-363 AD,	
Stratum VII:	363-551 AD,	Byzantine
phase a.	363-447 AD,	
phase b.	447-551 AD,	
Stratum VIII:	7th-8th c. AD.	Early Arab

Nabratein (tentative)

Stratum I:	27th/24th c. BC,	Early Bronze II-III
Stratum II:	8th/6th c. BC,	Iron II
Stratum III:	5th/4th c. BC,	Persian
Stratum IV:	3rd/1st c. BC,	Hellenistic
Stratum V:	50 BC-135 AD,	Early Roman
Stratum VI:	135-250 AD,	Middle Roman
Stratum VII:	250-350/63 AD,	Late Roman
phase a.	250-306 AD,	
phase b.	306-350/63 AD,	
Stratum VIII:	ca.500-640, AD.	Byzantine
Stratum IX:	640-700, AD.	Early Arab
Stratum X:	12th century,	Medieval

Figure 2

BYZANTINE *INSTRUMENTA DOMESTICA* FROM ANEMURIUM: THE SIGNIFICANCE OF CONTEXT.*

James Russell
(University of British Columbia)

During recent years Canadian excavations have been conducted at the ancient site of Anemurium on the coast of Rough Cilicia. Located on the east side of Cape Anamur, the southernmost promontory of Asia Minor, the city reached its greatest prosperity in the second and first half of the third century A.C. To this period belong the large public buildings of the Roman city and the extensive necropolis outside the walls, whose ruins still dominate the scene and which have provided the principal focus of attention. The investigations, however, have also shed much light on the community's history during the early Byzantine period, when it continued to flourish well into the sixth century. Towards the end of that century a marked decline set in, probably precipitated by an earthquake and aggravated by the unsettled conditions that prevailed during the following decades. The churches and other public buildings of Byzantine Anemurium, with the considerable expanses of well-preserved mosaic flooring still *in situ*, inevitably attract the greatest interest, but examination of the secondary uses to which the earlier Roman buildings were put has yielded information of no less significance about the city in its later phases.[1]

Of particular interest is the spacious baths-palaestra complex, which represents the most monumental expression of the city's prosperity around the mid-third century. The stable conditions that encouraged such an ambitious project were cut short by the Persian occupation of the region under Shapur I, shortly after 260,[2] and within a century structures of humbler purpose began to encroach on the open spaces of the palaestra. Meanwhile the vaulted halls of the adjacent baths, doubtless now stripped of their marble decoration, were gradually invaded to accommodate a variety of industries that eventually included a lime-kiln, flour-mills, potteries and a lamp-factory. These presumably provided a livelihood for the inhabitants of the houses in the palaestra and its environs. This community of artisans and their families was long-lived and still going strong during the first half of the seventh century, at a time when the city's churches were already in ruins or only in partial use, and when other amenities of city life, such as baths and aqueducts, were no longer functioning. The walls of the houses of these last inhabitants of the palaestra, though of coarse construction, remain standing several courses high. The presence of stairs suggests a second storey in one establishment, while earthen ovens, the *tandir*, to be seen in use even today in various parts of Turkey, are found in several. The best preserved is a rectangular building, constructed in a technique still practised in the neighborhood. This consists of a skeletal structure of corner and interval piers composed of well-mortared masonry, the intervening gaps filled in dry stones. A doorway in the east wall leads into a corridor that divides the house into two halves. A large room occupied the south half of the building, evidently a kitchen with enclosed hearth covered by a cooking slab built against the north wall. Into this was inserted a chimney similar to one found in a house of the same general period at Arif in Lycia.[3]

Shortly after the middle of the seventh century even this modest community had ceased to exist, victim no doubt of the razzias of Arab marauders setting forth from Cyprus, a mere forty miles away.[4] Since there is no sign of violent destruction or last-ditch struggle, we may presume that the site was evacuated gradually and in an orderly manner in favor of the security of the mountains that surround the plain. A handful of coins dated after 660 indicates that some form of limited activity continued on the site into the early eighth century, but for all practical purposes life had already come to an end about that date.[5] With the passage of time the pisé or tile roofs of the abandoned houses caved in followed eventually by the walls, sealing in any coins, pottery and assorted odds and ends rejected or overlooked by the last occupants at the time of their departure. The significance of coins and pottery discovered in contexts such as these hardly requires comment. For this reason both genres of evidence have traditionally received preferential treatment. Much less favored, however, are the miscellaneous bric-à-brac brought to light in the excavation of a typical Byzantine habitation site, often in considerable quantity. At Anemurium for instance the inventory of small finds amounts to some 500 individual items, which does not include countless copper and iron nails, links of chain and other unidentifiable pieces of metal. Consisting for the most part of broken fragments of tools, harness, furniture and dress, or stray objects, such as weights, seals, gaming pieces and the like, this heterogeneous collection contains next to nothing of artistic merit. When the rare *objet d'art* does appear, it tends to be singled out for special treatment, as in the case of a molded bronze steelyard weight in the form of Athena, discovered in 1970 and promptly published.[6] Other objects found in the same vicinity and in a similar context on the floors of the Byzantine houses of the palaestra, however, still await publication.

This state of affairs reflects the regrettable practice in Byzantine archaeology to regard objects as cream or whey in proportion to their artistic quality or condition of survival. But from an archaeological point of view neither condition nor artistic quality can compare in importance with the context of the object when found. Unfortunately the recognition of this principle, readily honored in the treatment of coins, lamps, pottery and even glass, has rarely been applied to the study of small finds from Byzantine sites, as I have recently become aware while preparing the catalogue of small finds from Anemurium. To do justice to this category of evidence one depends heavily on comparative material from other sites of the same general period. Yet the only full-scale publication of Byzantine small objects from an archaeological excavation is Chavane's comprehensive catalogue of material from Salamis in Cyprus, published in 1975.[7] More typical are the cases of Antioch, Beisan (Scythopolis), Gerasa, Ephesus and the Athenian Agora, all major excavations, the latter two still in progress, each producing enormous quantities of miscellaneous objects still largely unpublished. Apart from the Salamis volume, the archaeological works of primary resort too frequently remain Déonna's *Délos* XVIII and Davidson's *Corinth* XII, published in 1938 and 1952 respectively, both admirable catalogues for description and illustration, but quite deficient in their attention to context and association.[8] The prospect for students of *instrumenta domestica* from Byzantine contexts promises to improve appreciably, however, with the imminent publication of substantial collections of such material from three major excavations in Turkey, Sardis, Saraçhane (St. Polyeuktos) in Istanbul, and Alahan in Isauria.[9] Another publication of importance currently in progress is of a large collection of Byzantine small bronze objects purchased by the Menil Foundation of Houston, Texas.[10] This collection, assembled originally by an Istanbul antiquities dealer, with its wide range of specimens of everyday items such as keys, belt-buckles, weights and crosses, provides typological sequences that should complement the contextual information from excavations.

Although archaeological scraps of the sort discovered amidst the destruction levels at Anemurium may appear trifling at first sight, the cumulative total, drawn from so many facets of daily life affords, if carefully analysed, a detailed documentation of Byzantine economy and society within the setting of a specific community. In the past only the Russian excavators of Cherson and the surrounding region have come anywhere close to realizing the enormous potential of this genre of evidence from Byzantine contexts.[11] Yet even a brief aperçu of some of the material from the early Byzantine levels at Anemurium will demonstrate the sheer variety of the evidence at the disposal of the student of Byzantine social and economic history. Industry and crafts are represented by a variety of tools, the farmer's iron dolabrum (fig. 1.1) and the carpenter's chisel; the fish-hook (fig. 1.2) and netting needle of the fisherman; the stone-mason's plumb-bob (fig. 1.3), and the lead stamp of one Sergius, probably a tile-maker or potter (fig. 1.4); the tailor's thimble (fig. 1.5) and the heavy needle used by a sail-maker or leather-worker (fig. 1.6); the bronze balance-arm and small pan of a jeweller's scales (fig. 1.7–8). A considerable range of leaded bronze weights in standard Byzantine denominations (fig. 1.9–11) and the collar and U-shaped suspension bar from a steelyard weighing apparatus (fig. 1.12) betray the world of retailing and merchandise.[12] Evidence for how these same artisans and shop-keepers furnished their homes is also to hand. From the heavy wooden chests that stored their dowries and other treasures we have the decorated hasps and hinges with typical punched circle designs (fig. 2.13–14); from their furniture come fragments of copper-sheathing worked in a chip-carved type of decoration (fig. 2.15) and elegantly turned balusters of polished bone (fig. 2.16); evidence for the way in which homes and strongboxes were secured survives in a lock-plate (fig. 2.17) and keys of varying shapes and sizes (fig. 2.18–19). Clay lamps manufactured on the site were probably the normal form of illumination,[13] but bronze lamps with finely turned hinged lids (fig. 3.20) were also in use, as were conical shaped glass lamps inserted into polycandela. This latter form of lighting is more commonly associated with churches, but the abundance of broken glass lamps, along with some 50 copper wick-holders belonging to them, as well as the fragment of a polycandelon (fig. 3.21) and several suspension hooks and chains (fig. 3.22) found in the ruins of the houses, point to their frequent use also in a domestic context.[14] Fragments of kitchen utensils survive in a skillet-handle with heat-guard (fig. 3.23), the detached handle of a bronze jug with the lower attachment plaque decorated with a cast head (fig. 3.24) and an iron fire-lighter (fig. 3.25). Dice and gaming counters (fig. 4.26–29), including on occasion fish vertebrae, are reminders of how leisure hours were spent. Loom-weights (fig. 4.30), spindle-whorls and hooks (fig. 4.31–32) bear witness to female occupations; while female vanity was indulged in copper and bone hair-pins, both plain and decorated (fig. 5.33–34), and in various shapes and sizes of kohl-sticks, cosmetic scoops and spatulas (fig. 5.35–37). Jewellery took the form of silver earrings, bronze finger rings (fig. 5.38–40), pendants attached by chains, ranging in quality from a silver bulla (fig. 5.41) to a local coin of Anemurium minted in the second century, but pierced in the seventh for reuse as a charm.[15] The religious devotion of Christians is reflected in pendant crosses, one of gold with glass paste en cloisonné (fig. 4.42), others of silver and bronze, while that of the Jew found expression in a phylactery, a thin inscribed silver scroll, enclosed in a bronze tube suspended from the neck by a chain (fig. 4.43). People protected themselves from the Evil Eye by wearing amulets such as a pair of copper plaques, one depicting Solomon as a horseman striking down a prostrate female demon (fig. 4.44), the other representing the Evil Eye being assailed by a variety of sharp instruments and wild animals, with the legend KYPI BOHΘI above (fig. 4.45); small bronze bells, *tintinnabula* (fig. 4.46–47), were hung in doorways or above the baby's cradle to ward off the Evil Eye.[16]

This selective, and perforce superficial, résumé has demonstrated in general terms the range of the evidence to hand. To illustrate the wider potential of this type of material when related to a known context for illuminating certain interesting aspects of contemporary society, therefore, I have selected the belt-buckles as a group for detailed discussion. A total of 32 has appeared, one of silver (no. 1), one of iron (no. 6), and the remainder of various copper alloys. The majority were found in the destruction debris of the abandoned houses of the palaestra complex or in the earth fill from the open areas between them. A significant number were also found in the rubble from the collapse of the hypocaust system of a small early Byzantine baths erected in the fifth century (but no longer functioning as such by the end of the sixth). In its final phase its three vaulted rooms seem to have been used as shops.[17] In both locations the considerable quantities of coins and pottery found in the same contexts suggest a date in the first half of the seventh century for most of the buckles. Full particulars of each specimen will eventually appear in the catalogue of small finds from Anemurium, currently in preparation, but a summary conspectus of the various types will demonstrate the wide range of designs in circulation in a single community.

The Anemurium buckles fall into three distinct categories: 1) those comprising only the two essential components of a buckle, the tongue and the buckle-frame proper, to which the belt would be attached; 2) those equipped with an attachment plate, in which plate and buckle-frame are cast as a unit; and 3) those in which buckle-frame and plate, separately manufactured, are attached to each other by a hinge.

In group I four types are distinguished, based on the shape of the buckle-frame.

1. Simple circular or oval frame, varying in thickness in some instances, around which the tongue is looped (fig. 6.1–3).
2. Ogival frame of varying width with marked thickening at the pointed end and thin cross-piece opposite to which the tongue was fastened by an open loop (fig. 6.4–5).
3. Buckle-frame consisting of a circular ring joined to a rectangular opening; the tongue would have been attached to the bridge between circle and rectangle. The sole example is of iron (fig. 6.6).
4. Rectangular frame composed of three elements, a U-shaped bar terminating in eyes to receive a pin, circular in section, the ends of which are splayed to hold it in place. The tongue is looped loosely around the U-shaped bar (fig. 6.7–8).

In the second group the shape and decoration of the plate are the distinguishing characteristics, the buckle-frame in each case being elliptical in shape. From the underside of the plate project perforated lugs, normally in pairs, but occasionally in threes, for insertion through the leather of the strap. In most instances the upper surface of the plate carries an incised design. Where relevant, correspondences with Werner's and Csallány's typologies are noted.[18]

5. Square plate perforated to receive the tongue, and decorated with an incised line parallel to the edge, with oblique strokes along the margin in one case (fig. 6.9–10).
6. Shield-shaped with small projection at bottom edge opposite the tongue-hole. Decoration consists of various shapes of open-work or incised circles arranged to simulate a mask (fig. 6.11–13). Included amongst Csallány's "maskenmuster" plates.[19]
7. Solid heart-shaped plate terminating in a rounded projection, its surface incised with stylized rosette or vegetable motif (fig. 7.14–16). Werner, Syracuse type; Csallány, Group 2.[20]
8. Lozenge-shaped plate incised with simple herring-bone pattern (fig. 7.17).
9. Plate in the shape of a cross with flaring arms, but no incised decoration (fig. 7.18–20).
10. Long, narrow plate with ornate profile of sharp, projecting moldings and pointed end. Decoration comprises an incised saltire beneath the tongue-hole and at the opposite extremity one incised circle and a circular perforation (fig. 7.21–22). Csallány, Group 20.[21]
11. Long narrow plate with wide blunt termination, decorated with two incised circles side by side immediately below the tongue-hole; the most distinctive feature is the pair of stylized duck's heads, with large circular incised eyes, projecting from each side of the oval buckle-frame (fig. 7.23). Csallány also includes this in his Group 20.[22].

In the third group, in which buckle and plate are hinged, a pair of pierced lugs projects from each element to receive a pin around which the tongue also was looped. As in the previous group, types are distinguished by the form and decoration of the plates.

12. Shield-shaped plate with two projecting pierced lugs at the upper corners for hinge-attachment to the buckle-frame now missing; incised ivy leaf decoration, flanked by two punched dots, set within a broken incised border that follows the outline of the plate (fig. 7.24). Csallány, Group 6.[23]
13. Triangular plate with rounded corners; incised outline frames open-work in the shape of a heart. Hinge takes the form of a pin passing through the projecting loops of the buckle on the inside, and the

plate on the outside (fig. 7.25). Werner, Bologna type; Csallány, Group 9.[24]

14. Plate has a complex profile of sharp and rounded moldings terminating in a rounded extremity. Decoration comprises open-work of varying shapes (circle, rectangle, figure of eight) and punched or incised circles. Two projecting lugs form the hinge-attachment (fig. 8.26–27).

15. Triangular plate with rounded projections at upper end and widening at lower extremity, now broken off, but probably rounded. Incised decoration includes chevron on shoulder and circle on each of the side projections. The surface between the shoulder and the terminal is framed on the flanks by three parallel incised lines enclosing a simple interlaced cable design. Plate is hinged to an oval shaped buckle-frame curved in section with punched strokes as decoration (fig. 8.28).

In addition to the types listed above in group three there are four buckle-frames with hinge attachments no longer joined to their plates. Three have a single kidney-shaped frame (fig. 8.29–31), while a fourth has a double kidney-shaped frame with circular perforation in the central bridge (fig. 8.32).[25]

This collection of belt-buckles discovered at Anemurium is remarkable for both quantity and range of types represented. The French excavations at Salamis, for example, have yielded only 13 examples;[26] while at Sardis, where excavation has been conducted on a far more extensive scale and over a much longer period, the early Byzantine contexts have produced only 25 buckles and belt fittings;[27] and although a total of 28 buckles emerged from the excavation of Saraçhane (St. Polyeuktos) in Constantinople, a site rich in the general bric-à-brac of Byzantine daily life, only 16 specimens at most fall within the chronological limits under consideration.[28] Moreover, with fifteen distinct types of design represented, Anemurium far surpasses these three sites in the variety of buckles. Indeed, of Byzantine city-sites with fully published inventories of small metal objects found during excavation, only Corinth exceeds Anemurium in quantity and variety of buckles found.[29]

The significance of the belt-buckle as evidence has long been recognized in the archaeology of central and western Europe where buckles have appeared in vast numbers in the excavation of graves in south Russia, the Danube region, north Italy, the Rhineland, Gaul, Britain and Scandinavia.[30] Buckles were designated by type as Avar, Bulgar,

Lombard, Merovingian etc. according to their find-spot or association with other objects in graves of known identity. When buckles of similar type appeared during the 1930s in excavations in Greece or elsewhere in the eastern Mediterranean their existence was felt to betoken some form of barbarian presence. The phenomenon was most thoroughly investigated in the case of Corinth. There the appearance in post-Roman graves of buckles and other objects normally associated with barbarian graves of the Danube region was ascribed by Gladys Davidson to an invasion of the Avars in the first half of the seventh century,[31] and by Kenneth Setton (citing texts referring to Bulgaric belts from the early seventh century) to the presence of Onogur Bulgars.[32]

The frequency with which buckles of "barbarian" type kept turning up in other parts of the Byzantine Empire, including Constantinople itself, however, eventually convinced others, especially Joachim Werner and D. Csallány, that the buckles were in fact derived from Byzantine prototypes.[33] This case has been further strengthened by the considerable numbers of similar buckles included in the Menil collection, most of which must have been found either in the capital itself or in the hinterland of Thrace or Bithynia. In his forthcoming publication of the buckles in this collection, Gary Vikan points also to the use of Greek inscriptions and monograms with Greek names and Christian invocations on some of these types and the degree to which the design and ornament of all the major types are interrelated as proof of the existence of a centralized workshop tradition.[34] The widespread distribution of certain types beyond the confines of the Empire could thus easily be explained by the ease with which these small objects, with their relatively simple designs, could have been cast from molds made from specimens imported in the first instance from Constantinople and other major centers of the Empire.

This explanation of the phenomenon is largely borne out by the increasing numbers of buckles of types once categorized as barbarian that have appeared from secure Byzantine contexts of the sixth and seventh centuries in the excavation of a number of sites in the eastern Mediterranean. An excellent illustration is provided by Werner's Syracuse buckle-type (Anemurium type 7, fig. 7.14–16), one of the commonest in circulation. With the exception of two specimens from Constantinople and one from Achmin in Egypt, Werner's examples were found either in frontier regions where barbarian influence was already dominant, such as the Balkans, Greece, the Pontic Chersonese, Italy, Sicily and north Italy, or from regions well outside the Empire, including the central and upper Danube, the Rhineland and even southeast England.[35] In a revised version of Werner's find-spot map of Syracuse buckles (fig. 9), however, we may now add, without exhaustive search, two instances from Monastir (Macedonia), five further examples from Constantinople, one from Pergamon, two from Sardis, one from Samos, one from the Yassi Ada shipwreck (near Halicarnassus), three from Anemurium and one other of uncertain provenance from Asia Minor; individual specimens from Salamis on Cyprus, Antioch, Apamea and Byblos in Syria, Pella and Scythopolis, both cities of the Decapolis, and one each from Ctesiphon (Mesopotamia) and Edfou (Egypt).[36] Clearly, distribution of this type was as widespread within the Empire as beyond its frontiers. The same is true also of Werner's Bologna buckle (Anemurium type 13, fig. 7.25). Previously represented only at Athens, Corinth and Constantinople within the Empire,[37] this type is now reported also from Anemurium, Salamis (with two specimens), Lesbos, Cherson, in addition to one further example from Constantinople and two from Athens.[38]

The case for an original place of manufacture within the Byzantine Empire is even stronger for some of the other buckle types found at Anemurium. This is particularly so with the simple designs with no attached or hinged plate. Examples of the distinctive Anemurium type 4 (fig. 6.7–8), for instance, are recorded also from Delos, Constantinople, Sardis, Yassi Ada, Midas City (Phrygia), Salamis (Cyprus), Antioch (Syria) and Nebo (Palestine), but never, to my knowledge, from any barbarian context outside the Empire.[39] This is the case also with Anemurium type 3 (fig. 6.4–5), which seems to show up only at sites within the Byzantine world, including Corinth, Delos, Constantinople (four examples), Sardis, Salamis, Antioch (Syria), Nessana (Palestine) and the Pontic Chersonese.[40] Even some of the more ornate buckle types with decorated plates occur rarely outside the Byzantine Empire. This is perhaps understandable in the case of Anemurium type 9 (fig. 7.18–20), examples of which are also recorded from Constantinople, Athens, Antioch (Syria), Scythopolis (Palestine) and Cherson, still probably a Byzantine city in the early seventh century when these buckles were in circulation.[41] The shape of its plate as a flared cross, a motif not likely to find favor with pagans, probably explains its apparent absence from barbarian graves. This hardly accounts for the rarity of other relatively common types in barbarian contexts, however, such as the hinged buckle with shield-shaped plate incised with leaf patterns (Anemurium type 12, fig. 7.24), which is now recorded from Constantinople, Sardis, Antioch (Syria), Achmin (Egypt) and Cherson.[42] Even the buckle with elongated plate (Anemurium type 10, fig. 7.21–22), associated with the Avars by Davidson when it first appeared at Corinth, occurs far more frequently at Byzantine sites (e.g. Athens, Constantinople, Sardis, Midas City [Phrygia], Antioch) than in barbarian graves, where it assumes a somewhat different form.[43]

The evidence thus far adduced from Anemurium and other sites within the Byzantine Empire, therefore, points decisively to the vigorous mass-production of belt-buckles of many different types within the Empire. At the same time, however, the appearance of some of these types in considerable numbers beyond the frontiers speaks of intensive commercial interaction between the Byzantines and their barbarian neighbors during the period of production in the late sixth and first half of the seventh century. Until a fair sample of buckles from a representative range of sites from both inside and outside the Byzantine Empire has been subjected to metallurgical trace analysis, we cannot, of course, be certain whether the buckles found in barbarian graves are Byzantine imports or local imitations.[44] But even if we assume that a large proportion of the buckles found in the barbarian world were cast at one or two removes from an original Byzantine product, we must still account for the carriage of prototypes or the molds themselves in sufficient numbers to stimulate local craftsmen to reproduce them over an area extending from south Russia to Spain and north Africa to Scandinavia.

On the whole, as witnessed in the burial of their dead, the barbarians eschewed the simple utilitarian buckle-forms that turn up regularly in the Byzantine cities from Asia Minor, Syria and Palestine, such as Anemurium types 2, 4, 5, in favor of the more flamboyant types with decorative plates, such as Werner's ubiquitous Syracuse and Bologna types and Csallány's "Maskenmuster" type, all represented at Anemurium (types 6, 7, 13), and others such as Werner's Sucidava and Corinth types that have not yet appeared at Anemurium.[45] The process of casting metal buckles and other belt fittings by local craftsmen is well documented by the discovery in barbarian graves of the actual terracotta or bronze molds. Indeed, nothing illustrates more vividly the eclectic character of barbarian tastes than the grave of an Avar goldsmith from Kunszentmárton in Hungary.[46] This contained all the equipment of his trade, hammer, anvil, whetstone, spoons, soldering-iron, tin-snips, and balance scales, along with bronze and stamped glass weights of standard Byzantine type. Of particular interest, however, are the bronze molds assembled from various sources, including Byzantium, for the manufacture of gold, silver or copper belt and harness fittings.

If the data considered so far from Anemurium and elsewhere tend to confirm the theory of an outgoing trade in buckle-types from Byzantine centers to the peoples beyond the frontier, we must also reckon with evidence for a reverse trade, leading to the circulation of buckle-types of unmistakeable barbarian origin within the Empire. This possibility is certainly implied by a papyrus text from the Fayum in Egypt, dating from the beginning of the seventh century, which confirms the delivery of a consignment of Bulgarian belts ($\beta ov\lambda\gamma\alpha\rho\iota\kappa[o\hat{v}$ $\kappa\alpha\rho\tau\alpha]\lambda\alpha\mu\acute{\iota}ov$).[47] We cannot tell what the Bulgarian belts actually looked like, to be sure, but, if modern belts are any guide, we may assume that the buckle would have been one of their most distinguishing features. As for archaeological evidence there is a strong likelihood that at least two of the buckles from Anemurium are of barbarian origin. One is Anemurium type 15 (fig. 8.28), with a design clearly derived from the Merovingian art of western Europe. With its simple interlaced pattern and incised circles protruding from its extremities, it is a humble imitation of the magnificent triangular buckles, often of gold and silver, with their intricate cable patterns and prominent bosses, that traveled throughout Europe during the Dark Ages.[48] Anemurium type 11 (fig. 7.23) is no less perplexing. Its jaunty pair of ducks' heads projecting from each side of the buckle-frame seems to betray a distinctly "barbaric" touch. Furthermore, the only recorded parallels for this particular design known to me are from Avar sites of the early seventh century in Hungary, including the grave of the goldsmith of Kunszentmárton already mentioned.[49] This fact in itself, as we have learnt from the false premises of earlier scholarship, is not conclusive proof of an Avar origin. Nevertheless, the discovery at Anemurium of a second object indisputably connected with the Avars strengthens the likelihood of such an association. This second object is an iron fire-lighter, shaped to form a small eye into which was inserted a flint for sparking a light (fig. 3.25). Such instruments have been found in large numbers in the Avar graves of central Europe,[50] but I know of only two secure occurrences within the Byzantine Empire, both from graves in Greece of the early seventh century, one at Corinth, the other at Olympia. In each case the occupant was probably of barbaric origin, for, besides the fire-lighter, the pottery and other objects found were identical to the contents of Avar graves in Hungary.[51] How did such objects find their way to Anemurium? Were they perhaps left behind by some wandering mercenary or by some seaman from a ship originating from a remote port *in barbarica*? Or are they local imitations of barbarian originals? The answer eludes us, but there are enough indications to discourage the formulation of simple answers to explain the circulation of belt-buckles both inside and outside the Byzantine Empire.[52]

Turning from the question of where the belt-buckles originated, I shall conclude with some remarks on the function of the belt-buckle in Byzantine society and the status of those who wore them, so far as these may be determined from archaeological contexts. It is clear from the frequency with which buckles occur at urban sites that the leather belt, of which they form the most distinctive component, was a standard item of dress throughout the Byzantine Empire during the sixth and seventh centuries, when most, if not all, of the buckle-types in question were in general circulation. Although its use on occasion to fasten a loose-fitting tunic or similar garb should not be ruled out, the principal raison d'être of the buckled belt in antiquity, as in modern times, was to secure a pair of trousers or tights, a garment originally associated with barbarians or barbarized elements in the Roman army. Already in the early Empire trouser-wearing barbarians, especially Gauls, Sarmatians and Osrhoenians were serving in the auxiliary units of the army, and in the course of time trousers, or rather tights, were adopted as a practical garb for use, especially in the country districts of the western provinces.[53] By the late fourth century trousers had taken a strong hold in the cities of the west also, including even Rome, where stringent penalties, a sure sign of ineffectiveness, were prescribed in the Theodosian Code curbing the use of trousers (braccae) in favor of the traditional toga.[54]

Literary sources from the Byzantine east, however, are generally silent on the wearing of trousers, reflecting perhaps their heavy emphasis on the imperial court and the church, precisely the two classes that continued to favor the ceremonial dress of the past. There is nevertheless considerable evidence for the acceptance of trousers or leggings as normal men's wear throughout the eastern Mediterranean during the late Empire. They are worn by a wide range of individuals in scenes depicted on wall-paintings and mosaics alike,[55] while trousers themselves (τὰ βράκια) and the name of the tailor who specialized in making them (βρακάριος) are listed in Diocletian's Price Edict,[56]

Individuals identified as trouser-makers are named in Egyptian papyri from the fourth century and later[57] and tomb inscriptions, also of late date, record the names of men practising the same craft at Sardis, Aphrodisias and Corycos, a Cilician city 170 kilometres east of Anemurium.[58] The archaeological evidence tells a similar story. The contexts that produced the belt-buckles at both Sardis and Anemurium point to the general use of belted trousers as normal dress amongst the artisans and small shop-keepers of both cities. At Sardis the largest number of buckles comes from the Byzantine shops that lined the colonnaded street, where they were found along with a wide variety of other objects.[59] This material reflects the modest status of the owners of the various establishments, the restaurateur, locksmith, toolworker, dyeworker and the like who conducted business in the shops below and probably lived on the second floor above.[60] At Anemurium the buckles found in the small baths were doubtless worn by those engaged in the retail business conducted there in their final period of reuse; those found amidst the ruins of the humble houses of the palaestra area must have belonged to their last occupants, workmen employed in the industries of the large disused bath-building close by. Even at sea standard garb for the ordinary mariner was probably some form of tights, to judge from the discovery of belt-buckles and a belt-tab in the contemporary ship-wreck off Yassi Ada, dated ca. A.D. 625.[61] The evidence from these sites and others, therefore, argues strongly for the widespread adoption of trousers and tights throughout the Byzantine world amongst the lower classes at least. The fact that buckles were manufactured in gold or silver suggests that they were used by more affluent members of society as well. The potential of the belt-buckle to proclaim the status of its wearer not only through the metal employed, but also through the complexity of design and decoration of the plate, which could even include a personal monogram, was no doubt an important factor in attracting the interest of a wealthier clientele.[62]

*The excavations at Anemurium began in 1965 under the direction of Professor Elisabeth Alföldi-Rosenbaum, University of Toronto. I assumed the direction of the project in 1971, since when the work has been sponsored by the University of British Columbia, Vancouver, and financed for the most part by research grants from the Canada Council and, since 1978, the Social Sciences and Humanities Research Council of Canada. Much of the research for this paper, which was presented in an earlier version at the Fifth Byzantine Studies

Conference held in Washington, D.C. in 1978-79, was accomplished during my tenure of a Senior Fellowship at Dumbarton Oaks.

I am deeply obliged to the following persons for providing access to their unpublished manuscripts, Margaret V. Gill, Museum Curator, Tunbridge Wells, for her catalogue of the small finds from Saraçhane (Istanbul), Jane Waldbaum, The University of Wisconsin, Milwaukee, for her catalogue of the metal objects from Sardis, Gary Vikan, Dumbarton Oaks Center for Byzantine Studies, for his essay on the belt fittings of the Menil Collection. For assistance in enabling me to view unpublished material, I am grateful to Mary Jane Victor of the Menil Foundation Collection, Houston, Texas, Frances Follin Jones of the Princeton University Art Museum, Richard Teitz of the Worcester Art Museum, and Caroline G. Dosker of the University of Pennsylvania Museum, Philadelphia.

I also acknowledge with gratitude my debt to Hilary Stewart for drawing the illustrations and preparing them for publication.

Notes

1. For a description of the ruins of the city before excavation, E. Rosenbaum, G. Huber and S. Onurkan, *A Survey of Coastal Cities in Western Cilicia* (Ankara, 1967), 1-27. For summaries of the history and antiquities of the site on the basis of subsequent fieldwork, J. Russell, "Anemurium—eine römische Kleinstadt in Kleinasien," *AntWelt* 7:4 (1976), 2-20; idem, "Anemurium: The Changing Face of a Roman City," *Archaeology* 33:5 (1980), 31-40. Preliminary reports of excavations have been published *Türk Ark Derg* 15:1 (1966), 1-12; 17:2 (1968), 177-184; 18:2 (1969), 37-58; 20:1 (1973), 201-219; 21:2 (1974), 153-165; 22:2 (1975), 121-139; 23:1 (1976), 93-96; 24:2 (1977), 109-123; 25:1 (1980), 263-290. Shorter summaries have also appeared regularly in "Recent Archaeological Research in Turkey," *AnatSt* and in M. J. Mellink, "Archaeology in Asia Minor," in *AJA*. For the necropolis, E. Alföldi-Rosenbaum, *Anamur Necropolü* (Ankara, 1971), J. Russell, "Restoration, Conservation and Excavation at the Necropolis of Anemurium, Turkey, 1974-75," *JFA* 4 (1977), 45-62.

2. Anemurium appears in the inscription recording the Res Gestae Divi Saporis from Naqš-i Rustam as one of the cities of Asia Minor captured by the Persians after the battle of Edessa. E. Honigmann and A. Maricq, *Recherches sur les Res Gestae divi Saporis* (Mém. Acad. Roy. de Belg. 47, fasc. 4) (Brussels, 1953), 14, 149, 153.

3. The palaestra area is indicated as E III 2 B in plans of the site. For secondary structures, *Türk Ark Derg* 20:1 (1973), 204-205, figs. 1, 7, 10, 11. For chimney at Arif, R. M. Harrison and G.R.J. Lawson, "An Early Byzantine Town at Arif in Lycia," *Yayla* 2 (1979), 17 (illustration p. 15).

4. Striking new evidence for the Arab invasions of Cyprus has come to light in an inscription discovered in 1974 in the Christian basilica of Soloi on Cyprus. It records the first invasion as occurring in A.D. 649 and dates to 655–56 the repair of the basilica desecrated in a subsequent invasion. I am grateful for this information to Professor V. Tran Tam Tinh (L'Université Laval, Québec) who will include a detailed discussion of the text in his forthcoming publication of the basilica.

5. The list of datable coins (all copper) of the seventh century A.C. discovered at Anemurium up to 1979 shows the following distribution:

Phocas (602–610)	24
Heraclius (610–641)	203
Constans II (641–668)	111
Constantine IV (668–685)	2
Justinian II (685–695)	1
Leontius (695–698)	0
Tiberius III (698–705)	1
Total	342

A breakdown of the coins of Constans II by DOC classes illustrates the marked diminution of frequency after ca. 660.

Classes 1–4 (641–648)	56
Classes 5–8 (648–658)	50
Classes 9–11 (658–668)	5

6. C.W.J. Eliot, "A Bronze Counterpoise of Athena," *Hesperia* 45 (1976), 163–170, pl. 26.

7. M.-J. Chavane, *Salamine de Chypre* VI: *Les petits objets* (Paris, 1975).

8. W. Déonna, *Exploration archéologique de Délos* XVIII: *Le mobilier délien* (Paris, 1938). G. R. Davidson, *Corinth* XII: *The Minor Objects* (Princeton, 1952).

9. Sardis, Jane Waldbaum, *Sardis Monograph 8: Metalwork from Sardis: The Finds through 1974* (Cambridge, Mass., Harvard University Press, 1983). Saraçhane, M. V. Gill, "The Small Finds," chapter 11 of R. Martin Harrison, *Excavations at Saraçhane in Istanbul* I, to be published by Dumbarton Oaks, Washington, D.C.

Alahan, catalogue of small finds prepared by Mary Gough as a chapter in the late Michael Gough's report of excavations at Alahan to be published by the Pontifical Institute of Mediaeval Studies, Toronto.

10. A complete catalogue of the Menil collection is being prepared by Gary Vikan and John Nesbitt. For a short treatment of certain genres of objects in the Menil collection (keys, locks, seals, rings, stamps, weights and scales),

G. Vikan and J. Nesbitt, *Security in Byzantium: Locking, Sealing and Weighing* (Washington, D.C., 1980).

11. See especially A. L. Yacobson, *Srednevekovy Khersones* ("Materialy i Issledovaniya po Arkheologii SSSR" = *MIA* 17) (Moscow-Leningrad, 1950); *idem, Rannesrednevekovy Khersones (MIA* 63) (Moscow-Leningrad, 1959). For a summary in English of research at Cherson, J. Smedley, "Archaeology and the History of Cherson: A Survey of Some Results and Problems," *Archeion Pontou* 35 (1979), 172–192.

12. A similar apparatus in complete condition is illustrated in M. C. Ross, *Catalogue of the Byzantine and Early Mediaeval Antiquities in the Dumbarton Oaks Collection* I (Washington, D.C., 1962), no. 71, pl. 44.

13. A local lamp industry may be assumed from the discovery of terracotta lamp-moulds in the fill of the large Roman baths (III 2 B). One belongs to a type represented in a hoard of some 650 clay lamps found concealed in the disused hypocaust system of another bath building (II 7 A), Hector Williams and Peter Taylor, "A Byzantine Lamp Hoard from Anamur (Cilicia)," *AnatSt* 25 (1975), 77–84.

14. A virtually identical example of a triple suspension bracket, also from a secular context, was found in the Kornos Cave on Cyprus, occupied during the second half of the seventh century, H. W. Catling and A. I. Dikigoropoulos, "The Kornos Cave: an Early Byzantine Site in Cyprus," *Levant* 2 (1970), 50–51, no. 18.

Copper wick-holders for glass lamps occur frequently in early Byzantine sites of the eastern Mediterranean, but their purpose is not always recognized; so Chavane (*Salamine* VI, 40 no. 114, pl. 13), who reports large numbers without comment from one of the Byzantine houses, and the excavators of Hama who refer to them as 'pincettes' (G. Ploug *et al. Hama: Fouilles et Recherches 1931–1938* IV: 3 [Copenhagen, 1969], 76 fig. 29.5). Two forms of wick-holder may be distinguished. One found principally in Palestine (e.g. Gerasa, Mt. Nebo, Nessana) consists of a single thin strip of metal of varying length, one end folded around to form a tube to contain the wick, the other end bent to hang over the rim of the lamp (see description and illustrations in S. J. Saller, *The Memorial of Moses on Mount Nebo* [Jerusalem, 1941], 310, nos. 188–220, pl. 135, fig. 1; pl. 137, fig. 1, nos. 3, 5; p. 126, fig. 18.3; and in H. Dunscombe Colt (ed.) *Excavations at Nessana* I [London, 1962], 54, pl. 22, no. 27). The second type differs from the first in having a second strip of copper extending from the tube, thus providing additional support for the wick. Besides Anemurium, examples of this type are reported from Alahan, where they were found in association with fragments of glass lamps, from Salamis and Hama, as mentioned above. In addition, numerous examples, as yet unpublished, were found at Antioch, now in the Princeton Univ. Art Museum, and I have seen an example in the museum at Annaba (ancient Hippo Regius), where it is wrongly labelled 'objet de toilette'. For the best description of how metal wick-holders actually functioned in practice, G. M. Crowfoot and D. B.

Harden. "Early Byzantine and Later Glass Lamps," *JEA* 17 (1931), 207–208; also P.V.C. Baur in C. H. Kraeling (ed.), *Gerasa* (New Haven. Conn., 1938), 517.

15. The inventory number is AN 76-12. Obverse bust is probably of M. Aurelius or Lucius Verus.

16. These and other apotropaic objects from Anemurium are discussed in detail in my article "The Evil Eye in Early Byzantine Society: Archaeological Evidence from Anemurium in Isauria," in *XVI Internationaler Byzantinistenkongress: Wien, 1981: Akten* (*JÖB* 32 [1982] in press).

17. The baths, indicated as III 15 in the site plan, are described in *Türk Ark Derg* 22:2 (1975), 125–126, fig. 13; 25:1 (1980), 266–267, figs. 6, 7–10.

18. J. Werner, "Byzantinische Gürtelschnallen des 6 und 7 Jahrhunderts aus der Sammlung Diergardt," *Kölner Jahrbuch für Vor-und Frühgeschichte* I (1955), 36–48 (hereafter Werner); D. Csallány, "Les monuments de l'industrie byzantine des métaux I," *Acta Antiqua Hung* 2 (1954) 311–348 (in Russian with French résumé, 340–348) (hereafter Csallány, 1954); *idem*, Les monuments de l'industrie byzantine des métaux II," *Acta Antiqua Hung* 4 (1956), 261–291 (in Russian with French résumé, 290–291) (hereafter Csallány, 1956); *idem*, "Byzantinische Schnallen und Gürtelbeschlage mit Maskenmuster," *Acta Antiqua Hung* 10 (1962), 55–77 (hereafter, Csallány, 1962).

19. See especially Csallány, 1962, 65, nos. 1–3; pl. 1, nos. 1, 2, 4.

20. Werner, 37, fig. 2; pl. 5, nos. 8, 9, 11, 12, 14–16; Csallány, 1954, 326–330, 343–344; pl. 2, nos. 7–9; 3, nos. 1–7; 8, no. 14.

21. Csallány, 1956, 285–288, especially no. 20, pl. 7, no. 1.

22. Csallány, 1956, 287, nos. 6, 8; pl. 7, nos. 3, 5.

23. Csallány, 1954, 333, 345–346; pl. 2, no. 6; 3, no. 9; 4, no. 1.

24. Werner, 40, fig. 5, pl. 5, no. 3; Csallány, 1954, 338–340, 348; pl. 6, nos. 10–11; 7, no. 5.

25. Like the other small objects from Anemurium, all of the buckles listed, except no. 3, are housed in the Alanya Museum. A concordance of the numbers listed here with the excavation inventory numbers follows:

1. 78–109	9. 71–16	17. 73–296	25. 73–306
2. 79–18	10. 70–168	18. 71–388	26. 73–109
3. not inventoried	11. 72–35	19. 76–81	27. 78– 14
4. 79–5	12. 72–1	20. 71–57	28. 70–112
5. 76–30	13. 76–334	21. 70–40	29. 71–106
6. 70–10	14. 71–20	22. 71–434	30. 71–145
7. 70–53	15. 73–260	23. 71–435	31. 71–114
8. 76–176	16. 73–108	24. 71–220	32. 71–379

In addition, two further fragments may be noted, a hinged tongue (72–78) from a larger buckle, and a fragment of an oval buckle-frame (72–25).

26. Chavane, *Salamine* IV, 161–166, nos. 463–475, pls. 46–47, 69.

27. Waldbaum, *Metalwork* catalogue nos. 689–712 (buckles); 713–714 (belt ends).

28. M. V. Gill "Small Finds" in Harrison, *Saraçhane* I, nos. 553–564, 566–569.

29. Davidson, *Corinth* XII, 266–273, especially nos. 2174–2212, pls. 113–114.

30. The writings of Joseph Hampel are particularly influential, *Alterthümer des frühen Mittelalters in Ungarn* (3 vols., Brunswick, 1905); also N. Åberg, *Die Franken und Westgoten in der Völkerwanderungszeit* (Uppsala, 1922); *idem, Die Goten und Langobarden in Italien* (Uppsala, 1923); H. Zeiss, *Die Grabfunde aus dem spanischen Westgotenreiche: Germanische Denkmäler der Völkerwanderungszeit* (Berlin-Leipzig, 1934); Gy. László, *Contributi ai rapporti antichi cristiani dell'arte industriale dell'epoca avara* (Budapest, 1935); N. Fettich, *Das Kunstgewerbe der Avarenzeit in Ungarn* (Budapest, 1926).

31. "The Avar Invasion of Corinth," *Hesperia* 6 (1937), 227–239. In a more recent article Davidson, although still arguing for barbarian associations, has modified her opinion that the buckles and related objects found in graves belonged specifically to Avars. G. Davidson Weinberg, "A Wandering Soldier's Grave in Corinth," *Hesperia* 43 (1974), 512–521 (especially 513, note 3); also *Corinth* XII, 5, n. 8.

32. "The Bulgars in the Balkans and the Occupation of Corinth in the Seventh Century," *Speculum* 25 (1950), 502–543, especially 520–524. For criticism of Setton's opinion, Davidson, *Corinth* XII, 5, note 8 and P. Charanis "On the Capture of Corinth by the Onogurs and its Recapture by the Byzantines," *Speculum* 27 (1952), 343–350, with Setton's reply *ibid.*, 351–362.

33. This theory was first proposed by H. Zeiss, "Avarenfunde in Korinth?" *Serta Hoffileriana* (Zagreb, 1940), 95–99. Werner, *passim*, and Csallány, *passim*, but especially 1962, 70–72. For the most recent discussion of this and related problems, see D. Pallas, "Données nouvelles sur quelques boucles et fibules considérées comme avares et slaves et sur Corinthe entre le VIᵉ et le IXᵉ s.," *Byzantino-Bulgarica* 7 (1981), 295–318.

34. Vikan, introductory essay to the catalogue of belt fittings C1–C52 in the Menil Collection, currently in preparation.

35. Werner, 45–47, map 1.

36. Monastir, Metr. Mus. of Art, New York, acq. 20.118. 1–2 (unpublished); Constantinople, Vikan, Menil Collection, C21-22; Constantinople (Saraçhane), Gill, "Small Finds," nos. 560, 561, 563; Pergamon, A. Conze *et al., Altertümer von Pergamon* I:2 (Berlin, 1913), 326, fig. 118; Sardis, Waldbaum, *Metalwork* nos. 689–690; Yassi Ada (example without decoration), S. W. Katzev, "Miscellaneous Finds" in G. F. Bass and F. H. van Doorninck, Jr. *et al., Yassi Ada I: A Seventh Century Byzantine Shipwreck* (College Station, Texas, 1982), 275–76, 278–79, MF 19, figs. 12.5–6; Anemurium, nos. 14–16 above; example from Asia Minor, provenance unknown, Johns Hopkins Univ. Mus. H. T. 849 (unpublished); Salamis, Chavane, *Salamine* VI, 162–163, no. 466, pls. 46, 69;

Antioch, Princeton Univ. Art Mus. excavation ref. DH-27-Θ (unpublished);
Apamea, J. Napoleone-Lemaire et J. C. Balty, *Fouilles d'Apamée de Syrie* I: I
L'Eglise à atrium de la grande colonnade (Brussels, 1969), 107, fig. 25; Byblos,
Ashmolean Mus., Oxford (unpublished); Pella, R. H. Smith (ed.), *Pella of the
Decapolis* I (Wooster, Ohio, 1973), pl. 68, nos. 15, 352; Scythopolis (Beisan),
Univ. of Pennsylvania Mus., Philadelphia, acq. 31.50.261 (unpublished);
Ctesiphon, J. H. Schmidt, "L'expédition de Ctésiphon en 1931-32," *Syria* 15
(1934), 22, pl. 6a; Edfou, Paris, Louvre, dépt. des antiqu. égypt. AF 1136
(unpublished).

37. Werner, 47-48, map 2.

38. Anemurium, no. 25 above; Salamis, Chavane, *Salamine* VI, 164, nos.
470-471, pl. 46; Lesbos, *BCH* 79 (1955), 284-285, fig. 5; Cherson, Yacobson,
MIA 63 (1959), 273, fig. 139, no. 9; Constantinople, Vikan, Menil Collection,
C25; Athens, J. Travlos and A. Frantz, "Church of St. Dionysius," *Hesperia* 34
(1965), 167, nos. 4, 5, 6, pl. 43a.

39. Delos, Déonna, *Délos* XVIII, 296, no. B1163, pl. 88, 758; Constantinople (Saraçhane), Gill, "Small Finds," no. 558; Sardis, Waldbaum, *Metalwork*, no. 704; Yassi Ada, Womer in Bass, *Byzantine Shipwreck*, 277, 279-80.
MF 21, figs. 12, 5-6; Midas City, C.H.E. Haspels, *Phrygie* III, *La cité de
Midas: céramique et trouvailles diverses* (Paris, 1951), 95, 151, pl. 41 d4; Antioch, Princeton Univ. Art Mus. excavation ref. 3890.U2777 (unpublished);
Nebo, Saller, *Memorial of Moses on Mt. Nebo*, 312, no. 269, pl. 137, fig. 2.4.

40. Corinth, Davidson, *Corinth* XII, 266, 270, nos. 2176, 2177, pl. 113;
Delos, Déonna, *Délos* XVIII, 296, no. B1310-6022 bis, pl. 88.760; Constantinople (Saraçhane), Gill "Small Finds", nos. 553-556; Sardis, Waldbaum, *Metalwork*, no. 710; Salamis, Chavane, *Salamine* VI, 162, no. 465, pl. 46; Antioch,
Worcester Art Mus. Mass. acq. 1940.327b (unpublished); Nessana, Dunscombe Colt *Nessana* I, 53, no. 12, pl. 23; Pontic Chersonese, G.M.A. Richter,
Greek and Roman Bronzes (Metrop. Mus. of Art) (New York, 1915), 331, 333,
no. 1075 (from Kertch); also N. Riepnikoff, "Quelques cimitières du pays des
Gothes de Crimée," *Bull. de la Comm. Imp. Arch. St. Petersbourg* 19 (1906),
67, pl. 12.3.

41. Constantinople, Vikan, Menil Collection, C9-C18; Athens, Travlos and
Frantz, *Hesperia* 34 (1965), 167-168, nos. 7-8, pl 43a; Antioch, Princeton
Univ. Art Mus. excavation ref. 45-265 (unpublished); Scythopolis (Beisan),
Univ. of Pennsylvania Mus., acq. BY 1713a (unpublished); Cherson, Yacob-
son, *MIA* 63 (1959), 253 fig. 139.10-12, fig. 140.3.

42. Constantinople, Csallány, 1954, 333, 345-346, pls. 3.9, 4.1; Antioch,
Worcester Art Mus. acq. 1940.330 (unpublished); Achmin, Csallány, 1954, pl.
2.6; Cherson, Yacobson, *MIA* 63 (1959), 276, 273, fig. 139.15.

43. Corinth, Davidson, *Hesperia* 6 (1937), 236, fig. 6F; *Corinth* XII, 272,
nos. 2209-2210, pl. 14; Athens, Setton, *Speculum* 25 (1950), pl. at p. 523 (lower
left); Constantinople (Saraçhane), Gill "Small Finds," no. 565 (differs in hav-

ing a rectangular frame projecting at right angles to receive the belt end);
Sardis, Waldbaum, *Metalwork*, no. 697; Midas City, Haspels, *Phrygie* III, 8,
13, 18, 95, 150, pl. 41c2; Antioch, Princeton Univ. Art Mus., small objects tray
10 (unpublished). For variants of this group from barbarian contexts, Csallány, 1956, 285–288, pl. 7.

44. To my knowledge the only spectrographic analysis of Byzantine belt
buckles from an archaeological context has been conducted on seven specimens from Sardis. Waldbaum (*Metalwork*) reports that they varied considerably in composition, from leaded tin bronze (691) to zinc bronze (689) to
brass (690, 694, 698, 701, 702). No conclusions could be drawn as to their
origin.

45. For find-spots, Werner, 45–46, map 1 (Sucidava), 47–48, map 2
(Corinth).

46. J. Werner, "Zur Verbreitung frühgeschichtlicher Metallarbeiten,"
Antikvarist Arkiv 38: *Early Medieval Studies* I (1970), 71–73, pls. 5, 6 A–B.

47. Setton, *Speculum* 25 (1950), 523–524. In this article Setton also cites a
passage from the *Tactica* of Mauricius dealing with the clothing of footsoldiers.
His version of the text, ζωνάρια δὲ λιτὰ καὶ οὐ βουλγαρικά (i.e. simple belts
and not Bulgarian ones), however, is inaccurate. In Mihăescu's critical text the
phrase reads ζωνάριά δὲ λιτὰ καὶ οὐ βουλγαρικὰ σαγία (i.e. simple belts not
Bulgarian cloaks); H. Mihăescu (Ed.) *Mauricii Strategicon* ("Scriptores
Byzantini" 6) (Budapest, 1970), 314 l. 17. I owe this information to Prof.
Alexander Kazhdan of Dumbarton Oaks.

48. For close parallels dated securely to the seventh century, R.
Moosbrugger-Leu, *Die Schweiz zur Merowingerzeit* (Bern, 1971), 130–133, pl.
25, nos. 55, 58; pl. 55, nos. 2–5a. A belt-buckle of unmistakable "barbaric" type
was also found in the shipwreck off Yassi Ada. Though without close parallels
amongst belt-buckles, its zoomorphic decoration, related generally to "Migration Style" metalwork of the sixth and seventh centuries, has affinities with
motifs used on belt-tabs in Hungary during the same period. See Katzev in
Bass, *A Byzantine Shipwreck* I, 279, MF20, fig. 12.7.

49. Werner, "Verbreitung" (note 46), pl. 6B.13; also examples from Pápa
and Keszethely in Hungary, Csallány, 1956, 286–287, pl. 7, nos. 3, 5.

50. Anemurium 71–316. Numerous examples from Avar graves are illustrated in E. Garam, I. Kovrig, J. Gy. Szabó, Gy. Török, *Avar Finds in the
Hungarian National Museum* (Budapest, 1975), e.g. 53, fig. 2; 165, fig. 5; 174,
fig. 14; 176, fig. 16; 172, fig. 12

51. Corinth, Davidson, *Hesperia* 43 (1974), 512–521, fire-lighter, 517, pl.
111c; Olympia, N. Yalouris, "Chronika," *Deltion* 17 (1961–62), 107 pl. 117.
One further possible example from Sardis may be noted, but the object, now in
the Fogg Art Museum, is somewhat different in appearance and has no known
context, Waldbaum, *Metalwork*, no. 1016.

52. The inadequate state of our knowledge of belt-buckles of the period is

measured also by the presence at Anemurium of two types which, to my knowledge, still lack convincing parallels, type 8 (fig. 7.17) and type 14 (fig. 8.26-27). The latter in particular, with its distinctive design of open-work and punched circle decoration, represented in two variant forms, can hardly be unique to Anemurium.

53. On trousers generally see the article "bracae" in Daremberg-Saglio I, 746-47; also R. MacMullen, "Some Pictures in Ammianus Marcellinus," *ArtB* 46 (1964), 446, especially note 3.

54. *Cod. Theodos.* XIV 10.2,3 (dated A.D. 397 and 399 respectively). The use of *braccae* as gladiatorial garb in the amphitheatre may also have affected popular fashion in the cities as early as the time of Septimius Severus (D. Levi, *Antioch Mosaic Pavements* [Princeton, 1945], 336, note 82).

55. Levi, *ibid.*, 336-37. For an excellent illustration of trousers, see the tomb-painting from Durostorum (Silistra) in Moesia, dated probably in the second half of the fourth century. This depicts a servant carrying over his shoulder a pair of tights equipped with a buckled belt (R. F. Hoddinott, *Bulgaria in Antiquity* [London, 1975], 141, pl. 93).

56. *IG* V: 1.1406, 1. 23 (βράκια), 1.18 βρακαριος from Asine in Messenia. From its use in this passage of the Price Edict and elsewhere the term βρακαριος appears to have acquired a wider range of meaning, the βρακαριος being responsible for the cutting and finishing of garments of coarser cloth, while the ραπτης undertook the sewing of garments of finer materials, M. N. Tod, "A New Fragment of the Edictum Diocletiani," *JHS* 24 (1904), 195-202; E. Hanton, "Titres byzantins dans le *RICAM*," *Byzantion* 4 (1927-28), 70-71.

57. POxy. 1341 (fourth century A.C.); PLond. inedit. 2176 (βρεκαπριος, century A.C.).

58. Sardis, W. H. Buckler and D. M. Robinson, *Sardis* VII: *Greek and Latin Inscriptions* (Leiden, 1925), no. 167; C. Foss, *Byzantine and Turkish Sardis* (Cambridge, Mass., 1976), 18-19, 110, no. 12.

Aphrodisias, T. Reinach, "Inscriptions d'Aphrodisias," *REG* 19 (1906), 298, no. 219; H. Grégoire, *Recueil des inscriptions grecques-chrétiennes d'Asie Mineure* (Paris, 1922), 91 no. 262.

Corycos, J. Keil and A. Wilhelm, *MAMA* 3 (1931), 160, no. 406 (βρεκαριος), 187, no. 597 (βρικαριος).

59. Eleven out of 23 buckles, Waldbaum, *Metalwork*, nos. 692, 695, 696, 698, 700-702, 705, 707-8, 710.

60. Foss, *Byzantine and Turkish Sardis*, 16, 43.

61. Katzev in Bass, *A Byzantine Shipwreck* I, MF19-22, figs. 12.5-7. Katzev suggests (p. 278) that light sleeveless tunics tied at the waist by rope belts were used on shipboard, while leather belts were part of the mariner's shore dress.

62. For interesting observations on the hierarchy of metals, A. Cutler, "Art in Byzantine Society: Motive Forces of Byzantine Patronage," *XVI Internationaler Byzantinistenkongress, 1981* (*JÖB* 31: 2[1981], 772-776). Note especially his reference to a bronze buckle in the Menil Collection closely resembling one in gold at Dumbarton Oaks (p. 773 n. 71, figs. 4-4a).

Figure 1. *Instrumenta domestica* from Anemurium,
nos. 1-12 (Scale 1:1, except where otherwise marked).

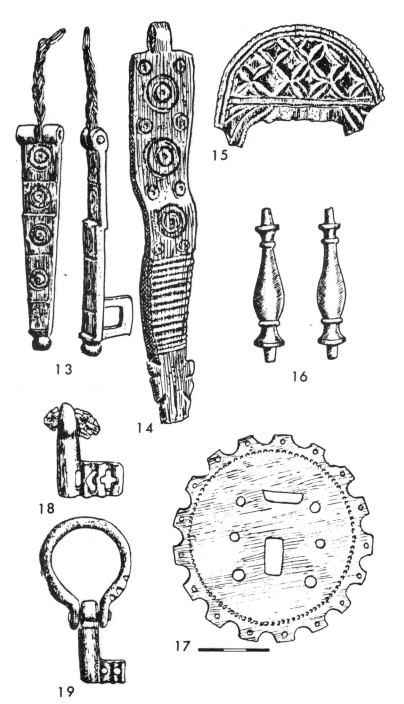

13　14　15　16　17　18　19

Figure 2. *Instrumenta domestica* from Anemurium, nos. 13-19 (Scale 1:1, except where otherwise marked).

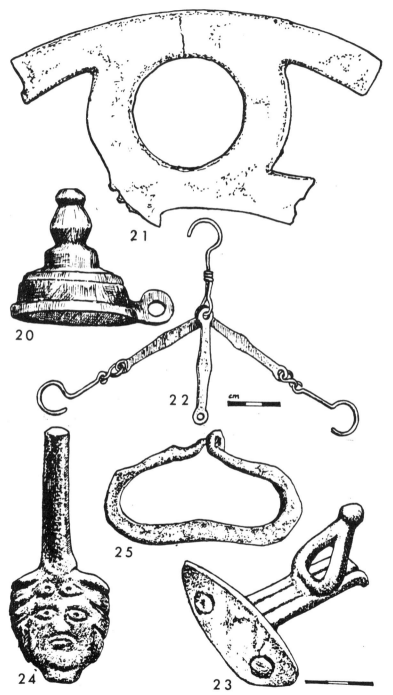

Figure 3. *Instrumenta domestica* from Anemurium. nos. 20-25. (Scale 1:1. except where otherwise marked).

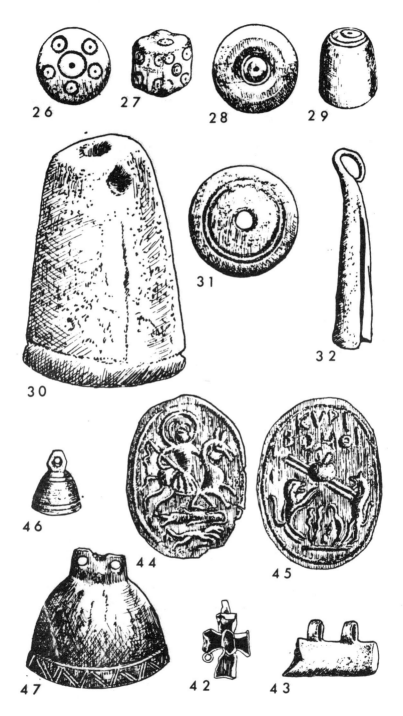

Figure 4. Instrumenta domestica from Anemurium, nos. 26-32, 42-47 (Scale 1:1).

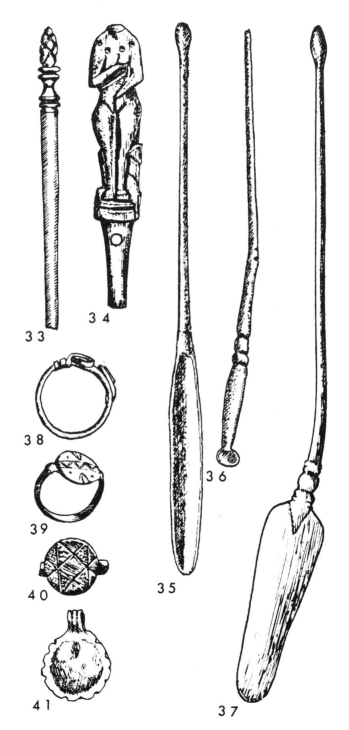

Figure 5. *Instrumenta domestica* from Anemurium, nos. 33-41 (Scale 1:1).

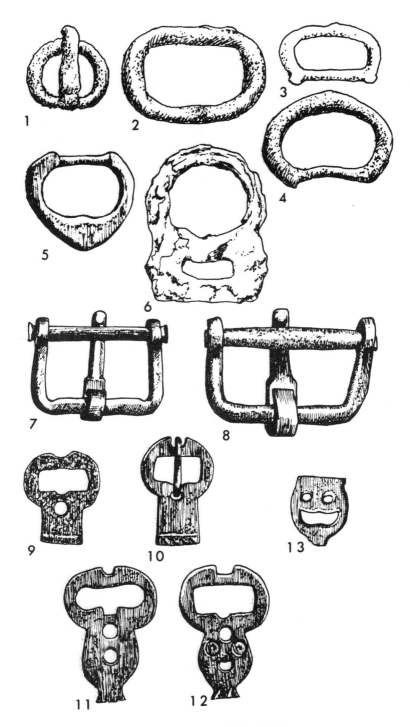

Figure 6. Belt-buckles from Anemurium. nos. 1-13 (Scale 1:1).

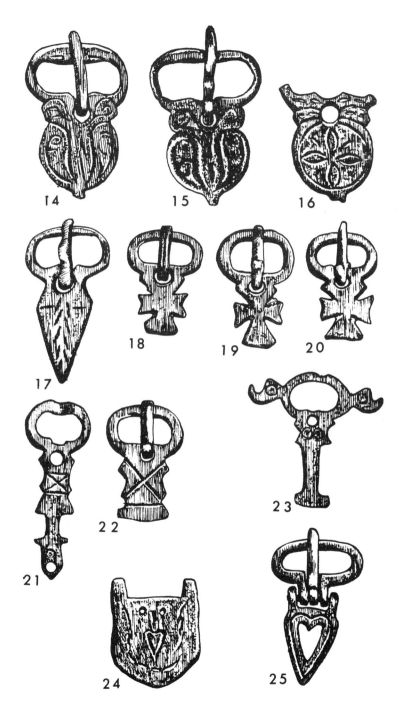

Figure 7. Belt-buckles from Anemurium. nos. 14-25 (Scale 1:1).

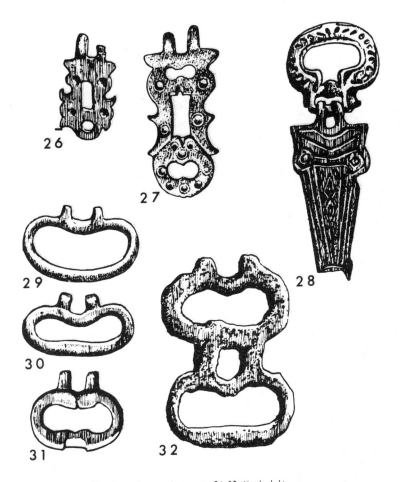

Figure 8. Belt-buckles from Anemurium. nos. 26-32 (Scale 1:1).

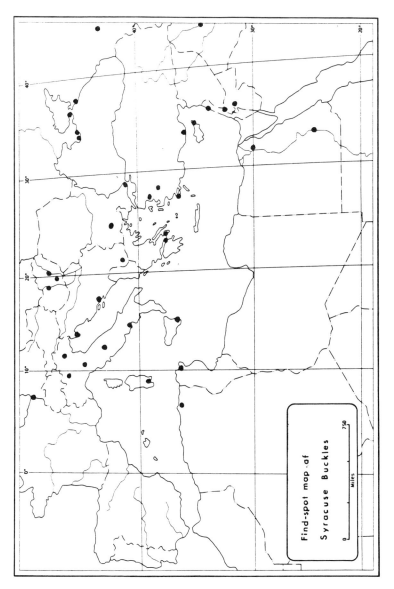

Figure 9. Revised fine-spot map of syracuse-type buckles.

8

BYZANTINE STREET CONSTRUCTION
AT CAESAREA MARITIMA

Robert Lindley Vann
(University of Maryland)

Streets are ubiquitous with the remains of ancient cities yet they have received little, if any, attention in the publications. The obvious features—alignment, dimensions, and materials—might be noted in the text but too often the street itself is drawn simply as a vacant space between curbs or adjacent buildings. At Jerash, for example, although excellent stone for stone drawings exist for streets leading into the great oval plaza, one must refer to the detailed description of the city gate to discover even the width of the streets. No probes beneath the paving were mentioned at that site.[1]

The limited archaeological evidence is matched by a meager literary record as well. Historians might record the construction of a city or the erection of a public monument but fewer references were made to the constant series of repairs necessary to keep the public services of a city in acceptable condition for its citizens. Although detailed descriptions exist for the construction of a concrete floor or major highway, we do not have a comparable source for street construction.

The current excavations at Caesarea Maritima now have provided an opportunity to ask pertinent questions.[2] Two major phases of street construction have been uncovered, one rather surprisingly late in date.[3] The preliminary dating of these phases, the third century and the late sixth century, provides a possibility to investigate the construction and continuity of streets in major city of the early Byzantine period. What was the pattern or patterns of the streets throughout these centuries of use? Did the various phases represent the repaving of earlier (Herodian?) streets in identical positions or were they built *de novo* as part of the original pattern or according to another, modified system? To answer these and other questions surveyors located a single long trench, C/23–24, on line with the southern extension of *Cardo* II West and the western extension of *Decumanus* I South (Figs. 1–3).[4] Excavations in 1978 in this area uncovered the intersection of these two streets. The next campaign focused on the open tract of farmland south of Field 'C.' In 1979 survey teams established fields 'K,' 'L,' and 'M' thus defining the entire area between the theater and crusader city for future excavations. More evidence of the streets came from K 2, K 3, M 1, and L 1. Finally, during the 1981 season, another stretch of Cardo II appeared in C 30.

Sub-Phase 7a, Late Roman (A.D. 200–300)

Evidence of streets of the Late Roman Period, Phase 7a, appeared in two areas during the 1979 season (L 1 and K 2) and one area (C/30) during the 1980 season. The largest portion of Roman paving was from L/1 (locus 1035) (Fig. 4). Pavers of hard Mount Carmel limestone, known locally as 'mizzi,' extended from the north baulk and covered an area with maximum dimensions of 5.45 x 1.50 m. Blocks varied in size and shape; many were square, measuring 0.50 m. on a side, while others were rectangular with a maximum length of 0.85 m. Upper surfaces were worn smooth by years of exposure to the elements and traffic. By contrast in the undersides were left roughly cut and often the entire block pyramidal in shape. This toothlike profile helped firmly anchor the block into the bedding. That roadbed consisted of two compact layers of fine sand. An analysis of the pottery within this matrix revealed fragments of Arretine ware, eastern *terra sigillata*, Pompeian red slip, and a few sherds of Nabataean ware. In addition, two lamp fragments discovered were also of late Roman date.

The pavement of the road also appeared in K 2. Pavers emerged in the southwest probe at a level of 6.20 m. a.s.l. while foundations, presumably for the curbing or stylobate, were found in a north central probe at 6.08 and 5.79 m. respectively.

More substantial remains of this earlier street emerged in C/30 during the 1980 campaign. The pavement of hard 'mizzi' limestone was 0.65 m.

beneath the surface of the higher street. Blocks were rectangular with a maximum size of 0.35 x 0.65 x 0.20 m. laid with tight-fitting joints and worn smooth by years of use. A manhole, now identified with the later road, was a feature of the original one as well. The shaft, 0.82 x 0.49 m., changed size at a level of 6.54 m. a.s.l. We assume this was the point at which the new shaft was built above the older one in order to join with the higher level street. One only needs reconstructed manhole cappers 0.25 m. thick to bring the level of its covering flush to that of the adjacent pavers (locus C 30023). The channel associated with the manhole was 0.45–0.50 m. wide and was filled to within 0.35 m. of its roof with debris. Slabs of stone covering the channel, 0.32 x 0.46 m., opened into the manhole shaft from the east at a level of 6.30 m. a.s.l., or 0.30 m. above the channel. A sondage dug in the last days of the season failed to provide suitable dating evidence for this subpavement construction.

Sub-Phase 6a, Late Byzantine (A.D. 550–614)

There was little evidence of street building during the early and middle Byzantine periods, sub-phases 6c and 6b (A.D. 330–550). There were, on the other hand, extensive remains of a flurry of mid-sixth century building activity. The most important evidence was *Cardo* II, the major colonnaded street from the area of the inner harbor (now within the crusader city) to the theater.

Remains of the street first appeared in C 13 during the 1974 season. The portion excavated was immediately east of Structure I (the Archives Building) (Fig. 5). The western curb was well preserved, 0.55 m. wide and adjacent to the stylobate which had been robbed but the limit of the street was clearly defined by the extent of preserved powers. The blocks averaged 0.60 m. in length by 0.40 m. in width and were 0.10 m. thick, set in a herringbone pattern pointing to the north. A north-south drain, 0.43 m. wide and 0.40 m. high, ran beneath the center of the street. The floor of the drain was at an elevation of 6.03 m. a.s.l., approximately 1.75 m. beneath the paved surface and sloped in a northerly direction. Access to the drain came through a covered manhole.

Excavators found two column bases on the stylobate, set with an interaxial distance of 3.10 m. Fragments of three limestone columns appeared on the street pavement. Their diameters, 0.60 m., fit conveniently on those bases and no doubt belonged to the street portico. A battered Corinthian capital found nearby may have been part of the order. Beneath the roof supported by these columns was a mosaic-paved sidewalk, 5.35 m. wide. An 18 m. stretch of this tessalated floor was uncovered east of the Archives Building.

Another portion of *Cardo* II West appeared in C 30 during the past season. Blocks were rectangular, average examples measured 0.60 x 0.33 x 0.17 m. and set with their long sides perpendicular to the flow of traffic. The material was not the hard Mount Carmel limestone but softer varieties subject to more rapid deterioration. The resulting quality of the road surface was not as good and in some areas the pavers were fragmented. Blocks had smooth vertical faces but with their undersides left rough.

The bedding consisted of three distinct strata: (1) a bed of sand and pebbles, c. 0.15 m. thick; (2) a layer of sandstone and limestone chunks, also set in sand, 0.06 m. thick; and (3) a level of varied composition that included cobbles set in cement. Below this third level was a bed of sand that overlaid the surface of the 7a street.

The manhole discussed above in conjunction with the 7a street was a feature that was incorporated by the Byzantine builders. By doing so they also were able to utilize the major and minor drains of the earlier system.

The most substantial remains of Cardo II came from C 23–24 during the 1978 campaign (Fig. 6). A sequence of features similar to that in C 13 consisted of tessalated paving, stylobate, curb, and roadway. The mosaics (loci 23048 and 24009) were not fully uncovered for definition of their widths but can be assumed to have been 5.35 m. on the basis of similar border dimensions with the floors found outside the Archives Building in C 13. Stylobate and curb widths, 0.80–0.85 m. and 0.57 m., were consistent with those uncovered to the north. The roadway proper, 5.40 m. wide, was laid in a herringbone pattern and the total reconstructed width of the street with flanking colonnades was 17.50 m.

The excavations in C 23–24 greatly increased our knowledge of the street system. For example, the architect's reconstruction of two column fragments provided the height of the order (Fig. 7). The shaft was 3.74 m. tall, the base from C 13 was 0.26 m. tall, and the capitals from the Sdot Yam museum 0.55 m. tall. Other features found in C 23–24 were semicircular installations set within the line of the stylobate. Their interior widths averaged 1.05 m. There was no evidence of their function although one might expect to find some connection with the public water system as was commonly the case for street foundations in cities of the ancient world. A tile conduit (locus C 24004), found 0.25 m. below the level of the paving, was not completely excavated. To date no evidence connects these two features.

We can further clarify our knowledge of the original terrain by noting the top levels of the street pavement. The elevation of the crown in C/13 was 7.74 m. a.s.l., 7.10 m. in C/30, 6.89 m. in C/23, and 6.28 m. in the intersection with the *decumanus* in C/24. From that point the road continued to rise slightly to the south.

Field 'K' produced additional remains of the streets. Pavers in K/2 were not of 'mizzi' but less durable limestones and calcareous sandstones, laid perpendicular to the flow of traffic, and set in a bedding of packed earth. Excavations also revealed a poorly preserved tessalated floor, 5.35 m. wide that corresponded exactly in size with those in C/13, C/23, and C/24. Additional blocks of the stylobate appeared in the north baulk.

K/3 produced the next intersection between *Cardo* II and *Decumanus* II (Figs. 8–9). This east-west thoroughfare was more narrow than that found in C/23, measuring 2.50 m. from curb to curb or a total of 3.30 m. including the curbs. Ceramic evidence dated the mosaic pavement (locus K 3001) to phase 6a. Of exceptional importance was the fact that this street was not associated with an earlier one but instead stood on sterile soil.

The most prominent feature of *Decumanus* II was the complex system of drains feeding into a manhole 4.35 m. west of the intersection with Cardo II (Figs. 10–12). A major east-west channel could be entered through a vertical shaft identified on the surface by its different arrangement of capstones. The shaft measured 0.65 m. square and was 1.95 m. deep from the street paving above to the floor of the drain below. The walls of the shaft were made of ashlar masonry; two subsidiary channels entered it from the north and south at 7.27 m. and 7.42 m. a.s.l. These channels, although their exact sources were not discovered, probably collected runoff water from street gutters and the courtyards of nearby structures.

The channel of the major east-west drain was 0.65 m. wide and 1.05 m. high with a roof consisting of single slabs set across the width of the sewer. The underside of these stones was cut in an arched profile similar to those in C/30. The length of the channel investigated was insufficient to indicate the slope. The direction of flow could have been either east or west. The latter direction would have led directly to the sea. If that were the case, this would have a major storm sewer of the city, designed to facilitate rapid drainage of rainwater. If, on the other hand, the gradient fell to the east, water from this channel would join that of the large drain beneath *Cardo* II (uncovered in C/13) that sloped gently to the north and the area of the inner harbor. A probe within the channel directly beneath the manhole contained ceramic evidence in its lowest level dating to the Late Byzantine period (phase 6a). As noted earlier, beneath the walls of the drain was sterile sand.

Two stretches of ceramic pipe appeared in Field 'K,' one in K/2 (Fig. 12) and the other in K/3. The former (K 2067), ran north-south beneath the sub-phase 6a pavement and the latter, east-west beneath the same pavement. Both appeared to connect with a vertical shaft (K 3024). The pipes, 0.11 m. in diameter, were tightly sealed and set into a bed of stone and mortar. Conduits of this type generally carried fresh water for public or private use. The shaft probably served a double function of relieving pressure to facilitate the flow of water at the same time it provided a means of clearing the channel of any accumulation of debris.

Decumanus III South appeared in a probe in M/1 (Fig. 13). No systematic excavations continued beneath the pavement but a lack of any pavers above and similarities of blocks with those of the other sectors indicated that this stretch also belonged to phase 6a. Whether or not it overlaid an earlier Roman street or whether it too was built *de novo* remains to be seen. Its width was the same as that of *Decumanus* II located in C 23–24. The roadway was 3.80 m. wide; the total width of 5.20 m. including the curbing. There was no evidence of stylobates or tessalated floors. The level of the crown was 9.10 m. a.s.l., indicating the continuation of a gentle slope uphill from K/2.

The final evidence for the streets came from L/1 where excavators have identified the intersection between *Cardo* II West and *Decumanus* IV South (Figs. 14–15). Rectangular paving blocks, set perpendicular to the flow of traffic, indicated the different directions of the *cardo* and *decumanus*. Robbing had removed both curbing and stylobates.

The Literary Evidence

Turning from the archaeological record to literary *testimonia* we learn from the descriptions of Josephus that the streets of Herod's city that converged on the harbor were set at equal distances from one another.[5] This statement suggests the use of an orthogonal plan with arteries parallel to one another and intersecting at right angles. The resulting grid was always the most common type of formal planning for building new cities in antiquity. Josephus also stressed the importance of the design of the sewage system.

> . . . But below the city the underground passages and sewers cost no less effort than the structures built above them. Of these some led at equal distances from one another to the harbor and the sea.[6]

In other words, the system of drainage and streets were integral parts of a single construction program.

Another reference from the fourth century commented upon the quality of the city plan.[7] Otherwise the record is silent. Clearly the excavated evidence discussed above does not date from the Herodian period but our lower level of streets, sub-phase 7a, could represent the orderly continuation of that original plan—thoroughfares that would have been in service by the fourth century and perhaps commented upon by our late source mentioned above. The relationship between paving of phases 6a and 7a clearly indicated that in many areas Byzantine builders did retain earlier patterns. On the other hand, *Decumanus* II South was evidently a new street not conforming to that original scheme.

Unfortunately we do not possess a technical document of the Hellenistic or Roman period that discussed street or road construction specifically. But there does exist a well-known and valuable passage from Vitruvius on floor construction that is applicable in this case.

> If this concrete floor is to be laid level with the ground, let the soil be tested to see whether it is everywhere solid, and if it is, level it off and upon it lay the broken stone with its bedding . . . After the bedding (*statumen*, or broken stones of at least fist-size) is laid, mix the broken stone (*rudus*) in the proportions, if it is new, of three parts to one of lime: if it is old material used again (brick or stone), five parts may answer to two in the mixture. Next, lay the mixture of broken stone, bring on your gangs, and beat it again and again with wooden stamps, and let it be not less than three-quarters of a foot in thickness when the beating is finished. On this lay the nucleus consisting of pounded tile mixed with lime in the proportions of three parts to one, and forming a layer not less than six inches thick. On top of the nucleus, the floor, whether made of slabs or mosaic, should be well and truly laid by rule and level.[8]

Another interesting passage comes from Statius, the poet-laureate of Domitian, describing the building of the *Via Domitiana*.

Now the first stage of the work was to dig ditches and to dig a trench in the soil between them. Then this empty ditch was filled up with the foundaton courses and a watertight layer or binder and a foundation was prepared to carry the pavement. For the surface should not vibrate, otherwise the base is unreliable or the bed in which the stones are rammed is too loose. Finally the pavement should be fastened by pointed blocks and held at regular intervals by wedges.[9]

Although the preceeding passages described the construction of a concrete floor within a house and a major highway outside the city, their application to street construction is clear when comparing their contents with the excavated material from Caesarea. To what extent can we identify threads of continuity between Roman and Byzantine traditions in street building from what we know of the archaeological and literary records? The final step is to consider the following areas for comparison: composition of the setting bed, types of materials selected as pavers, patterns employed in setting pavers, and finally, the way in which the Byzantine streets were coordinated with the existing late Roman pattern of distribution.

When preparing the bedding for the street in C 30 Byzantine crews first set a layer of sand over the earlier Roman paving (Figs. 16–17). They next added a bed of cobbles in mortar both to hold the aggregate in place and to provide a waterproofing to counteract seepage from the ground below. Next, this bed was covered with two layers of finer composition including crushed pottery that served as the final setting bed for the new sixth century street surface. The sequence, however, was not consistent throughout; in other sectors such as K 2, the pavers were set directly into beds of sand. Construction, then, varied according to the local needs and or conditions.

Additional information comes from an inspection of the building materials. The better built roads of the Roman period used pavers of hard Mount Carmel limestone throughout. But the sixth century street builders employed this same type of stone in more limited quantities. The possibility arises that much of the hard limestone was, in fact, spoils from earlier streets or buildings. Was there less concern about the quality of materials employed? Or was the issue a question of availability due, perhaps, to the rising costs of transportation of materials from the quarry?

The selection of a paving pattern was an important consideration for the stability of the street. A regular grid of stones of equal sizes aligned in such a way that their joints were continuous was avoided. Instead, it was desirable to break joints, thereby creating an interlocking system to prevent individual stones from shifting. Herringbone patterns, as seen in C 13 and C 23–24, were very popular throughout the Roman world and remained so during the sixth century as well. But the most common pattern of arranging pavers in the areas investigated at Caesarea was in rows perpendicular to the flow of traffic. By setting the stone in a transverse position and by implementing a sequence of breaking joints, there would be fewer continuous grooves or ruts (created by the joints between pavers) parallel to the direction of traffic. It should also be pointed out that the visual pattern of blocks set with their long dimensions parallel to the direction of the street, that is in a longitudinal fashion, would have provided a significantly different impression from blocks set with the long sides in a transverse direction. The former pattern would emphasize the perspective character of the street thereby creating a visually long, narrow space whereas the latter would create lines across the width of the thoroughfare, emphasizing that dimension.

The various streets, both *cardines* and *decumani*, were found to be of different widths corresponding to what we know from literary sources and comparative examples from other sites. Augustus had limited the sizes of streets in Rome during the first century thereby creating a hierarchy of importance: forty feet for *decumani*, twenty feet for *cardines*, twelve feet for the *vicinae*, and a maximum of eight feet for lanes.[10] The integration of streets of different widths was a common element in the plans of Roman cities. A traditional pattern might include a wider *cardo maximus* and *decumanus maximus*. At Caesarea there seems to be a wider *cardo* within the series of streets uncovered to date. Does the wider *cardo* indicate that we have, indeed, discovered the *cardo maximus* of the city? Despite the fact that we cannot, at this time, equate with certainty the position of this *cardo* with the *cardo maximus* of the city or with the original Herodian plan, there can be no doubt that it was one of the major thoroughfares of Caesarea.

The variety of measurements for our roadways is not surprising considering the long period of time during which the system was built and repaired. The dimensions of the streets appear to be consistent with those of other Palestinian cities as well. For example, the width of *Cardo* II West uncovered in C 23–24 is 5.40 m., or eighteen feet (*podes*), exactly the same measurement as that identified by Broshi as the standard width for streets in Jerusalem for the Roman and Byzantine periods.[11] The unit measure at both Caesarea and Jerusalem was 0.30 m., or one hundredth of a *plethron*, shorter than the official Byzantine foot of 0.312 m.[12] Therefore, the *decumani* at Caesarea measured eight 'feet' and twelve 'feet' respectively (*Decumanus* II in K 3 and *Decumanus* III in M 1) curb to curb and eleven 'feet' and seventeen 'feet' including the curbing. The suggestion has been made that this street, leading from the theater to the area of the inner harbor (and the forum?), is appropriate for the *cardo maximus* of the city. Certainly its location is an important one and the continuation of that line to the north (beyond the crusader fortification) leads one to the north gate of the city. But this identification must be seriously questioned on the basis of width, 5.40 m. for the roadway and 17.50 m. including the flanking porticoes. As a means of comparison, the major colonnaded streets at Samaria-Sebaste and Gerasa are 11 m. and the overall dimension with the porticoes, 22 m. That is exactly the size found in Jerusalem, multiples of the same 5.40 m. width of the smaller streets.[13]

On the basis of streets uncovered in the southwest quarter to date, we can reconstruct the cadestration of the sixth century as a series of small, squarish blocks, 80 x 90 m. The pattern is a familiar one with parallels as early as the fifth century B.C. at Miletus and Priene. Later examples from the Roman world were widely spread: Trier, Verulamium, Thamugadi (Timgad), and Augusta Raurica in the west.[14] Another city closer at hand for comparison is Jerusalem where the *insula* measured either 225 m. or 300 m. on a side.[15] Of those listed above only the *insulae* at Timgad were smaller in size than those at Caesarea. Rectangular blocks were more characteristic of cities in the East. Should we expect to find at Caesarea a system of larger *insula* that were divided by additional streets the later centuries? That certainly might be the case in the example of *Decumanus* II South that was laid down in the late sixth century on sterile ground. Likewise, might we expect a different arrangement of streets along the ocean front? If the Herodian plan for Caesarea was organized on a larger grid this question might be answered by further probes in the southwest quarter. Did these streets uncovered in K 3, M 1, and L 1 continue to the east?

Despite the fact that we cannot, at this time, equate with certainty the position of this *cardo* with the *cardo maximus* of the city or with the original Herodian scheme, there can be no doubt that this colonnaded street was one of the major thoroughfares of the Late Roman and Byzantine city. In addition, even if we remain uncertain of the original urban plan of the city during the first century, we do understand more clearly the organization of the area south of the artificial harbor. Finally, the opportunity to investigate the street programs of the sixth century has demonstrated the continuity of the site not only from the reuse of many of the streets and associated drains, but also in the application of similar building material and techniques of construction.

Notes

1. C. Kraeling, *Gerasa, City of the Decapolis* (New Haven, 1938) 119 ff. and 149 ff. For an introduction to roads and streets of the ancient world see R. J. Forbes, *Studies in Ancient Technology*, vol. II, 2nd ed. rev. (Leidon, 1965) 131–92; *Notes on the History of Ancient Roads and their Construction* (Amsterdam, 1964). Of more general nature is N. E. Lee, *Travel and Transportation through the Ages* (Cambridge, 1955). For earlier references to roads in Palestine see M. Avi-Yonah, "The Development of the Roman Road System in Palestine," *IEJ* 1 (1950–51) 54–60 and R. G. Goodchild, "The Coastal Road of Phoenicia and its Roman Milestones," *Berytus* 9 (1949) 91–27.

2. For earlier studies of the urban plan at Caesarea see A. Reifenberg, "Caesarea: A Study in the Decline of a Town," *IEJ* 1 (1950–51) 20–32 and L. Levine, *Roman Caesarea: An Archaeological-Topographical Study* (Jerusalem, 1975) 5–9. For activity in Field 'C' refer to a forthcoming article by R. Weimken and K. Holum, "The Joint Expedition to Caesarea Maritima: Eighth Season, June 24–July 27, 1979." *BASOR* 244 (1981) 27–52. The present study will not include the materials excavated in other sectors of the city (Fields 'A,' 'B,' or 'G'). The assignment of chronological phases of the city's use, based on archaeological data, follows Lawrence E. Toombs, "The Stratigraphy of Caesarea Maritima," *Archaeology in the Levant: Essays for Kathlean Kinyon*, eds. P. Moorey and P. Parr (Warminster, 1978) 223–232. Discussion of these streets is found in the unpublished field reports for 1971–76, 1978, and 1980. I am grateful to the General Research Board of the University of Maryland for its financial support during the summer of 1981 when several sites mentioned in the paper were visited. Many friends have read the paper but I would like to thank in particular Kenneth G. Holum of the University of Maryland for his helpful criticisms and suggestions and Robert L. Hohlfelder of the University of Colorado for offering the opportunity to include this study in the present volume.

3. Current excavations have demonstrated a dramatic level of building activity during the century before final conquest of Caesarea by the Arabs. Not only were streets being repaired and built but throughout the excavations of Field 'C' we have uncovered new building phases, often with the addition of magnificent mosaics. On this point one should refer to upcoming studies by M. Spiro. Previous historical accounts of the city have suggested that the city fell upon hard times. See the five pages that Levin reserves for this late period in *Caesarea Under Roman Rule* (Leiden, 1975).

4. The report of the 1978 season is contained in manuscript form. Robert J. Bull, "The Joint Expedition to Caesarea Maritima, 1978." The numbering system of the *cardines* and *decumani* is that of the Joint Expedition. In order to facilitate their identifications, the streets have been numbered according to which sector of the city they cross. From an arbitrary point near the southwest corner of the crusader fortifications, the site has been divided into four sectors. Field 'C' lies in the Southwest Zone. Judging from the intervals of our streets one assumes that the *cardo* in question is the second from our base reference point. Therefore the street is named *Cardo* II West. Somewhere on the opposite side of the modern road that leads from the car park to the restored theater and kibbutz is a street running parallel to ours that will be identified as *Cardo* II East (assuming the cadestration of the city remains uniform). Likewise the *decumani* being uncovered in the southwest zone are numbered according to their positions south of the base point.

5. Josephus, *Wars*, I. 21.7. For formal planning in the Greek and Roman world see F. Castagnoli, *Orthogonal Planning in Antiquity* (Cambridge, 1972); A. von Gerkan, *Griechische Städteanlagen* (Berlin-Leipzig, 1924); and K. Lehmann, "Städtebau Italiens und des römischen Reiches," *PW*, III-A, 2016–2124. A popular source is J. B. Ward-Perkins, *Cities of Ancient Greece and Italy: Planning in Classical Antiquity* (New York, 1974).

6. Josephus, *Antiquities*, XV, 9.6.

7. *Expositio totius mundi et gentium*, XXVI (J. Rougé, ed.) (Paris, 1966) 160.

8. Vitruvius VII, 1,1.

9. Statius, Silvae IV, 3. See also P. Fustier, Etude technique sur un texte de l'empereur Julien relatif à la construction des voies romaines," *RevEtudAncFr* 65.1 2 (1963) 114–21.

10. Forbes, *Studies in Ancient Technology*, vol. II, 2nd ed. rev., 169.

11. Magen Broshi, "Standards of Street Widths in the Roman-Byzantine Period," *IEJ* 27 (1977) 232–5. A street excavated at the House of Caiaphas on Mount Zion was 5.40 m. wide, a dimension that recurred six times elsewhere on Mount Zion as well as in other examples elsewhere in the city. F. J. Bliss and A.C.D. Dickie, *Excavations in Jerusalem, 1894–1897* (London, 1898) 52, 78–81, and 333. Also see B. Bagatti, *Nuovi Elementi di Scavo alle 'Torre' del Sion* (1895). Other examples are to be found in J. Germer-Durand, "La Maison de Caiphe et l'Eglise St. Pierre à Jerusalem," *RB* 11 (1914), new series, 244–5 and J. W. Crowfoot and G. M. Fitzgerald, *Excavation in the Tyropoeon Valley, 1927* (London, 1929) 41. More recently excavated is the example of a north-south street of the Byzantine period from Akko. "News and Notes," *IEJ* 24 (1974) 276–9.

12. E. Schilbach, *Byzantinische Metrologie* (Munich, 1970) 31.

13. J. W. Crowfoot, et al., *Samaria-Sebaste, I: The Buildings at Samaria* (London: 1942) 50–52. Kraeling, *Gerasa*, 119. The *cardo maximus*, portions of which were excavated by N. Avigad, is reported in Broshi, 234. Other locations

with street on the same standards are Palmyra Dura-Europas, Damascus, and Antioch. K. Michalowski, *Palmyra* (New York, 1970) 16–22. F. E. Brown, *Excavations at Dura-Europeas, Preliminary Report of the Ninth Season* (New Haven, 1944), 23–6. J. Sauvaget, "Le plan antique de Damas *Syria* 26(1949) 327; W. A. Campbell, "Archaeological Notes—The Sixth Season of Excavation at Antioch-on-the-Orantes, 1937" *AJA* 44(1940) 417.

14. G. Kleiner, *Die Ruinen von Milet* (Berlin, 1968). M. Schede, *Die Ruinen von Priene* (Berlin, 1964). R.E.M. Wheeler and T. V. Wheeler, *Verulamium: a Belgic and two Roman Cities* (London, 1936). E. M. Wightman, *Roman Trier and the Treveri* (London, 1970). R. Laur-Belart, *Führer durch Augusta Raurica*, 2nd ed. (Basel, 1948). A. Ballu, *Les Ruines de Timgad (antique Thamugadi)*, 3 vols. (Paris, 1897, 1903, 1911).

15. J. Wilkinson, "The Streets of Jerusalem," *Levant* 118–36.

ADDENDUM

Three publications have appeared since this article was completed that concern measurements of streets in Jerusalem, the identification of the *Cardo Maximus* in Caesarea, as well as the identification of a *decumanus* in that same city. The first article refers to recent excavations of the *Cardo Maximus* in Jerusalem under the direction of Professor Nahman Avigad (Doren Chen, "Dating the Cardo Maximus in Jerusalem," *PEQ* 114.1(1982) 43–5). Excavators date the initial construction of this portion of the *cardo*, located in the Street of the Jews, to the Byzantine period on the basis of architectural analysis of the Corinthian capitals and by the large amounts of Byzantine ceramics found beneath the paving. The architect, Doren Chen, observes that the *Cardo* has been laid out according to a unit measurement of 0.32 m., the length of a Byzantine foot that he identifies elsewhere as a standard early Byzantine *podes*, seen first at Philippi and later in Illyricum was well as in nearby Bethlehem. See Doren Chen, "The Design of the Ancient Synagogues in Galilee," *Liber Annuus* 28(1978) 193–202. P. Lemerle, *Philippes et la Macédoine orientale* (Paris, 1945) 346. N. Spremo Petrović, *Proportions architecturales dans les Plans des Basiliques de la Préfecture de l'Illyricum* (Beograd, 1971) 63–5, 66–71. D. Chen, "Justinian's Church of the Nativity at Bethlehem: Unit measurement and proportions of the plan," A paper delivered at the 5th Archaeological Conference in Israel (Jerusalem, 1978).

Excavations reveal a flanking portico 5.12 m. wide (16 *podes*) with evidence for column bases set at an interaxial distance of 5.77 m. (18 *podes*) (for two bays?). Although the opposite stylobate (curb) and colonnade have not been uncovered, the relative positions of street drains running parallel to the curbs as well as structures beyond the portico indicated a symmetrical arrangement of flanking porticoes and street passage. Doubling the distance from the south curb to the central rows of paving slabs (Chen's spina) produces a width of 12.16 m. (38 *podes*) for the street passage. Thus the overall width of the *Cardo Maximus* in Jerusalem (at this point) is 32 *podes* for the two flanking porticoes and 38 *podes* for the central roadway, or a total of 70 *podes* (22.40 m.). Chen continues by stating that the width of the *Cardo* varies from 22.50–23.50 m. toward its southern extremity and postulates that the street, as designed, would have been laid out with ideal measurements of 15 and 40 *podes* respectively for the width of the colonnades and roadway (also a total of 70 *podes*).

Chen's system works only with this section of the street where the exact total is 22.40 m. On the other hand, there remain many examples of streets, including ours in Caesarea and at least six examples from Jerusalem, that follow another system of measurement based on a *podes* of 0.30 m. (see above 169–170).

In a second article Professor Robert J. Bull, Director of the Joint Expedition excavations at Caesarea, identifies *Cardo* II West as the *Cardo Maximus* of the Late Roman and Byzantine city: "Caesarea Maritima, the Search for Herod's City," *BAR* VIII.3(1982) 25–40. Although excavations have not yet reached Herodian levels at any portion of the street in Field 'C,' a comparison of street alignments with those of the Herodian vaults facing west toward the ancient harbor complex suggests that the later streets followed an earlier Herodian plan.

But is this the *Cardo Maximus* of either the Herodian or late Roman city? Comparison of street dimensions (see above 170) with those of other cities in the Roman east clearly indicates that despite the addition of colonnades, the roadway remains relatively narrow, the standard size of smaller streets in the roadway remains relatively narrow, the standard size of smaller streets in Jerusalem, Jerash, and Dura-Europas. Is it not more likely that the nature of the street changed during the course of its long history? Excavations reveal the remains of important public buildings of the late Roman and Byzantine periods in the *insulae* west of our street in Field 'C.'

Was this an area for public buildings and colonnaded streets during the Herodian period or, as its position near the vaulted horrea suggests, might not the structures here be more closely associated with the harbor activities? It might be more appropriate to consider a position further inland for the major thoroughfare similar to relative positions in cities like Ephesus or Carthage. With so few clearly identified remains of Herodian Caesarea uncovered it is too soon to label *Cardo* II as the principal north-south street even though its subsequent development would suggest that at a later date it did become a principal street, *perhaps* the most important for the Byzantine city of Caesarea.

A final article concerns the northern part of the city but raises several interesting points worthy of note here: Duane Roller, "The Wilfred Laurier University Survey of Northeastern Caesarea Maritima," *Levant* XIV(1982) 90–103. The survey identifies a principal *decumanus* running east from the northern wall of the crusader fortress. Roller suggests that the fragments of columns found in three locations at intervals of 80 m. are the remains of a colonnaded street. This interval of 80 m. is the width of *insulae*, the same dimension of *insulae* uncovered in the southwest quarter (see page 170). This northern *decumanus* is 275 m. north of the paved road which approaches the site from the east. This modern highway is often associated with the *Decumanus Maximus* of the ancient city. The interval between these two streets can be divided into two blocks of 137.50 m. The resulting *insulae* of 80 by 137.50 m. are larger than those found in the southwest quarter during the late Roman period but are consistent with this author's suggestion that the orginial Herodian plan might have consisted of longer *insulae* that were reduced in size at a later date by the addition of more *decumani* (see page 170).

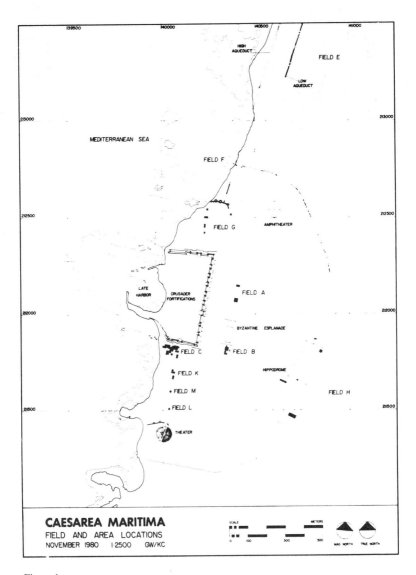

Figure 1

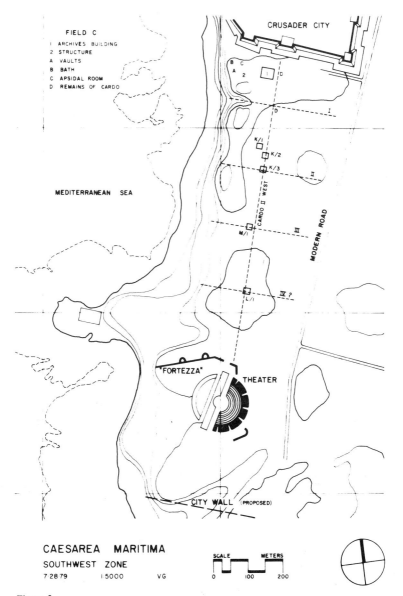

FIELD C

1 ARCHIVES BUILDING
2 STRUCTURE
A VAULTS
B BATH
C APSIDAL ROOM
D REMAINS OF CARDO

CRUSADER CITY

MEDITERRANEAN SEA

CARDO II WEST

MODERN ROAD

"FORTEZZA"

THEATER

CITY WALL (PROPOSED)

CAESAREA MARITIMA

SOUTHWEST ZONE

7·28·79   1·5000   VG

SCALE   METERS
0   100   200

Figure 2

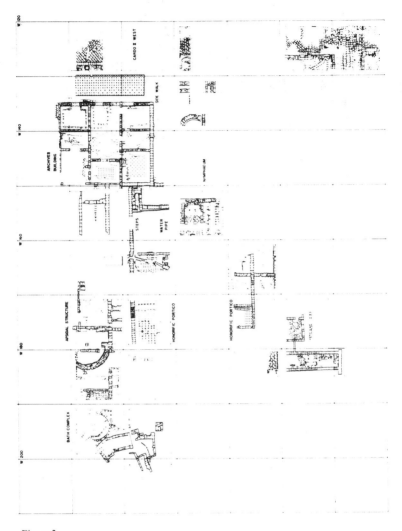

Figure 3

Figure 4

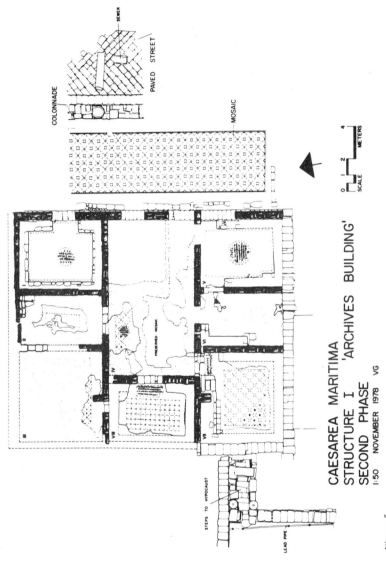

CAESAREA MARITIMA
STRUCTURE I 'ARCHIVES BUILDING'
SECOND PHASE
1:50   NOVEMBER 1978   VG

Figure 5

Figure 6

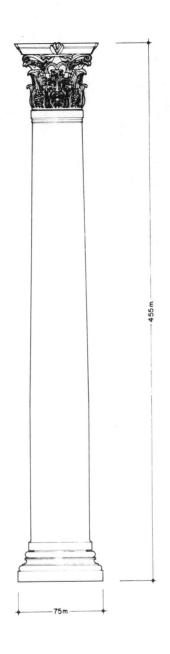

455 m

75 m

CAESAREA MARITIMA
KARDO II WEST
RECONSTRUCTED COLUMN   1:10
VG   7.25.79

Figure 7

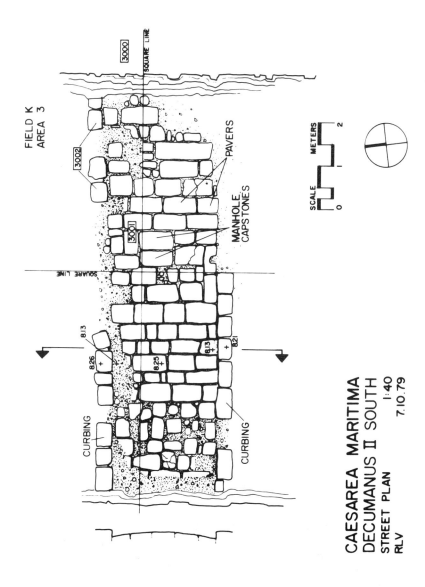

CAESAREA MARITIMA
DECUMANUS II SOUTH
STREET PLAN   1:40
RLV   7.10.79

Figure 8

Figure 9

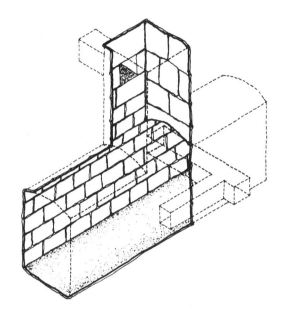

CAESAREA MARITIMA
AREA K/3
SEWER ISOMETRIC   1:20
AMB   6.14.81

Figure 10

Figure 11

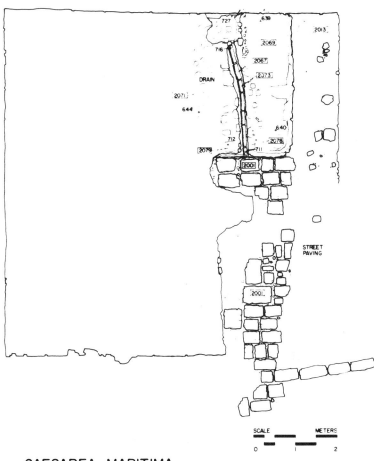

727 639
2069
716
2067
2073
DRAIN
2071
644
640
712 2078
2079 711
2001
2013

STREET
PAVING

2001

SCALE ▬▬ METERS
0   1   2

CAESAREA MARITIMA
AREA K/2
PHASE 6A EAST   7.28.79
1:20   GRW/RLV

Figure 12

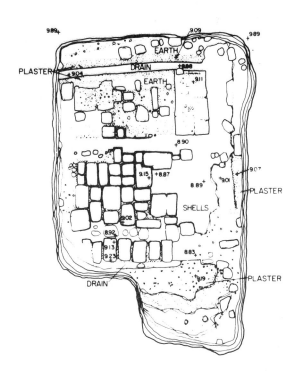

CAESAREA MARITIMA
AREA M/I
STREET PLAN   1:40
RLV   7.16.79

Figure 13

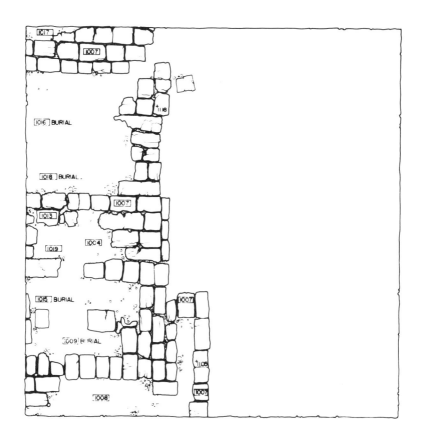

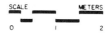

CAESAREA MARITIMA

AREA L/I

PHASE 6A STREET   7.28.79

1:20   VG/RLV

Figure 14

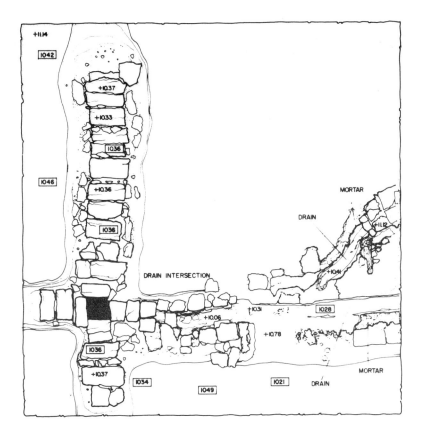

CAESAREA MARITIMA
AREA L/I

PHASE 6A SEWERS   7 2879
1:20   VG/RLV

Figure 15

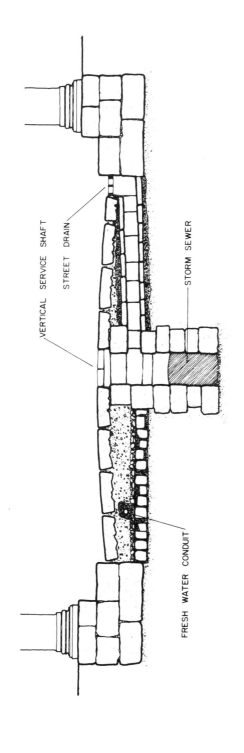

VERTICAL SERVICE SHAFT

STREET DRAIN

STORM SEWER

FRESH WATER CONDUIT

SCALE

METERS

0   4   8   16

CAESAREA MARITIMA
KARDO II WEST RECONSTRUCTION
1:20
6.15.81
SUBPHASE 6a: BYZANTINE
AMB

Figure 16

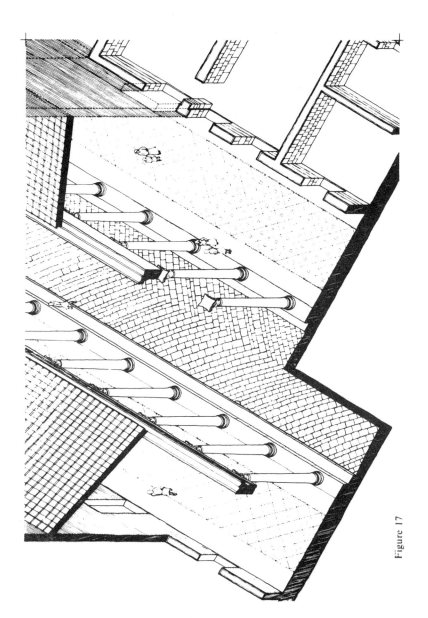

Figure 17

9

THE JUSTINIANIC FORTIFICATION
OF INTERIOR ILLYRICUM

Frank E. Wozniak
(University of New Mexico)

In his work *De aedificiis* (On the Buildings), Procopius listed the fortifications of interior Illycrium which were built or restored by the orders of the Emperor Justinian.[1] A majority of the forts and cities were simply refortified or had their walls strengthened while new constructions seem to have been kept to a minimum. The preponderance of refurbished older structures over new foundations testified to the exigencies of the moment; in addition, the restoration of old defenses appears to have been less costly than the beginning of new ones. The proportion of restored to new constructions also indicates that the Byzantine government accepted most of the existing forts, listed by Procopius, as adequate to meet the existing strategic needs of the Empire in Illyricum. Was this system of fortification strategically adequate for its avowed purpose of defending the interior Illyrian provinces? Did the forts in fact defend the provinces of Illyricum when put to the test by subsequent barbarian invasions?

That Procopius did not include some very considerable fortifications, such as those at Thessalonika, creates some anomalies in his list. Due to damage from earthquakes or decay from neglect, Thessalonika was extensively refortified in the first half of the fifth century.[2] Because the capital of the prefecture was already securely protected and because Procopius confined himself to listing those places for whose fortifications

Justinian's government was responsible, Thessalonika and some other cities were left out of his lists.

A most serious problem in dealing with Procopius' lists is our general lack of knowledge concerning the location of the large majority of the new and refortified sites except in their very appropriate regional distribution.[3] For the major cities that survived from the third and fourth centuries, we are comparatively well informed but for the rest we are largely at a loss. Most of the sites, whether refurbished or newly constructed, seem to have been small in size. Too few of these Justinianic forts have been excavated or are extant in Illyricum to assert more than has Diehl that the forts varied in size and form in relationship to their importance.[4] To compare the fortifications of the times from one area of the empire to another seems possible; however comparisons of the interior arrangements in Illyricum with those in the North Africa or Syrian fortifications are tentative and have tended to ignore the important topographic and constructional distinctions between the Balkans and these other areas.

Whatever the form of the forts, most of them can not have been very large. The cost of numerous major fortifications would have been prohibitive and contrary to the economic necessities that had in part impelled these constructions.[5] Also, many of the forts were probably relatively unsubstantial given the short time in which they seem to have been constructed as well as the nature of the barbarian threat which they were meant to withstand. These forts were not intended to hold out against an attack by people with a knowledge of siegecraft; they were simply built to impede a direct assault on the occupants. It would seem likely then that most of these forts were refurbished or newly constructed by the local population at their own expense from locally available materials. The admonitions of earlier Roman governments to the officials and people of Illyricum to see to the proper repair of their walls seem to have still held.[6] The central government sent down its directives but officials at the local level had to implement these instructions as best they could with impoverished local resources in order to provide places of refuge in emergencies for the rural population of interior Illyricum. In some major instances the resources of the central government seem to have been employed at particularly vital points as Thermopylae but such instances were rare.[7]

While it is likely that the imperial government had some overall strategic plan which it wished to implement, there are few indications in Procopius as to how any such plan was carried out. Except in a very few cases as Thermopylae or the Isthmian wall or the larger and more easily identifiable cities where the comprehensive nature of the fortifications indicates a professional military presence, the involvement of military engineers in the fortification of interior Illyricum is not indicated by available archaeological or literary evidence. (In fact our sources on military engineers are lamentably sparse for this vital period.) Central supervision of the refortification of Illyricum seems to have been minimal, consequently the integration of defenses at the Procopian district level is hard to define, if it existed. Even at the provincial level there seems to have been only a haphazard integration of the fortifications and at the prefectural level a minimal attention to strategic integration. Recent archaeological and historio-geographical work seems to confirm the presence of a large number of refuge fortifications in the interior of Illyricum as a reading of Procopius would lead one to expect but this research also indicates the general lack of strategic integration.

Though we cannot give names from Procopius' lists to most of the extant 6th century fortifications, Justinian's government quite certainly insured the covering of the interior with fortified and refortified sites; however, the further implication of Procopius that these constructions made the interior unaccessible to the barbarians is more difficult to support—the strategic importance and integration of the Illyrian fortifications has not been proven only assumed.[8] Before one can deal with the comprehensive question of a viable and integrated defense of the Illyrian provinces, the more narrow problem of the immediate defense of each site must be confronted.

Once built or refortified, the question arises as to who was to defend these places. For the larger towns and cities, small regular garrisons seem to have existed, supplemented at need by the urban population as had been the case in the fifth century. On the immediate frontiers what was left of the *limitanii* would have served, possibly augmented by barbarian federates. At such extensive positions as Thermopylae and the Isthmus, local militias or regular soldiers were used to garrison their systems of walls and forts.[9] However, for the majority of sites, which were clearly of only local significance there were no regular garrisions. These fortifications were intended not only to provide places of refuge for the local population in case of a successful breaching of the frontier lines by the barbarians but also to relieve the regular army of its responsibilities for local defense.

The strategic and tactical mobility of the field army in Illyricum was vital for Justinian on two counts: one, the limited manpower and effectiveness of the *limitanii* required a mobile field army (*praesentalis* in the fourth and fifth century) to restrict the penetration of the interior by barbarian forces and second, Justinian needed forces that were immediately available to carry out his plans for reconquest in Dalmatia and Italy. The wars against the Ostrogoths and the diversion of the prefectural field army to defend Thrace left Illyricum seriously strapped for manpower and dangerously exposed to constant barbarian raids. The interior provinces of Illyricum were studded with dozens of fortifications to protect the population left particularly vulnerable by the extensive use of the magistral forces outside of the prefecture for purposes that the Imperial government had determined to be more strategically vital. But the burden of local defense was now shifted onto the shoulders of the local population. Though they now had walls to provide a refuge and the barbarians were fortunately unskilled in the taking of fortifications,[10] how were they to defend themselves? Walls without defenders are useless, and the barbarians while not masters of siegecraft could and did capture Byzantine fortresses.

In order to limit crime and out of fear for armed insurrections, the Justinianic government like its predecessors made serious efforts to keep military arms out of the hands of private individuals. In addition, arms were only to be manufactured and distributed under close government supervision and deposited in central arsenals.[11] For the major cities immediate defense presented little problem; they had garrisons and arsenals or access to both, but the situation was very different for the ungarrisoned and unsupervised forts spread over the Illyrian landscape.[12] If these places were to have any hope of resistance they needed arms, but could the government permit the deposit of weapons in these forts where their security and distribution would be difficult to control? Local self-help seems to have been the result, either officially countenanced evasion of the imperial decrees on private arms holding or the extension of the *limitanii* or rural militia into the interior. The former seems the most likely as there is some evidence for non-enforcement or selective enforcement of the Justinianic law on arms but there also is some intriguing, if difficult to interpret, evidence for the existence of rural militia in sixth century interior Illyricum.

As in most of the provinces of the late Roman empire, the local aristocratic landowners seem to have taken local defense into their own hands.[13] In part they were given these responsibilities by the Imperial government as in the case of being held responsible for the maintenance and repair of city and town walls. On the other hand they seem to have assumed responsibility in activities and areas where the central government could no longer fulfill or had abdicated its responsibilities.[14] The Imperial admonitions against the employment of *bucellaroi* by local aristocrats are well known, particularly as these relate to the illegal actions of the aristocrats and their retainers. The *bucellaroi* were not only flunkies but trained and armed soldiers.[15] However they came into the service of the landowners, they were present in large numbers within the provinces of the empire including Illyricum. The repetition of government prohibitions on their employment simply reiterates the fact of their continued presence as armed bodies outside the control of the government.[16]

The landowners had need of them not only to influence tax collectors and judges or to intimidate small landholders but also to provide protection for their properties from local brigands and barbarian raiders.

As an anomaly in its prohibition on private arms holding, the government encouraged local populations to arm and defend themselves against brigands.[17] Whatever their ethnic background brigands both Roman and barbarian were a plague against which the central government was unable to defend its citizens. This fact produced a government sanctioned exception to the arms laws that recognized the government's ineffectiveness and the reality of locally initiated self-protection probably led by landowning aristocrats backed by bands of technically illegal *bucellaroi*. The anti-brigandage laws provided a major loophole through which the *bucellaroi* could be legitimized.

Because of narrow self-interest and the broader problems of a lack of local policing and military forces, the wealthy landowners developed private armies. Though a potential threat to the central government and its bureaucracy, the simple inability of that government to provide elemental order and security in the provinces compelled the local aristocrats to depend upon their own resources, often to the further detriment of public order and in defiance of imperial laws but nonetheless filling a vacuum left by the central government itself. While the government could not countenance the intimidation of its tax collectors by the private armies of the landowners, it was willing to throw on the shoulders of the local population the costly and dirty task of rooting out brigandage which was threatening to become entrenched in the provinces.[18] If the *bucellaroi* of the magnates could be used against brigands, it was but a small step to leave responsibility for local defense in the hands of the magnates; their *bucellaroi* could combat bands of barbarians as well as brigands.

In Illyricum, the local aristocracy was already responsible from the fifth century for good repair of the walls of cities and towns; it seems likely from the character of most Justinian fortifications in the interior provinces that these were also constructed by local initiative. The limited nature of current archaeological research in much of the interior of Illyricum makes it difficult to ascertain the extent to which the magnates fortified their own residences or whether they simply depended upon the major local fortifications which have been located. Even if prompted ultimately from Constantinople, the local landowners certainly had their own interests enough at heart to defend them. Local initiative seems also to have provided the defenders to make walls effective; the *bucellaroi* of the magnates were the men who held the walls in case of an emergency and defended the local population in these local refuges.

On the question of local militias who were not part of the *limitanii*, there is some good evidence for their existence near the more exposed frontiers for the fifth and late sixth centuries, i.e., the case of Asemus.[19] Some sort of the local urban militia also seems to have existed in Thrace early in the fifth century.[20] Further, repeated prohibitions on private arms holding merely indicates its persistence. Local participation in the defense of cities and towns seems to have been assumed by the imperial government on numerous occasions. The one major example of a functioning rural militia was in the case of Thermopylae but there, Justinian's government replaced them with a regular garrison due to their ineffectiveness.[21] The existence of formally organized and sanctioned rural or local militias in the interior provinces of Illyricum is possible but not probable given the state of the evidence. In any case the magnates and the *bucellario* are the most likely defenders of the fortifications which the central government wished to be spread thickly throughout Illyricum.

At the strategic level, the question of the defensive value of Justinian's fortification system in Illyricum hinges immediately on the underlying purpose of these walled sites (however large or small they might have been). Most commonly, the system has been called a defense-in-depth, largely by analogy with the defenses of the Byzantine territories in North Africa and Syria.[22] But does the defensive organization of Illyricum warrant such a characterization of its fortifications, especially since such a defensive system implies not only walls but also a military structure to make this a realistic strategy? Before we can explore how Illyricum was being defended, it is necessary to examine what was being defended. Was this diverse collection of walled sites a defense of communications, the urban and rural population, supply centers, strategic resources, military deployment centers, a deep frontier, or all of these or a combination of some of these possibilities? From the small number of sites that have been located and examined, it would appear that the refortification of Illyricum was a curious mixture of overlapping intentions. The fortifications from Dyrrachium to Thessalonika had the apparent purpose of defending the *Via Egnatia*, i.e., preventing permanent breaks in communication between Constantinople, the Adriatic coast, and the West.[23] These fortifications were intended not only to defend the *Via Egnatia* but also to obstruct barbarian use of the route; it is likely that other roads in Illyricum were similarly defended with road forts, fortified cities, and forts at fords and passes.

Wherever the topography permitted, the Byzantines seemed inclined to build long walls, the most famous being that in Thrace but Illyricum had its share at Dyrrachium, Potidaea, Thermopylae and Isthmia.[24] Long walls were a burden to build and maintain but they did make possible a preclusive defense of extensive territory within the walls so long as they were provided with a garrison, either a local militia or regular troops. Events proved that only a regular garrison could insure the defense of such extensive fortifications; at Thermopylae, Justinian had to station 2000 men to secure central and southern Greece against attack.[25] For the other long walls in Illyricum we do not know what the Emperor provided for their garrisons, if anything.

Despite the long walls, the road defenses and the other fortifications, large rural areas of Illyricum were left open to barbarian raids. To call the Justinianic constructions a defense-in-depth would require more than numerous walled sites even if they had garrisons, such a designation would have necessitated the existence of a regularly available, mobile field army to intercept the barbarians and render rapid assistance to endangered positions. Only on rare occasions did Justinian have or make available such a force in Illyricum after 535. The whole system of enumerated fortifications for Illyricum has the *ad hoc* qualities that characterized most of Justinian's actions in the Balkans.

B. H. Warmington in a paper "Frontier Studies and the History of the Roman Empire: some Desiderata" read at the Ninth Congress on

the Roman Frontiers (Bucharest, 1972) presented some tentative
assessments which are of immediate application in this instance.[26]
According to Warmington, the Imperial government could not or
would not prevent the barbarians from disrupting the economy and
communications of the interior provinces. Such continual exposure of
the infrastructure of the Balkan provinces damaged the continued
capacity for provincial or regional defense. Further, the reaction of the
Roman army to barbarian raids was dangerously slow. The greater
part of the population escaped by taking refuge in existing or hastily
revived forts but the barbarians were left free to plunder the countryside. Even more pointedly, he raised the question of the placement of
the fortifications. Many of them he alleges to have been poorly located
and once fortified in stone the sites continued to be used even if badly
placed. While referring to the third and fourth centuries, Warmington
seems correct when we carry the analysis into the sixth century.

Quite clearly, Procopius' own evidence in his history of the Justinianic wars testifies that the fortifications of Illyricum did not effectively
hinder the marauding by foreign tribes anywhere north of Thermopylae during the sixth century. The Byzantine army was notoriously slow
in reacting to barbarian raids, a habit which was not improved by the
depletion of the magistral forces to supply other fronts. Most of the
military resources of Illyricum were diverted to Italy or Thrace, leaving
the prefectural population to shift for themselves with little hope for
assistance or relief by regular military forces. Consequently, the rural
and small town populations tended to seek refuge in the larger and
more secure cities because they could not survive indefinitely in their
isolated and often inadequate local forts. After the population of Illyricum had become concentrated in the cities or had taken to the hills,
the Avars arrived with the siegecraft to take cities. This precipitated a
stampede to the coastal cities in the late sixth and early seventh centuries.[27] Since they had access to supplies and Imperial aid by sea, the
maritime cities could in many cases provide a refuge and a measure of
security which had been systematically denied the interior cities
because of their location or Imperial preoccupations elsewhere.

The preponderance of refortifications in Justinian's defensive
scheme would seem to indicate that most sites were chosen because
they had been previously utilized rather than because they fit into an
integrated system for the defense of Illyricum. The majority of forts on
Procopius lists were refurbished older forts[28] The new constructions
were kept to a minimum and even then, from the limited archaeo-

logical evidence now available, they were not wholly new in their sighting as many of these new forts seem to have been placed on the sites of fortifications abandoned earlier in antiquity.[29] (A fact which raises the question of the correlation of the military needs of earlier times with those of the late Roman period.) It was easier and cheaper to reuse a site or strengthen existing fortifications than to begin afresh on a new site. The pre-existence of constructions in stone in a number of places, particularly from the third and fifth century emergencies, strongly encouraged the continued occupation or rebuilding of fortifications whether well located or not.

Because of the rapidly accumulating emergencies of the 540's and 550's the whole fortification system of Justinian in Illyricum was hastily conceived and executed with a minimum of careful strategic planning. The result was an impressive number of fortifications in Illyricum but a poorly integrated system of defense that was repeatedly shown to be inadequate. Even before the Justinianic constructions, the experiences of the third and fifth centuries had demonstrated the deficiencies of such defensive preparations both in the fortifications and the tactical and strategic allocations of manpower. In addition, the Byzantine government seriously miscalculated the nature and the extent of the new barbarian threat in the sixth century; consequently the interior provinces were left exposed to constant raids which gradually destroyed the economic, military and administrative infrastructure of Illyricum and ruined the empire in the Balkans by the mid-seventh century. The emperor Justinian sought to compensate for the continued lack of adequate garrisons and field forces by a massive building program which hoped to protect the Illyricum population if not their property but which also enshrined the past inadequacies of the Illyrian fortifications in ever greater accumulations of masonry.

Financial necessities, conservatism, dreams of reconquest and historical precedent caused Justinian to leave the population of Illyricum to depend upon its own resources with a minimum of central direction or assistance; the result was a haphazard innundation of the countryside with fortifications and inadequate preparations for the threat presented by the Slavs, Bulgars and Avars.

Notes

1. Procopius. *De aedificiis*, ed. J. Haury (Leipzig, 1913) IV, i–iv.
2. Michael Vickers. "Further Observations on the Chronology of The Walls of Thessaloniki," *Makedonika*, 12 (1972), 228–33.
3. See the provincial and regional grouping of Procopius' lists for Illyricum (*De aedificiis*, IV, iv.); also on the problem of locations for Thrace, see V. Besevliev, *Zur Deutung der Kastellnamen in Prokops Werk "De Aedificiis"* (Amsterdam, 1970).
4. Charles Diehl. *Justinien et la civilisation byzantine* (Paris, 1901), 240.
5. The economic constraints on the empire are well known even if one does not accept the charges of Procopius (*Anecdota*, xix–xxvi).
6. *Codex Theodosianus*, ed. Th. Mommsen and P. M. Meyer (Berlin, 1905) VII, 15.1.34 and 1.49; see also *Codex Iustinianus*, ed. P. Krueger. *Corpus Iuris Civilis*, 2 (Berlin, 1928) VIII, 12, 12, and 18; and Justinian, *Novellae*, Ed. G. Kroll. *Corpus Iuris Civilis*, 3 (Berlin, 1895) XVI, 4.
7. Procopius. *De aedificiis*, IV, ii, 1–15.
8. Procopius. *De aedificiis*, IV, i, 13–14.
9. Procopius. *De aedificiis*, IV, ii, 13–14 and 28.
10. E. A. Thompson, *The Early Germans* (Oxford, 1965), 133–40.
11. Justinian, *Novellae*, 85.
12. While Procopius (*De aedificiis*, IV, i, 6) states that Justinian placed innumerable garrisons in Illyricum, his reference is characteristic of panegyrical exaggeration.
13. The law codes of the fifth and sixth century clearly give the landowners such responsibilities; further examples from the western part of the empire, especially from Gaul, serve as an excellent analogy to the situation which was slowly developing in the interior of Illyricum, see K. F. Stroheker, *Der senatorische Adel in Spätantiken Gallien* (Tübingen, 1948).
14. Ramsay Macmullen *Soldier and Civilian in the Later Roman Empire* (Cambridge, Mass., 1963).
15. On the *bucellaroi* in general see R. Grosse, *Romische Militergeschichte* (Berlin, 1920), 283–91 and O. Seeck, "Bucellarii," *R. E.*, 3:1 (1897), 934–9.
16. Theodosius II. *Novellae*, XV, 2; *Codex Iustinianus*, IX, 12, 10. The problem was especially serious in Egypt but prevalent everywhere.
17. *Codex Iustinianus*, III, 28, 1 & 2; *Codex Theodosianus*, VII, 18,14; IX,14.2.
18. See the anti-brigandage laws in the fifth and sixth century law codes which are partially listed above.
19. Priscus, frg. 5 and Theophylactus, VII, 3.
20. See the resistance of the Thracian towns to Gainas in 400 A.D. [Zosimus, *Historica nova* (Austin, 1967) ch. 19].
21. Procopius, *De aedificiis*, IV, iv, 15.

22. Charles Diehl, *Justinien et la civilisation byzantine*, 234–40; J. B. Bury, *History of the Later Roman Empire*, 2 (New York, 1958) 308–10.

23. M. von Sufflay, *Städte und Burgen Albaniens*, (Vienna, 1924) 17; N.G.L. Hammond, *A History of Macedonia*, 1, *Historical Geography and Prehistory* (Oxford, 1972), 19–58.

24. M. von Sufflay, *Städte und Burgen Albaniens*, 20; Procopius, *De aedificiis*, IV, iii, 21–26; ii, 1–22; ii, 27–28.

25. Procopius, *De aedificiis*, IV, ii, 14–15.

26. B. H. Warmington "Frontier Studies and the History of the Roman Empire: Some Desiderata," *Actes du IXᵉ Congrès international d'études sur les frontières romaines*, (Bucharest, 1972; Köln, 1974), 291–296.

27. See the life of St. Demetrios for a description of the effects of the Avar invasions for this period: F. Barisić, *Cuda Dimitrija Solunskog* (Beograd, 1953).

28. Procopius, *De aedificiis*, IV, iv.

29. N.G.L. Hammond, *Epirus*, Oxford, 1967) 38–285; N.G.L. Hammond, *A History of Macedonia*, 1, 19–211; I Mikulcić, "Über die Grösse der spätantinen Städte in Makedonien," *Živa Antika*, (1974) 191–212.

PENROSE MEMORIAL LIBRARY WHITMAN COLLEGE